Total Quality Management

B.S. Sharma

ANMOL PUBLICATIONS PVT. LTD.
NEW DELHI - 110 002 (INDIA)

ANMOL PUBLICATIONS PVT. LTD.
H.O.: 4374/4B, Ansari Road, Darya Ganj,
New Delhi-110 002 (India)
Ph.: 23278000, 23261597

B.O.: No. 1015, Ist Main Road, BSK IIIrd Stage
IIIrd Phase, IIIrd Block,
Bangalore - 560 085 (India)
Visit us at: www.anmolpublications.com

Total Quality Management

First Published, 2006

PRINTED IN INDIA

Printed at Mehra Offset Press, Delhi.

Contents

Preface

"Total Quality Management" as a paper is being taught at M.Com., M.B.A. and Other Management Courses at various universities and institutions. This book is designed as an introductory text to the above paper, encompassing vital information on all pertinent aspects. Thus the material presented here would be of interest as well as of great use to the students, teachers and professionals of Business Management. This book will provide complete knowledge of basic concept of total quality, importance and components of TQM, quality planning, functional linkage of realiability, quality management process, functional linkage of quality system standards, quality costs and taguchi loss function, statistical process control, ISO-9000 standards and quality audits, management of quality control process, zero defects programmes; motivation for quality development, quality improvement teams and planning; marketing aspects of T.Q. services, quality audits; quality's function in testing etc. to the students.

The major topics dealt in this book are—Basic Concept of Total Quality; Importance and Components of TQM; Quality Planning; Functional Linkage of Realiability; Quality Management Process; Functional Linkage of Quality System Standards; Conceptual Approach to Source of Quality; Quality Costs and Taguchi Loss Function; Statistical Process Control; ISO-9000 Standards and Quality Audits; Management of Quality Control Process; Zero Defects Programmes; Motivation for Quality Development; Quality Improvement Teams and Planning; Marketing Aspects of T.Q. Services; Quality Audits; Quality's Function in Testing etc.

It is hoped that all those will benefit from the contents of this book for whom it is meant. The author will feel amply rewarded, if motive is achieved.

Editor

1

Basic Concept of Total Quality

Quality is viewed as one that requires every member of the organization to provide the next person in the process with an acceptable product or service. This means that everyone is responsible to perform a task in such a manner that the product can be used immediately and in the most efficient manner possible. Juran further identified four important parameters of fitness for use as:

1. Quality of design
2. Quality of conformance
3. The abilities
4. Field service

Quality is a term that has valuable meaning to both producer and customer. The producer views fitness for use in terms of the ability to process and produce with less rework, less scrap, minimal downtime, and high productivity.

Quality characteristics are elements of fitness for use that typify the variety of uses of a given product. Quality characteristics may be of several types:

1. Time-oriented (serviceability, reliability, maintain ability)
2. Sensory (colour, taste, beauty, appearance, and others)
3. Commercial (warranty)

4. Structural (including frequency, weight, length, and viscosity)
5. Behavioral or ethical (fairness, honesty, courtesy, and so on)

Improvements in quality are therefore made by examining the design and conformance phases with their associated characteristics through the application of techniques and methods. Productivity and quality management will be defined as follows. Productivity and quality management is an integrated process involving both management and employees with the ultimate goal of managing the design, development, production, transfer, and use of the various types of products or services in both the work environment and the marketplace. The process requires the total involvement of everyone in the planning, measurement, evaluation, control, and improvement of productivity and quality at the source of production or service center.

Productivity and Quality Management Triangle

The productivity and quality management triangle (PQMT) encompasses an information system that provides input of information relevant to the planning, performance, and measurement processes and implementation of corrective actions and techniques that improve productivity. For an organization initiating comprehensive productivity and quality management, measurement, control, and evaluation is the first stage in the PQMT triangle. Once a set of measures has been developed, plan targets and strategies are formulated. Based on these strategies, short-range objectives are formulated and operational improvement techniques are then used to implement short-and long-range objectives. In order to assess the extent to which the improvements were successfully implemented, measurements, control, and evaluation are performed again. This triangular relationship thus continues as long as the comprehensive productivity and quality programme exists in the organization.

The management of productivity and quality can provide the following benefits to organizations:

1. Productivity and quality management will enable the consumer to pay low price for goods and services because the cost of production is reduced owing to reduced rework and gains in productivity.

2. Productivity and quality management enable the effective utilization of resources. More goods and services are produced for a reasonable amount of expended resources.

3. Productivity and quality management provide the basis for higher real earnings for employees The reduction in the cost of production of goods and services can allow increases in wages without significantly offsetting gains in total productivity.

4. Productivity and quality management enable the public to realize greater social benefits through increased public revenues from organizations.

5. Productivity and quality management will enable an organization to be more profitable because quality improvement results in reduced rework, reduction in scrap, better utilization of tools and equipment, and less work in process inventory, which in turn leads to higher productivity. Minimization of the cost of manufacture for goods and services improves the profit margin. The production of good quality products also improves the market share because the satisfied customer will buy more and will recommend the product to another consumer.

6. Productivity and quality management components provide an organization with the strength to deal with internal operating weakness and external competition.

Deming discusses what top management must do to improve both productivity and quality. The fourteen points offered by Deming have been successfully implemented in Japan and most of the industrialized countries in the world. A summary of Deming's fourteen points follows:

1. Create constancy of purpose toward improvement of product and service, with a plan to become competitive and to stay in business. Decide to whom top management is responsible.

2. Adopt the new philosophy. We are in a new economic age. We can no longer live with commonly accepted levels of delays, mistakes, defective materials, and defective workmanship.

3. Cease dependence on mass inspection. Require, instead, statistical evidence that quality is built in to eliminate the need for inspection on a mass basis. Purchasing managers have a new job and must learn it.

4. End the practice of awarding business on the basis of price tag. Instead, depend on meaningful measures of quality, along with price. Eliminate suppliers that cannot qualify with statistical evidence of quality.

5. Institute modern methods of supervision of production workers. The responsibility of foremen must be changed from sheer numbers to quality. Improvement of quality will automatically improve productivity.

6. Find problems. It is management's job to work continually on the system.

7. Institute modern methods of training on the job.

8. Drive out fear so that everyone may work effectively for the company.

9. Eliminate work standards that prescribe numerical quotas.

10. Remove barriers that stand between the hourly worker and the right to pride of workmanship.

11. Break down barriers between department. People in research, design, sales, and production must work as a

team, to foresee problems of production that may be encountered with various materials and specifications. .

12. Eliminate numerical goals, posters, and slogans for the work force that ask for new levels of productivity without providing methods.
13. Institute a vigorous programme of education and retraining.
14. Create a structure in top management that will push every day on the other thirteen points.

Causes of Productivity Decline in Companies

Mali presented twelve causes for the decline of productivity in organizations:

1. The inability to measure, evaluate, and manage the productivity of white-collar employees can cause a shocking waste of resources.
2. Rewards and benefits given without requiring the equivalent in productivity and accountability causes spiraling inflation.
3. There is low motivation among a rising number of affluent workers with new attitudes.
4. Late deliveries may be caused by schedules that have been disrupted by scarcity of materials.
5. Diffused authority and inefficiency in complex organizations cause delays and time lags.
6. Organizational expansion that lower productivity growth results in soaring costs.
7. Unresolved human conflicts and difficulties in team work result in the firm's ineffectiveness.
8. Rapid technological changes and high costs result in a decline in new opportunities and innovations.

9. Increasing demand or leisure time causes disruption of time commitments.

10. Increased legislative intrusions or antiquated laws result in constrained management options and prerogatives.

11. Overspecialization in work processes results in monotony and boredom.

12. A practitioner is unable to keep pace with the latest information and knowledge.

Although Mali's points focus on productivity, much the same reasons are applicable to the decline of quality within organizations.

Quality Costs

Quality costs are those various categories of costs that are associated with identifying, avoiding, producing, maintaining, and repairing products that do not meet specifications. Quality costs are in four categories. Each quality cost category will now be described.

Appraisal Costs

Appraisal costs are associated with measuring, evaluating, or auditing products, components, and purchased materials to assure conformance to quality standards and performance specifications.

Prevention Costs

Prevention costs are associated with designing, implementing, and maintaining a quality system capable of anticipating and preventing quality problems before they generate avoidable costs. All costs related to efforts in design and manufacturing that are directed toward the prevention of non-conformance are in this category.

External Failure Costs

External failure costs are generated by defective products shipped to customers. The product generally does not conform to requirements and fails to meet the satisfaction of the customers.

Internal Failure Costs

Internal failure costs are associated with defective products, components, and materials that fail to meet quality requirements, and this failure is discovered prior to delivery of the product to the customer.

In order to improve productivity and quality, an effective management system must be in place. Such a management changes in policies, organizational structure, and procedures that allow a fertile environment for productivity and quality improvement. The following are basic requirements:

1. Management philosophy must be one that is geared toward continuous productivity and quality improvement at the source of production or service. Management of productivity and quality is not a one-time action. It is a continuous process that involves both management and employees, in producing and delivering good products and services.

2. Management philosophy must accept no levels of defect. Low productivity is not acceptable.

3. There must be a system in place for measurement, control and evaluation, planning and analysis, and improvement and monitoring of all activities.

4. Management and employee commitment to quality and productivity improvement can be translated into a written policy. There must be documentation of such a policy and clear specifications of all the necessary details to assure it.

5. There must be a data base for the strong and retrieval of information about the process.

6. There must be a clear definition of process parameters and variables. Input and output elements must be clearly identified.

7. All process parameters must be characterized with complete understanding of repeatability and variability.

8. The management information system must provide a real time feedback mechanism to everyone involved in the productivity and quality improvement efforts.

9. There should be a provision for ongoing management and employee training in productivity and quality improvement techniques.

10. There must be process ownership by everyone involved in the management process.

11. Productivity and quality improvement based on the implementation of key actions must be documented and rewarded on a timely basis.

12. There should mechanisms for the identification and removal of barriers between functional departments to facilitate open communication.

13. Management must provide clear guidance and clear goals and objectives, specify short and long term commitments, and set the direction for excellence.

14. The attainment of a good quality product should be through prevention of defects, not through detection of defects.

15. The removal of defects from a process should be done through root cause analysis and the implementation of proper corrective action. Cost inspections should be discouraged. The strategy should be that which utilize sampling inspection when necessary and no inspection when it is not warranted.

In order for a productivity and quality management system to provide useful and meaningful results, it is important for the level of emphasis to be clearly specified and understood within the productivity and quality management hierarchy (PQMH). The productivity and quality management hierarchy suggests thal productivity and quality management should start at the basic levels. If all the associated inputs and outputs are clearly identified and managed properly at this level, the results have tremendous impact. It becomes less cumbersome to quantify and manage productivity and quality at the other eight different levels.

The PQMH also provides a basis to identify the productivity and quality issues from a global perspective. Most importantly, it shows that the productivity and quality management of any nation starts from the basic units. At each level of the PQMH, techniques and methodology are required for the planning and analysis process, performance and measurement process, and improvement and monitoring process. Aggregation technique is usually applied to understand productivity and quality management issues at the higher levels. It is usually helpful if there are consistent and conducive policies affecting productivity and quality at the higher levels of the PQMH.

It has already been stated that Total Quality represents a competitive strategy. 'Quality', in terms, of 'Total Quality', is everything an organization does in the eyes of its customers, which will determine whether they buy from this company or from its competitor. Total Quality therefore is as much concerned with confidence and the 'overall impression' of the market as it is with specific measurable or quantifiable characteristics. Sometimes, the customer is adversely influenced by some quality deficiency which may even work in his favour. For example, if a supplier forgets to invoice his customer, this is clearly to the latter's advantages, but even so, the effect on him will almost certainly be negative. It may well occur to the customer that if his supplier is poorly organised in this respect, then he may also be weak in other areas. His confidence will be lowered and it is quite likely that he may put future business elsewhere, particularly when the service to be purchased is critical to the customer in some way.

A total Quality organisation must have four principal objectives, which are common to any organisation. A given organisation may also have many additional specific goals.

1. Continuous improvement of the organisation, which must be equal to or greater than that of any competitor.
2. Continuous and relentless cost reduction.
3. Continuous and relentless quality improvement.
4. To create an organisation whereby everyone is working towards making their organisation the best in its business, and to capitalise on the sense of achievement and working in a world-class organisation.

Let us look at each of these goals in turn.

Continuous Improvement

Many organisations take a natural pride in their progressive improvement activities, which is laudable and to be encouraged. It is amazing, however, to discover how few organisations have any idea as to how they are actually perceived in comparison with their competitors in the marketplace.

Many people mistakenly think that if you are not achieving customer satisfaction, you are causing its opposite, *i.e.*, customer dissatisfaction. By so doing, they forget the most important and dangerous situation of all customer indifference! It has been said that to be successful in business it is necessary to be better than your competitor at least something. Nowadays, even that may not be enough. We must be better than our competitor in every possible way. Just 'meeting the requirements of the customer' is not sufficient. Consider a restaurant as an example. Typically, the manager or head waiter will ask his customers whether or not they enjoyed their meal. In most cases, the response will be affirmative. Only occasionally do people complain, and then only when they are quite upset. Only occasionally do we give praise, and then only when we are very pleased. So in most cases, we do not provide feedback for the services we have received. It is easy to see how the restaurateur can be deceived. We told him the service was OK, and yet we probably will not go back. The service meets the specification, but some competitor does it better. Just meeting the requirements of the customer does not provide feedback for the services we have received. It is easy to see how not meet the exacting requirements of Total Quality.

On many occasions at seminars, one asks the audience. How many of you think that your company is good at what it does? Usually about 60 per cent of the participants will put up their hands. Very few can answer the subsequent question. 'How do you know'? What information do you have to support your belief? except to say. 'We get very few complaints'. For most, this is an indication that they are probably in the 'indifferent zone'. It is amazing how many companies in the same business think that they individually have over a 50 per cent share of the market!

Even when we do know our market share, and even if we find out that, yes, we are the best, and yes, we have the lion's share, there is no cast-iron guarantee that things will not change. Even as the reader is reading this book there is some organisation out ther conspiring to take away his livelihood because that is what modern competition on a global scale is all about. Dr. Juran claimed that the Japanese automobile industry overtook its Western competitors around 1975. Substituting company A and B in the example, we see that for a long time, Company A has the biggest share of the market and the best reputation. However, Company B introduces an aggressive Total Quality programme with the express intention of taking pride of place from Company A. In the words of Dr. Juran, 'The gap narrows until it closes. A time of trouble besets Company A'.

Generally speaking, the warning signals do not reach Company A until after the lines have converged. It is only when faced with plummeting market share and the onset of serious cash flow crises that Company A begins to realise that it is in trouble. In many cases, the realisation comes too late for the company to be able to respond the patient is too weak to withstand the operation! Even if company A can respond in time, if it has waited until after convergence it will be forced to improve at an even more rapid rate than Company B if it is ever regain its place in the market. Otherwise, all it can hope for is to progress at a parallel rate.

The lessons to be learnt from this are:

1. We must react before convergence, if there is still time left;
2. It is our rate of improvement relative to competitors which is important not simply the fact that we are getting better;
3. We must obtain the information from the marketplace to know where we stand in relation to the competition and monitor this continuously.

With regard to point 3 above, the majority of Japanese companies operate what they often refer to as 'Green Groups', which consist of key company personnel and selected leading customers. These groups are regarded as an extremely important part of a company's business strategy. The groups meet on regular basis to discuss the future plans of the business, progress with existing developments, and to solicit from the customers their thoughts and attitudes towards these developments, and their perceptions as to competitive advantages and disadvantages in the marketplace. Unfortunately, such activities are not commonplace in Western organisations, mainly due to a product-oriented mentality.

Depending on individual perceptions of the meaning of the word 'quality', these two points may seem to be in conflict with each other. Certainly, it is possible by reducing cost to cheapen a product or service, and of course regretfully, this often happens. The laudable concepts of value analysis and value engineering were brought into disrepute in the West for this reason. The confusion is due to different interpretations of the word 'quality' to some people the term refers merely to the specification of a product or service, and not necessarily to the processes which take place to achieve that requirement.

Consider the widespread advertisement for 'Quality Homes'. The intention of such advertisements is to convey to the world be purchaser that he will be getting something out of the ordinary in terms of the specification: for example, brass fittings, panelled doors, primary double glazing, and to forth. Whilst these items are clearly 'quality', the decision to produce homes to this higher specification is a marketing decision aimed to attract a particular type of customer. At the other extreme, it is an equally reasonable 'quality' decision to produce the most basic homes at the most economical price in order to attract the first-time buyer. Of course, in both cases it is necessary to identify very carefully the requirements of the intended customer, and then seek to provide that requirement. That would be a 'quality' decision, and a major element of business strategic thinking consistent with earlier comments it would also include the notion of pinpointing weaknesses in a competitor's strategy and exploiting a 'quality' advantage to the full for as long as it lasts.

Imagine the perfect company that never did anything wrong. Perfect raw materials or supplier support come in at one end; perfect processes take place such that there are no hold-ups, hiccups, or reasoning things because they were wrong or inadequate the first time. Everyone is properly trained and does their job well. There are no misunderstandings or inquests, and there is perfect provision of the product or service to the customer at the other end. In our perfect world there are no customer complaints, no warranty claims, and our reputation is second to none. In this situation we get the best of both worlds: better quality for the user, and lower cost for ourselves. In the context of points 2 and 3 this is the aspect of quality referred to. It can be seen that cost reduction, and improved quality in terms of the process, are totally iterrelated.

Quality concepts can be separated into two distinct categories: hard or logical, and behavioural. The 'hard' or logical aspects of quality include systems', 'process control' 'problem solving skills', and other organisational aspects. The majority of quality practitioners are likely to be basically left-brained thinkers. It is their attraction to logic, systems, procedures, organisation, measurements, calculations, problem-solving tools, etc., which drew them into the subject in the first place. Without balancing right-brained thinking, it is unlikely that such people would show much interest in the behavioural aspects of the subject, which are very much right-brained. On the other hand, the behavioural scientist is likely to be almost exactly the opposite. He will shrink away from what he regards as the mechanistic aspects, and will want to concentrate on the purely people-related features. Neither of these groups on their own can possibly get Total Quality into perspective, since Total Quality requires an equal appreciation and understanding of both aspects. In Western society such gifted people are not much in evidence in the field of Total Quality. That is not to say that they do not exist; the author of this book has conducted no research in this area, but it would be very useful if this was looked into. However, there is a distinct possibility that in Japanese management circles, a better balance exists.

It is clear that, whatever the characteristics of the key decision-makers and opinion influencers in any particular organisation, the benefits of Total Quality cannot be achieved purely through the introduction of techniques and skills. The high failure rate of Total Quality programmes in Western organisations is almost entirely due to a failure to understand the people factors, and virtually nothing to do with understanding the intricacies of the statistical method, BS 5750, or any such mechanical concept. Whenever discussions take place regarding failures of such programmes, it is almost always the much-maligned middle manager whom we hold to be responsible. On other occasions it may be 'lack of top management commitment' or 'union resistance', etc.

How can middle managers be collectively to blame? Much as some people may wish to argue otherwise, the middle manager is not genetically different from any other group of people. If he behaves in a certain way then it is the culture which is responsible. To blame any particular class or group of people provides no answer to the problem. If they behave in certain way, then that must be a symptom, not the cause. It is doubtful whether anyone behaves in a negative way because he wants to. Most people want to feel good about themselves and towards the society in which they live. If they became negative, then it is invariably due to either a real or a perceived threat. If middle managers are seen collectively or individually to be working against the will of the organisation then it may safely be assumed that they perceive their security or enjoyment of working life to be at risk in some way.

When studies of many orgqnisations' approach to Total Quality or Quality Circles are analysed, it is not usually difficult to see why one group or another is behaving in a negative, non-co operative way. More of this later. For now, we will consider how a positive approach will benefit an organisation. Total Quality is founded on the belief that people produce their best results when they enjoy what they are doing; enjoy the relationship they have with their colleagues; like, trust and respect those in higher positions; have belief in their organisation; and see in their jobs an opportunity for continuous self-development, and the feeling that their company is better for them being there. In the ultimate, people should feel on a Sunday night, 'Oh good, it's Monday tomorrow!' instead of the usual. 'Oh God, it's Monday tomorrow and I have to grind through a whole week to pick up a pay cheque'. We spend a significant part of our lives at work, and in terms of our social standing our job is very important to us. It sees fundamentally wrong that this should be painful experience for so many. Is it their fault, or does the collective blame lie with society? We cannot change society on our own, but we can change the organisation in which we work and live. The upper managers in any organisation can, within limits, create any culture they wish, provided of course that people are prepared to suffer at the worst end of the spectrum. In the Total Quality organisation, everyone is working towards making their company the best in its business.

Let's takes a sporting example. Consider two 16year-old boys, each of whom would like to be a professional footballer. One attends a trail at, say, Liverpool, who are top of Division 1 in the English league more often than not, and the other attends a trail at a fourth division club. Both are successful. The boy who is accepted at Liverpool will probably run home to tell his parent; the other may wall home, and still not be certain whether football is the right choice of career.

If the boy at liverpool ever gets the opportunity to run through the tunnel onto the field for a Division 1 game, with the roar of 40,000 Anfield supporters, he will probably run his legs off, because he will be thinking all the way through the game. 'I don't want to let my mates down'. Every one of whom will have been his hero only a year or so before. He will want to play up to this standards, and they will support him, because that is what teamwork is all about.

That example is directly analogous to the ideal Quality company. Any organisation which world class can, as a bonus, cream off the top of the universities, technical colleges, and local society because everyone wants to work for the 'best' company. Such companies hardly ever need to advertise for jobs because if they did, they would not be able to cope with the number of replies. Those who work for such companies will give their best efforts because they will not wish to let their colleagues or their company down. Hence the organisation gets the best of all possibilities, better quality work people and better quality performance.

Economic Justification of Total Quality

So far we have focused on the business strategies reasons for the introduction of Total Quality. It has been implied that the process can also be justified on the basis of cost reduction, and this is what must now be considered. A simple model based on our perfect company described earlier. This shows that not only does the perfect company operate at lower cost than its competitors, but it can command premium prices in the marketplace due to its reputation.

Most people will pay extra for something if they know it will be good. Even where this is not the case and where products and services are sold purely on lowest tender, it will be the most efficient organisation which will be able to undercut the price of its competitors. In addition to this, if the perfect company decides that it wants to increase its share of the market, and brings its selling price down below the cost of manufacture of its competitors, the result, may be 'exit" Company Average from the market'.

The cynical reply to the above argument would be, well, all this assumes two things:

1. that the cost difference between perfect and average is sufficiently large to make a difference, and
2. that significant reductions in total cost are possible to avoid a situation where the cure costs more than the disease.

In the first case, of course it is not possible through the pages of a book to identify the actual quality-related costs of any organisation. However, there is sufficient evidence to suggest the minimum such costs are likely to be in any organisation which has never before embarked on a programme to reduce these costs. It is fairly safe assumption that these costs will be at least 20 per cent of the turnover or sales revenue of any company, regardless of industry. In other words, we are paying at least 20p in every pound we spend for the internal inefficiencies of our supplier. Many companies find it hard to believe it is possible for such costs to exist in their organisation and not already have been picked up in the accounting system.

In one large high-volume food manufacturing company, the author was challenged on this point by the Finance Director, who said, 'I don't know what companies you have worked, in Mr. Hutchins, but they were not in the food industry. If we had figures like that, we would have poisoned half the population by now, and we would be out of business. It is more like 1½ per cent. Fortunately, my continued involvement with that company did not rest with him, otherwise the rest of the story would be lost. About four weeks later, we met again, after having both done some work on the topic. The Finance Director said, 'You were wrong about that 20 per cent'. When asked what he thought it was he replied.

The question then is why did he originally think 1½ per cent, only to discover so soon afterwards that it was as high as 35 per cent? This was a highly educated, highly articulate man who knew his job well, and who was at the height of his profession. The answer is that very few companies separate the consequential costs of poor quality from other accounting figures, which are usually lumped together as ledger coded overheads or direct costs. His 1½ per cent would have consisted of scrapped products, some rework but not by any means all, warranty claims, etc. However, each of these quality deficiencies, when they occur, create many other costs, often orders of magnitude higher than that which is accounted for. For example, most companies are aware of the value of stock, work in progress, and so forth.

In Western organisations, if a breakdown in plant or a process occur, it is normal to keep upstream processes running. Could one imagine a typical company closing down its entire production line because one of the final assembly operations has broken down? Usually, what happens is that all upstream operations continue to supply their output, with everything converging at the point of breakdown like a log jam. Of course, in a typical organisation there are multiple mini log jams occurring almost all the time. These create 'work in progress' which is a curious term since most of it isn't progressing at all. The same applies to 'working capital'; all too little of this is actually working either. A non-production example of quality-related costs which are not classified as such involves the R & D and Design departments of a well-known British company. In this case, the consultant was called in to conduct a company wide quality audit prior to assessment by a major customer. The company was aware that it had quality-related problems but it did not know what or where.

The audit indicated that in terms of manufacturing organisation, all appeared to be well. The same applied to supply quality. However, the company had altogether too many recorded customer complaints for such an apparently well-ordered organisation, and it was also losing market share rapidly. The customer complaints were analysed by using a matrix. A team comprising the consultant and three senior company personnel then identified which of the various functions was primarily responsible. If it was difficult to be certain, then ticks were put in the most likely areas. When all the complaints has been analysed in this way, the consequential cost for each was determined and assigned, and thus the proportion of quality-related cost could be estimated for each function.

Quite naturally, the engineering director responsible for the design function reached to the results. He was then askecd, how many of his 28 design staff were, at that time, actually engaged in creative work on new designs, and how many of them were doing reactive re-design of existing products for no other reason than that there was a known quality deficiency which should not have been there in the first place. He did not know the answer, but as it turned out, every single employed in that department was so engaged. How many companies, or finance personnel, would ever have considered putting the entire salaries of the design department down as a quality-related failure cost? Perhaps this was an extreme example, but the likelihood is that similar situations are all too common. In Dr. Meredith Belbin's famous paper 'Quality Calamities', published by the British Institute of Management, based upon research in the 1960s, he quotes very similar statistics. It appears that little has changed since those days. The cases quoted above are of course taken from manufacturing companies.

The more usual and effective means by which quality-related cost data is retrieved by companies who are successfully implementing Total Quality programmes is the brainstorming method. This participative technique can be used by a variety of different types of groups with a organisation, but at the top level, management can use it to identify the most important problems confronting the enterprise. Using brainstorming effectively, such groups have identified many hundreds of problems which can be resolved successfully using the improvement techniques.

The second step is to apply the Pareto principle in order to sort these problems and identify the important few. Further analysis will usually indicate that the biggest and most costly problems can only be resolved at the highest level in the organisation. This may come as an unwelcome surprise for many senior people since it becomes evident that the improvement process of Total Quality is one activity they cannot delegate.

Even a 50 per cent reduction of some of these problems may save more than solving a very large number of the smaller problems. Companies which have used this approach to failure cost identification have usually found that failure costs alone account for some 75 per cent of the total cost of poor quality. Having identified failure costs in this way, it then becomes possible to determine how much monitoring, inspection, and testing is carried out for no other reason that the existence of these failures. It is important to follow this sequence: failure identification first, followed by the identification of 'appraisal costs'. This is because the latter come in two categories:

1. Appraisal costs which will be there anyway, irrespective of failures.
2. Appraisal costs which are directly failure dependent. In other words, if the failures ceased to exist there would be no feed for the appraisal.

The third element of quality-related cost is represented by 'prevention costs'. This includes all the money spent on attempting to eliminate the failures. Again, as with appraisal cost, it is necessary first to identify failures, then to ask, 'how much do we spend attempting to reduce these failures?' This is because, with many prevention costs, it is difficult to judge whether they are just part of sound business practice, or are directly failure-related.

It can be seen that by selective attack on failure cost items, quality-related costs can be progressively reduced. Western companies which have seriously approached Total Quality in the past decade have found that quality-related costs can be reduced by some 50 per cent in 3-5 years through this approach. Using an investment appraisal approach, Total Quality can therefore be justified not merely on the belief that it will help increase market share; there are tangible, measurable, cold hard facts to justify its introduction.

For example, consider the following fictitious company:

Turnover	Rs. 100m
Capital employed	Rs. 50m
Cost of poor quality	Rs. 20m
Profit	Rs. 10m

In the normal way, assuming that the organisation is running close to capacity in order to double annual profit it would have to double the capital employed to Rs. 100m. If the statistics for quality improvement discussed above are any where near correct, then reducing the cost of poor quality by 50 per cent would also mean an increase of profit of Rs. 10m, since the saving in quality cost would go directly to profit. The cost of achieving this at Rs. 15 per cent of the cost of poor quality would be Rs. 3m. Even at 20 per cent this would still only be Rs. 4m, against the alternative of 50m through a more traditional approach.

Four Elements of Total Quality

Despite the obvious advantages of the new approach as evidenced by Japanese competitive success, the West in general still clings to some of the old ideas. Instead of Quality becoming everybody's job, as in Japan, it has been and still is seen by many as a kind of police force activity parallel to production rather than being inherently part of it. Throughout the 1970s and 1980s the advocates of this approach have stubbornly resisted any deviation from their belief that Quality Systems are the centre of the universe. Even now, when all the evidence points to the fallacy of this approach, and it has become self-evident that Total Quality along the lines of the Japanese experience is the only way to compete, they still argue that Quality Systems are the focal point of what they refer to as Total Quality 'Management.'

Of course systems and procedures are important of course there must be traceability, calibration, and so forth, but it does not matter how mnch focus one puts on systems, systems do not hold the pencil of the designer, not turn the handles on the machines. Quality control does not answer the phone every time a customer calls, nor it deliver the product or service to the customer. If the people involved do not really care, if they just do their jobs according to instructions, then it does not matter how much system you have, you will never remain in business in the face of international competition. Real quality is all about winning the hearts and minds of all of the people, and there has never been a quality control or quality assurance department capable of doing that. When the systems-focused approach has failed to produce the results, the advocates of this approach, instead of considering that they may be wrong have insisted that what is required is more of the same medicine with a larger spoon consequently, organisations which have suffered from this treatment have become more and more bureaucratic and people have become alienated from Quality, seeing it only as a negative self flagellation process rather than the stimulating, exciting concept that it really is.

In reality, systems are only one of four fundamental elements of Quality which are:

1. Systems. The principles of Quality Systems can readily be found in such documents as British Standard 5750; ISO 9000; Allied Quality Assurance Publications (AQAPs); Federal Drug Association of America Publications; and many variants created by some specific organisations, for example Ford QI.

Third Party Certification

This concept has been gaining popularity in the UK and Europe in recent years as a development of the Ministry of Defence 'Contractor Assessment' Scheme which started in June 1972 in the UK. Under these schemes, an organisation is assessed by an external audit team and judged on its systems and procedures, usually against the requirement of such standards as BS 5750, etc. The one merit of such schemes is that at least the assessed organisations, when they meet with the requirements, have a base level of organisation. This is all that can be claimed as a result of such assessments. They do not and cannot imply that the said company will produce high quality products. All that can be hoped for in that respect is that some of the worst disasters can be avoided. For example, it is unlikely that the Zeebrugge disaster would have occurred if the ferry company had operated to the spirit of BS 5750, because there would have been a procedure to ensure that the ship could not have left the harbour with the bow door open, or without the Captain knowing, which was apparently the case.

There is nothing which a third party audit can do under the terms of these standards which will put an organisation into a position of competitive advantage, which unfortunately is the mistaken, belief of many organisations who have enthusiastically introduced Quality Systems into their organisations. One company making gas appliances was recently awarded unqualified approval to BS 5750 and yet, on the admission of the plant manager, 40 per cent of the product was rejected on first submission to the customer, and 60 per cent reworked before it ever left the factory gates. The systems and procedures were apparently faultless; the processes were inadequate to say the least. Unfortunately, BS 5750 and its variants are not designed to evaluate processes. Even if this were changed, it is doubtful whether many of the auditors could be trained to conduct the process capability studies which would be necessary.

2. Processes. No matter how good the systems and procedures are, if the processes are not capable then quality cannot be achieved. Another fundamental difference between Japan and the West is the focus on process improvement and processes controL In Japan they have a saying, 'Look after the process and the product looks after itself!' Unfortunately in the West we lack the means to look after the processes, even if we had the desire. The reason is that to do so would require the harnessing of all the resources of all the people on a scale never dreamed of even today in Western organisations. In Japan, following the original introduction of Quality Circles in 1962, millions of workers have been educated, trained, and developed over the years to a level unheard of in the West.

Consequently, the only problem-solvers are the managers and engineers. The sheer volume of processrelated problems in even the simplest of organisations goes well beyond the capacity of such personnel, who in any case will be so involved in fighting day-to-day sporadic fires that in no way can they engage in consistent project-by-project process improvement on the scale of that being achieved in Japan.

3. Management. It is accepted that managers are also people!- but 'management' has a critical role to play in Total Quality. In fact this group can be regarded as the linchpin or power house in a successful programme. It is important to remember that managers as such do not make anything. Managers get results through people. Since managers can opt for several different styles of management, it follows that these must be studied very carefully if the performance of people is to be consistent with the exacting demands of Total Quality.

Basically, the two extremes of management style are:

(a) authoritarian

(b) participative

Of the two, the authoritarian style is the easier. Given a careful balance of threats, penalties, and regards, the approach makes few demands on the busy manager, and when span of control is wide, and the manager under pressure, he may feel that this is the only option available, even if he would prefer to manage in a more participative way. Participative management, on the other hand, at first sight would appear the opposite. If goals are to be achieved through loyalty, job satisfaction. and group activities, it is necessary to know the people on a more intimate level. This is demanding on the busy manager, and many would believe that the main resource of time is not available. Fortunately, experience with Quality Circles indicated that this could be a false impression, provided that the concept is introduced carefully, and is properly understood. Unfortunately in the West most companies appear to be either unwilling or incapable of doing this research first. The concept of Quality Circles is regarded to be of such great importance that much of this book is devoted to the subject.

Another aspect of the management role in Total Quality involves team-work. There was some discussion of the cross-functional problems related to the internal customer-supplier concept, and management 'professionalism'. This form of management involvement is the very essence of Total Quality and is very different from the systems approach controlled by the quality assurance department. The remedies to the problems identified by the managers using the Pareto principle referred to earlier will involve measures to:

(a) improve systems and procedures,

(b) improve processes,

(c) improve management organisation, or

(d) improve workers' methods.

The fact that it is the managers themselves who are finding the remedies is very different form those managers having remedies imposed upon them by quality assurance and others. the very fact that they have participated in identifying the theories of causes, testing the theories, and finding remedies, will motivate them to a degree far beyond that achieved through more traditional methods.

❑

2

Importance and Components of TQM

The acronym 'TQM' (short form of Total Quality Management) is perhaps one of the most widely used business expressions and has certainly been liberally used as a generic descriptor of the quality development efforts in recent years. In an academic sense, total quality is the integrated application of all the techniques described throughout this book with some kind of coherent implementation framework. In more simple language total quality management (TQM) can be thought of as 'involving' everyone and all aspects of an organisation in continuous improvement through team work'.

The application of all the various quality management techniques and systems and the involvement and motivation of the people within an organisation represent a significant management challenge requiring considerable sources. So then why so many organisations throughout the world identified quality development as the number one business priority?

The simple answer to this is again the competition. There is an old saying which states that in business there are only problems—'Customers and Competitors'. This message can be well summarized as:

* In the future there will be two kinds of company those who have gave implemented Total Quality and those who have gone out of business.

The timescales for this message are certainly not the same across all sectors of industry and commerce but the principle remains the same. As markets, products and technology mature then the basis of competitive advantage is quality. In the long term, orgánizations compete on the basis of their product or service quality; TOM is therefore seen as an approach to gaining or sustaining a competitive lead. We certainly have many examples of major (often international) organisations who have been able to demonstrate that quality development and business development go hand in hand. The other viewpoint, however, is that TOM is a 'winners' methodology only applicable to mature world-class organizations. If TOM is seen as being one end of the spectrum of quality development, then certainly: there is a requirement for such organizations to have reached a collective and individual state of maturity. TOM organizations need excellent systems, excellent techniques and, methods and above all, excellent people. The internal (in terms of cost base) and external, (in terms of market share) benefits of reaching the advanced state of quality development which is characterized by TOM are enormous.

All organizations, however, can benefit by quality development and the competitive pressures for quality in less mature markets or business section are just as important. Many of the total quality companies have reached their state of development due to a combination of:

(a) The pressure (usually cost driven) to improve internal effectiveness;

(b) The pressure (usually customer driven) to improve external performance.

Industries such as motor car manufacture; telecommunications, consumers electronics, etc., have faced intense international competition for many years and as a result many of the most mature, total quality organizations are to be found in these sectors. The need for quality development in other sectors of industry is just as important, however, and in many cases, it is the early recognition by senior management of the need to prioritize quality development that is the critical factor in ensuring long-term business viability.

For most organizations in the 1990s the only certainly about competition in the future is that is will become more fierce. As the European Union develops, as markets in South East Asia mature and as American businesses strive to retain their share of international markets so the competition for quality will intensify. In industry, many companies are now explicitly seeking fewer suppliers and increasingly selecting their supp.liers on their ability to produce quality products on time.

CHARACTERISTICS OF TOTAL QUALITY

So what does a total quality organization look? Certainly companies that have adopted TOM are:

(a) improvement orientated;

(b) customer focused;

(c) a quality driven.

But what do they actually do? What are the sort of activities which are talking place in TOM organizations that are absent from less developed ones? In simple terms these total quality organizations are using team-based quality management systems and techniques and they are involving their people in the process. The people in total quality organizatiors have two jobs:

(a) job number one is the work they do;

(a) job number two is finding ways of improving job number one.

This passion for improvement is part of the organization developing an improvement orientation. As the organization develops yet further and achieves a prevention orientation then a passion for the customer emerges and two rules are adopted.

(a) Rule number 1: the customer is always right.

(b) Rule number 2: if the customer is wrong see rule number 1.

In other words, the organizations always behaves in such a way as to promote excellence in customer service.

Internally, total quality organizations are characterized by their emphasis upon teamwork and a management style which is enabling rather than controlling. Quality improvement is seen as part of the process of running the business rather than as a separate activity. Decisions are made from the view point 'does this enhance quality' rather than simply 'does this cost less'.

Externally, total quality organizations are generally able to charge more for their products (research shows that typically this premium pricing is around 10%) and enjoy a greater customer loyalty. Everyone in the organization is focused upon the customer, seeking to understand and satisfy the requirements and monitoring and improving performance.

Quality Assessment Models

One of the main problems with quality development is that there is no single, prescriptive approach. The tools, techniques, systems and methods described throughout this book have to be applied in an appropriate way to suit the business priorities and the organizational challenge. The reason that there is no single route to quality development is that there is no single starting point nor a single destination. Certain elements of total quality, such as quality system implementation through ISO 9000, have a very prescriptive approach and a defined finishing point (accreditation). Similarly the stages in the implementation of SPC are well established and the final outcome is easily recognized (capable processes). Total quality management is a mature integration of systems, techniques and behaviour and consequently no single assessment criterion is available or appropriate.

There is a need, however, to be able to validate an organization's claim to total quality and also a need for companies to measure their own, comparative level of quality development. In response to these needs a number of international quality assessment mechanisms have been developed. The three most important of these are:

(a) the European Quality Award (primarily used in Europe);

(b) the Malcom Baldrige Award (primarily used in the United States);

(c) the Deming Award (primarily used in Japan).

The European Quality Award. The European Quality Award (EQA) is a quality assessment scheme developed and managed by the European Foundation for Quality Management (EFQM). The assessment criteria are divided into five basic areas as illustrate in Figure 1.

The EQA classifies the areas of assessment into either enablers or results. The enables are the business activities which are employed to prcduce the results. This represents an important approach to selfassessment by encouraging organizations to understood, appreciate and balance the efforts which are put in and the performances which result.

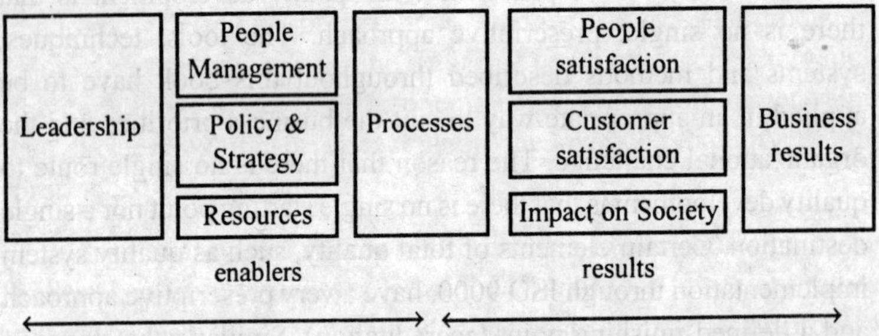

Fig. 1. The European Quality Award assessment model.

Each of the nine elements of the EQA model is assessed through a comprehensive self-appraisal questionnaire to measure and organization's quality development.

The Malcom Baldrige Award. The Malcom Baldrige Award (named after the US Secretary for Commerce) was established in 1987 to promote quality improvement and recognize achievement amongst American companies in the way the Deming Award had in Japan. The Baldrige Award assessment is based upon seven categories divided into leadership, system, measures and goals as shown in Figure 2.

In essence the Baldrige Award assesses qaality development by evaluating the foliowing:

(a) Leadership. Not only in terms of the role of senior managers in the management of quality but also the way in which quality policy is communicated throughout the organization and the way in which the quality responsibilities to the community are effected.

(b) Information and Analysis. The way in which information on quality performance is used to support the development of the organization, in particular competitive comparisons/ benchmarking and the company level use of data.

(c) Strategic Planning. The extent to which quality improvement plans are incorporated into the business planning process and the use and development of quality plans to sustain quality development.

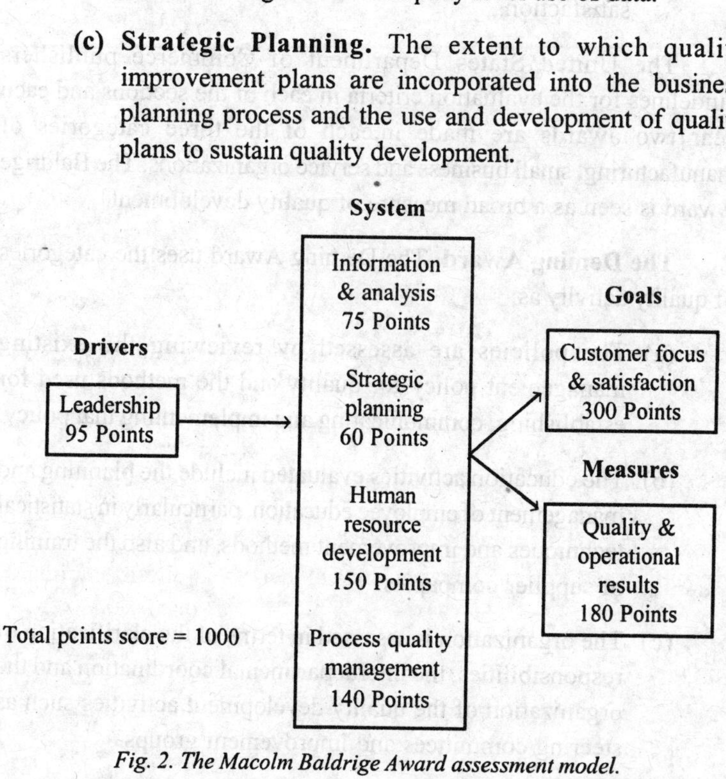

Fig. 2. The Macolm Baldrige Award assessment model.

(d) **Human Resource Development and Management.** The development involvement, education, performance, recognition and satisfaction of employees.

(e) **Process Quality Management.** Evaluation of the processes used within the company and the assessment of supplier organizations' processes to ensure ever-improving quality.

(f) **Quality and Operational Results.** Assessment of the quality performance of the organized terms and evaluation of how these results are used for comparison with competing companies.

(g) **Customer Focus and Satisfaction.** The most heavily weighted category which examines the relationships and commitment to the customers and evaluates customers satisfaction.

The United States Department of Commerce publishers guidelines for the evaluation criteria in each of the sections and each year two awards are made in.each of the three categories of manufacturing, small business and service organizations. The Baldrige Award is seen as a broad measure of quality development.

The Deming Award. The Deming Award uses the categories of quality activity as:

(a) The policies are assessed by reviewing the existing management policy for quality and the methods used for establishing, communicating and implementing that policy.

(b) The education activities evaluated include the planning and management of employee education, particularly in statistical techniques and improvement methods, and also the training of supplier compapies.

(c) The organization is assessed in terms of the clarification of responsibilities, the interdepartmental coordination and the organization of the quality development activities such as steering committees and improvement groups.

(d) The standardization category examines the establishment, and application of both systems and standards.

(e) The assessment of the collection and use of information within the organisation is evaluated in terms of the quality of communications and analysis of statistical data. The evaluation of the analysis methods also examines the utilization of statistical methods and the pinpointing of quality improvements.

(f) Under the heading of quality assurance the product and service development activities, including preventative measures are assessed together with customer satisfaction, process capabilities and the quality assurance system procedures.

(g) The assessment of control management includes a review of management systems, control points the application of control charts and the contribution to quality circles.

(h) Finally the organization's future plans are assessed in terms of problem reduction and longer-term planning.

Main Components of Total Quality

Whilst there is no single blueprint for how total quality should be developed within an organization, there are certain fundamental components which need to be present. In terms of approach TOM requires:

(a) senior management leadership;

(b) improvements orientation;

(c) customer focus;

(d) company-wide involvement;

(e) Ownership of the process;

(f) Emphasis on measurement and review;

(g) Commitment to training and education;

(h) Team work.

In terms of the activities these can be categorized into seven main components as shown in Fig 3.

Organizations need to develop in each of the areas shown in Fig 3 in order to exhibit total quality although progress in each of these elements will not necessarily be equal as organizations prioritize their development activities.

One of the key components is therefore ownership of the quality development process. Planning for total quality.requires people to understand the quality development process and to develop their own way forward on the basis of business priorities, customer needs and the prevailing management culture.

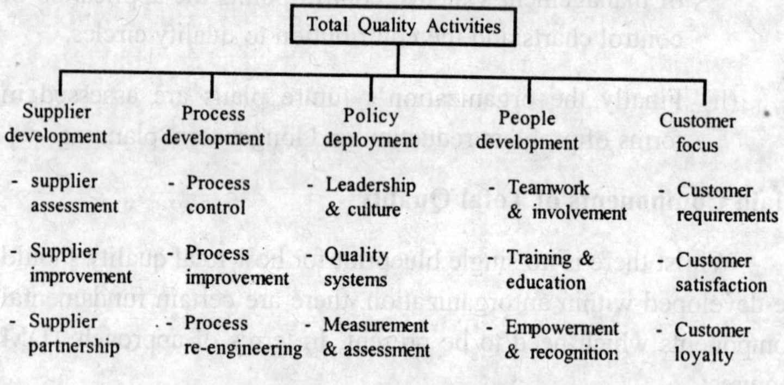

Fig 3. The main element of total quality development.

The Dimensions of Quality Development

Quality development is a three-dimensional process. Only if progress is made in all three aspects of development can total quality be used to describe the outcome. It is this problem of simultaneously progressing in three different dimensions that makes progress towards total quality so organizationally challenging. It is because each of the three dimensions supports the progress in the other two that this integrated approach is so important, as illustrated in Figure 4.

If progress is made only in developing the behaviour (people) then the quality development will be naive anq will not provide sustained improvement in business performance. Conversely if the developments only concern the systems and the techniques then the development will be brittle and when the business comes under pressure (say, from competitor reformance) then the attitudes may not support the organizational changes required. The skills required to simultaneously progress in each of these three dimensions are unlikely to be present in a single individual and hence company-wide involvement and a team-based approach are essential.

The management challenge with total quality is the simultaneous development of people, systems and techniques. The difficulty of this task requires sustained management commitment over a period extending beyond the next balance sheet. The long-term business benefits from the synergy of total quality are enormous in terms of operating efficiencies, customer satisfaction and employee motivation.

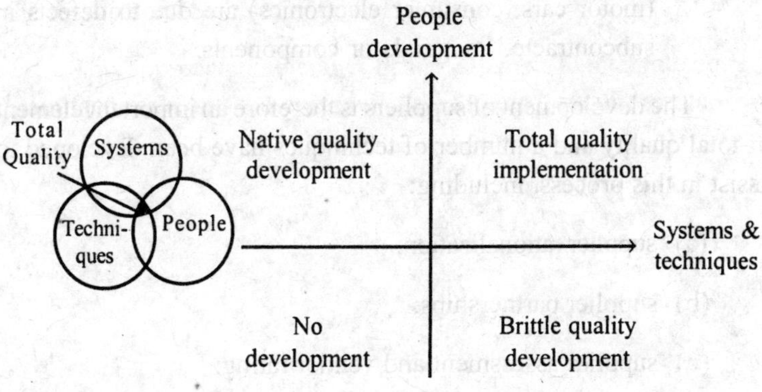

Fig. 4. The dimension of quality development

Supplier Development

The development towards total quality management involves the improvement of both internal and external business process as illustraied in Fig. 5.

The development of a customer orientation is therefore a critical aspect of total quality as described below in Section 5.4. Also important, however, is the development of suppliers particularly when considering that typically:

(a) over 50% of the manufacturing costs are due to raw materials and bought-in items:

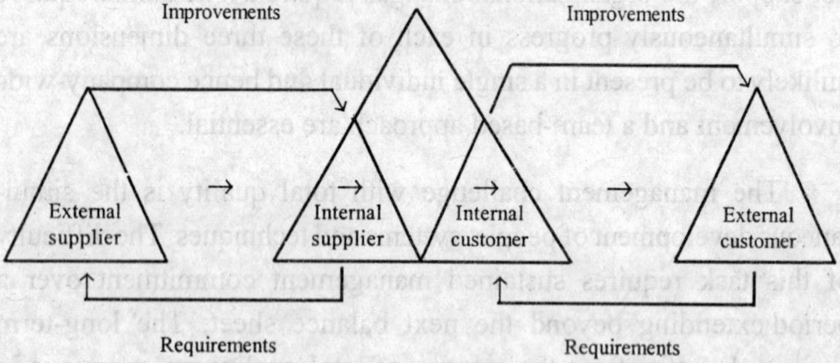

Fig. 5. The internal and external customer-supplier chain.

(b) over 60% of customer complaints on complex products. (motor cars, consumer electronics) are due to defects in subcontracted materials or components.

The development of suppliers is therefore an important element of total quality and a number of techniques have been developed to assist in this process, including:

(a) supplier rationalization;

(b) supplier partnerships;

(c) supplier assessment and vendor rating;

(d) supplier education;

(e) supplier awards schemes.

Supplier Rationalization. Supplier rationalization involves the adoption of fewer, better suppliers. Many organization as part of their quality development policy have reduced their supplier base typically by 60-80%. Instead of having four or five suppliers competing to supply on price, it is much better to have only one or two suppliers who optimize the oyerall cost of ownership of the raw material. Concern is sometimes expressed that having only one or two suppliers of a critical raw material of a component may leave the organization vulnerable both commercially and logistically. In most cases this is not the case as dealing with fewer suppliers enables much closer relationships to be developed and allows time for the effective planning of material supply (which generally has a greater impact upon the reliability of supply than does additional numbers of suppliers).

Supplier Partnerships. Supplier partnerships (sometimes referred to as co-makership) requires a much closer and earlier involvement of suppliers who should be viewed as an extension of one's own business rather than an outside organization with whom to 'do battle'. The foundation of partnership is a clear requirement as it is estimated that around 50% of the queries/rejections on incoming materials are due to unclear requirements. In order to develop organizations need to put proportionately more of their effort into clearly defining and agreeing requirements with suppliers ralher than the traditional adversarial relationship of inspection-rejection. Many quality developed organizations from improvement teams with their suppliers to clarify requirements, identify improvements and to implement corrective actions. As organizations mature to a prevention orientation. then suppliers are increasingly involved in the design process to ensure the requirements of their materials are clearly understood and that they are capable of providing reliable inputs to new products or services.

Supplier Assessment and Vendor Rating Systems. Supplier assessment and vendor rating systems are generally used as part of the development of a systems orientation and typical of the assessment approach to Supprier development is ISO 9000. Vendor rating schemes nonmally provide some form of scoring mechanism based upon the supplier's performance in terms of product quality, delivery, service and price. Typical vendor rating schemes are shown below.

	Quality	*Delivery*	*Service*	*Price*
Make out of	100	100	100	100
Weighting factor	0.7	0.15	0.05	0.1
Supplier categories	A = 80 and above			
	B = 50 to 80			
	C = Below 50			

Typical Vendor Rating Scheme

Supplier Education. Supplier education take the form of seminars and workshops in which suppliers are made aware of the methods, techniques, requirements and expectations of the purchaser. Typical of this approach are supplier training programmes in the application of statistical process control whereby supply companies are encouraged to use statistical methods and to dermonstrate process capability.

Supplier Awards. Supplier awards are used to reward suppliers, who have achieved certain quality, service and delivery goals during the year. This recognition can be used by suppliers to promote their products or services with other customers.

Total Quality Management Implementation Methodologies

As stated above, there is no single route to total quality because there is no single starting point. As yet, there is no internationally recognized "standard" approach to quality development although it is possible to identify key implementation factors which distinguish one approach to TQM from another. Research has shown that the three key factors are:

(a) organization;

(b) approach;

(c) motivation.

The organization of the total quality implementation programme can take a number of different forms. Among the critical organizational decisions are:

(a) How should the TQM process be steered?

(b) What type of improvement teams should be employed?

(c) What should be the mechanisms for creating culture change?

The approach adopted to the implementation of total quality focuses upon the main vehicles used in changing the way quality is managed within a company. Among the approaches which can be adopted are:

(a) techniques let—focusing upon the application of tools such as problem-solving, statistical process control or quality function deployment;

(b) 'guru' led—whereby 'established' programmes generally promoted by consultants who may have observed a number of quality development programmes and identified generic implementation approaches;

(c) vision led—in which the mission for the organization (for example, customer satisfaction) is enthusiastically communicated to all employees and becomes a focus for the quality developments within the company.

The motivation for the total quality implementation can be provided from a number of (not necessanly mutually exclusive) sources including:

(a) leader driven—normally from the chief executive;

(b) champion driven—normally the quality manager;

(c) quality council driven—led by a group of individuals;

(d) corporately driven—from external corporate level objectives.

The final major influence on the implementation of total quality is the timescale adopted by the organization. This timing element is in fact perhaps the most critical dimension of implementing total quality. The two most commonly observed pitfalls in terms of implementation timescales are as follows:

(a) Organizations employ a cautious, gradual approach whereby the understanding of the principles of total quality are allowed to slowly permeate down through the organization (usually in the form of training or awareness seminars) and the cultural changes are allowed to occur over some 'natural' timescale. Typically such an approach begins to peter out after about two years as the 'critical mass' needed for quality development never materializes and therefore the expected benefits are not realized and senior management enthusiasm wanes.

(b) Organizations employ a vigorous, breakneck approach whereby bold improvement objectives are set and employees are required to immediately become involved in the quality development process. Such an approach is often driven by some form of major organizational crisis (for example, market share or financial performance disasters) and total quality is seen as some form of panacea. With this type of implementation timescale, typically the quality development process 'stalls' and the discontinuity between the traditional approach to managing quality and the newly implemented total quality ideology come into conflict.

Organizations have an innate inertia and therefore the process of driving the change towards total quality should be applied at a rate which is fast enough to prevent the development grinding to a halt, but not too fast to create an insurmountable 'back-pressure'.

❐

3

Quality Planning

Quality planning is the business management portion of the total quality control effort, responsible for formulating the policies, procedures, techniques, and detailed plans necessary to achieve all quality control objectives. Time, in its November 6, 1964, issue, stated that "U.S. industry spends $35 billion a year on quality control." The magnitude of the business of quality control may surprise some people, but to professional quality control personnel it is a fact of life simultaneously appealing and frustrating. It is appealing because it offers an obvious professional challenge. It is frustrating because the much higher total cost of quality is still growing despite the efforts of the quality control profession to reduce it.

In addition to establishing the basic plan for the maintenance and improvement of product quality, planning for quality is aimcd directly at reducing, or at least minimizing, the total cost of quality. There are three ways by which total quality costs might be held to a minimum by the quality control organization; these are best envisioned as the three basic objectives of quality planning. The first is to make maximum use of available quality control effort; that is, to judiciously place the available controls where they can offer the most protection or prevention for the dollars spent. The second objective of quality planning is to exert maximum influence on the planning of others in an all-out effort to make the control of quality and the prevention of errors an inherent part of all company operations. The third objective is to review the results of the total effort periodically and present them to management in such a way that improvements can be forthcoming.

Visible evidence of the work of quality planning can be found in inspection plans, in documentation systems, in quality status reports, in procedures for the control of quality, and in the attitude of other planning groups with respect to the importance of quality control. When the total scope of the quality control effort is insufficient to support a separate planning function, the work of quality planning must be done by the available quality supervisors. No matter how small the total effort, the value of quality control will depend on how well it is organized as a function and how well it is utilized in a changing business environment. The quality planning output that must be constantly sought is the one which provides today's blueprint for success.

Taking inspection plans—the major task of quality planning—as a starting point, the business management of quality control begins to take shape. If planning for inspection is not effective, the entire function of quality control is ill-founded. All inspections should be carried out in accordance with a set plan and with established standards. The most effective inspection plans are those that are built or integrated into the manufacturing plans for a product. Such an integration of planning is the best guarantee that inspection will become an integral part of the manufacturing operation rather than a delayed side-effect of questionable significance. The only acceptable alternative to complete integration is to establish fixed points within each manufacturing process at which time individually planned inspections must be conducted.

When planning an individual inspection, whether it be a part of the manufacturing plan or a separate entity, many factors must be considered. A planned inspection is essentially a trade-off between protecting from errors and risking failure to find errors. The first factor to be considered begins with the engineering and specification requirements for the product, from which significant product parameters can be determined. The next factor is tooling to determine which significant characteristics will not be subject to excessive variation. Finally, there is the degree of manufacturing discipline that can be expected on the basis of past performance and problem history.

Once the parameters to be inspected have been defined, the next step in planning is to determine where to perform the inspections. To determine the best point within a manufacturing process for performing a particular inspection, the primary concern should be costs both inspection and manufacturing costs. From a manufacturing viewpoint, inspections should be performed at the earliest possible point in the process. This will preclude adding the cost of ensuing manufacturing operations to a part that may have to be scrapped or complicating the repair cycle for parts that can be repaired. From an inspection viewpoint, it is generally easier and more desirable to perform all inspections at the end of the line. In some cases, however, an inspection station at this point could be either costly or downright impossible. It would be costly, for example, if a duplicate of the manufacturing setup were required for inspection. It would be impossible if succeeding manufacturing operations covered up the area to be inspected, as is likely to happen in assembly operations.

The last step in planning is to determine how much inspection to perform. Certain critical parameters such as material condition for aircraft structural parts will always require 100 percent inspection and verification; there simply is no other way to determine a soft part except through failure in use. Dimensional errors, on the other hand, can be discovered in assembly. All critical parameters which will have no chance to be discovered in the future should require 100 percent inspection. All other parameters when the quantity of production permits can and should be sample inspected, although exceptions are usually made in specific cases where the future costs of repairs that would be incurred demands 100 percent protection.

Where the nature of the work would not normally require inprocess inspection such as the production of sheet-metal parts its incorporation on a small scale can help to prevent or minimize losses. In such cases, the in-process inspection performed is referred to as "surveillance" or "audit type" inspection; the extent of this additional effort should depend on the overall quality level of the work performed in the area. The criteria should be based on the results of final inspection of the total output. Planning should be specifically aimed at using today's knowledge to prevent, or at least to reduce, the production of scrap and rework.

In addition to direct cooperation with the manufacturing planners, initial certification of an entire manufacturing process can improve the quality level where people, equipment, material, and procedures are concerned. This begins with the physical and chemical certification of all raw material and with the establishment of controls to maintain its consistency. Next comes the validation of equipment and procedures through a complete examination of results, using laboratory support and any other means available to determine whether acceptable results can and should be produced. Finally, there is the certification of personnel in the proper use of equipment and procedures.

An equally important ingredient for each inspection plan is the documentation of results. In most cases, the result of an inspection is merely an official indication of the fact that an inspection was performed. But it should also indicate when acceptability could not be determined by referring to the rework or rejection tag that was prepared. The lone exception to this rule occurs when actual measurements must be recorded, as is sometimes required by engineering or contract personnel. Whenever possible, inspection results should appear on the original documentation for the work, such as the manufacturing process plan.

In many areas of industry, planning for inspection will not be come more complicated than the steps discussed so far as previously stated, it can be accomplished without a separate quality planning organization and with little additional documentation. But there are areas of industry where the documentation needs alone make the task infinitely more demanding and complex. For example, in areas where equipment is being assembled from many component parts, documentation of serialized component accountability and previous inspection or test history for each component is commonly found.

As assemblies become larger and more complex and particularly when they proceed into a test and use phase the need for the continuous availability of innumerable documentation requirements grows proportionately.

To meet the challenge of complex data requirements that are needed simultuneously, a means of quality documentation has evolved. This device-known as a quality logbook-appears to have started back in the early days of aircraft production. A logbook is the accumulation into one large package of specific pertinent data combined with information on the status of supplementary data physically filed elsewhere. Organized and indexed for the convenience of its many users, it may include in separate sections such documents and items of information as certificates of completion, acceptance summary report and configuration status, modification status, serialized component accountability, critical component accountability, calibration status and records, maintenance status, time-sensitive component records, test status and test procedure accountability, material review board decisions, discrepancy and failure history and status, and any specific customer-required documentation. The use of logbooks, where applicable, has simplified the overall quality planning effort and has improved inspection's ability to control total equipment status on a current basis. Without logbooks as they have been developed, the task would be far more cumbersome and costly, and timeliness would be almost impossible.

Like so many other developments throughout industry, the most recent refinements in quality documentation involve the use of computers. Many of the specific items in a quality logbook are now entered in the form of tab runs. In some cases, the entire log has been replaced by a tab run. Also, in certain sectors of industry, the growing importance of manufacturing process controls to longer life guarantees for products has led to the development of mechanized quality data. Here the computer is being utilized to schedule the many different inspection requirements as well as to detennine their status and verify the results. The next development may involve having the computer analyze the variations and trends in the results of process control inspections with an eye toward making more effective use of the results.

Inspection planning is not limited to manufacturing and test areas. It must become involved in all areas where work will be performed, including development work and, in particular, the work of planning. Whenever work can affect end-product quality, some inspection should be required and, therefore, inspection plans will be necessary. Integrating these inspection needs with the basic planning and the development of the work involved has already been stated as a basic objective of quality planning. In certain cases, however, quality planning must become integrated early enough in the flow of events that inspection will not inadvertently be guilty of delaying ensuing operations. For example, purchase orders must contain necessary quality requirements prior to their being placed with a vendor, and receiving inspection plans must be initiated prior to receipt of the material.

In the area of shipping, receiving, and storage, inspection plans follow requirements which differ from those followed in production. Shipping inspection is primarily concerned with the method of pack and the final handling of accepted material. Receiving inspection is a trade-off between the effectiveness of vendor quality control and the hazard of defective material in storage. In most cases, it may involve sampling plans. Storage inspection is concerned with the handling, protection, and rotation of stock, the removal of obsolete or discrepant material, and the accurate identification of all material.

Inspection plans for the development and building of production tools should be drawn up in exactly the same manner as are those for the development and building of the products of these tools. Historically, lack of sufficient inspection control in this important area has constituted a costly oversight for many companies. The ultimate cost of a single, fundamental error in a production tool can in many instances easily exceed the total cost of tool inspection, as can the expense incurred when a tool fails because of lack of maintenance. For this reason, all critical tools require a plan for periodic reinspection or formal incorporation into the company maintenance system. Of the utmost importance in this area are the tools and equipment that are used for determining acceptability.

Among the problems are the handy little gadgets commonly known as "assist tools" or "testing aids" which seem to pop up out of nowhere. The quality problem usually associated with them is that they are uncontrolled; that is, these gadgets do not appear on any official documentation and so are overlooked in updating production tools or test equipment to the latest product change. While they do not always cause problems, their uncontrolled existence makes them liable to do so, and they often do.

Where a requirement exists for the training and certification of inspection and other quality personnel, this task is usually assigned to quality planning because it already possesses the detailed knowledge needed to handle the necessary inspection planning. For the most part, its responsibility will begin with the establishment of training and certification requirements and end with the granting of certificates and the maintenance of certification records. It is not uncommon for this responsibility to be extended as well into total administration of the company's skill certification programme, including such processes as soldering, welding, X-ray, dye penetrant inspection, and so on. Requirements for skill certification are sometimes established by company practice, but for the most part they are imposed by contract. Quality planning's role in company sponsored certification programmes is a natural outgrowth of its knowledge of the need for and the value of certification in establishing work disciplines and thereby preventing problems.

In its unique role as business manager for quality control, planning must develop a close working relationship with the broadest possible spectrum of company activity. This is especially significant for large, complex companies, but it is essential even to the smallest. Wherever people become quality-conscions, companies profit. In each area it touches, quality planning properly contributes to all planning which can affect product quality and acts in a liaison capacity where a continuous relationship is required. As the emissary of quality control, it helps to sell total quality concepts and to bring back knowledge useful in promoting better quality control relations.

In the area of configuration control, for example, quality planning usually provides the quality control portion of the total plan and then stays on to insure that each modification work package leaving the area fulfills all requirements for quality. In this way, inspection merely has to verify the work and certify satisfactory completion back to configuration management; it should never have to become involved in problems of incomplete engineering, retest requirements, or contractual legality.

In association with material review procedures, quality planning should work with the responsible organization to establish plans and procedures for the salvage of useful material from items consigned to scrap and for the actual disposition of all waste. It should also work with engineering to establish and validate a standard repair manual. Standard repairs are used to eliminate the necessity of appealing to a formal material review board and, in addition, to serve as a guide for the work to be done. Whenever repairs are inherent in the nature of the work such as those associated with certain welding processes a standard repair manual should be used to save time and to provide consistent criteria and methods. Quality planning normally works with contract personnel in preparing plans for the verification of initial compliance with all contractual specifications. Such verification is a one-time inspection requirement designed to prove that the intent of each specification has been incorporated in both engineering design and manufacturing plans for the product. It is used whenever a verification requirement is imposed by contract. In such instances, quality planning determines inspection's role and prepares specification compliance inspection logs. Similarly, quality planning also works with the publications staff to detennine and provide the inspection plans necessary to insure the completeness and accuracy of all contractually required handbooks or other publications.

The magnitude and importance of the total quality control effort make cooperation between quality planning and other company planning groups mandatory. For programmes of the systems management type, quality control should participate in programme planning and should provide actual acceptance status. This close relationship creates many opportunities for learning new planning techniques, which in turn are used to improve quality control planning. It also creates an opportunity to influence the thinking of other organizations with regard to their responsibility for meeting all established quality requirements. Finally, it enables quality planning to contribute to company programmes in a strictly business sense. No single company department has a monopoly on all the best business practices, and quality planning's unique experience shauld place it in a position to provide many good ideas.

The type of contribution that an objective quality control organization is capable of making can be seen in a change that was designed and sold by quality planning in a major test activity at Cape Kennedy. Prior to quality planning's action, hundreds of components, meters, and gauges commonly were ratated periodically through a calibration laboratory. The first improvement was to have all meters and gauges not used for acceptance measurements marked "for indicating purpose only" and removed from the calibration schedule. Next, a plan was devised by which entire systems, including all previously calibrated components, could now be calibrated in place, with the frequency of calibration established as an integral part of the system check-out prior to launching. In addition to the obvious dollar savings, ultimate benefits included sustaining calibration integrity through the elimination of unnecessary handling and transportation, scheduling calibration requirements as close to the time of need as passible, and requiring calibration only when called for by a real need such as a scheduled launching. This approach to system calibration should be applicable to any major test activity.

Despite the importance of the work already described, one particular responsibility may well constitute quality planning's most important job. That is to design and establish the basic data system for all quality documentation the valuable objective evidence of company performance from origin and flow through distribution, accumulation into a useful data center, and final retention. The magnitude of this task obviously varies with the size of the total activity, but its importance remains constant. When the quality of a company's product is challenged, the company's quality control effort is valueless unless it can produce evidence of its useful existence.

A quality data center should be organized in such a way that, first, it receives all pertinent documentation. Next, it should be prepared to reproduce and distribute copies of any specific data required by other company groups or customer agencies. Then it should file all documentation in a manner designed to facilitate convenience and timeliness of retrieval, including cross-reference files where necessary. For major programmes, it should include a system for the control and status of all programme-required documentatian which clearly and currently identifies completions and delinquencies, or so-called open items.

The value of a quality data center is not limited to the insurance that it provides for company performance. The parade of performance history that passes through this center can be even more useful in terms of identifying areas most in need of improvement. For this purpose, many different types of reports can be prepared, at varying frequencies, for management's use. From the data received, quality planning is generally best able to analyze the results and to prepare the necessary documents. Typical are reports on quality-level ratings, trend analyses, data on costs related to quality, and summary reports of total results.

Quality planning has its fair share of special administrative responsibilities, including stamp control and administration of a technical library. A variety of quality stamps are in constant use, each one representing the personal "signature" of the person to whom it is issued. Absolute control of all quality stamps is essential to the maintenance of personal integrity for the entire inspection function. When a technical library is necessary, it is developed and maintained for the use of all quality control personnel. It usually contains standards manuals of all kinds, numerous government specifications, and other pertinent reference material associated with specific quality requirements. Quality control personnel are often accused of digging up requirements that are unnecessary, illogical, and invalid. The fact is that quality control personnel generally do the best job of learning what the company's commitments are, and this knowledge can be used just as effectively to eliminate unnecessary tasks as to enforce necessary ones.

Other administrative responsibilities of quality planning include the preparation of all quality control estimates for change proposals and new business proposals, as well as the preparation of statements of work in support of the estimates. When its sheer magnitude is considered the business of quality control can no longer be satisfied with seat-of-the-pants methods. It must be based on requirements to which a company is specifically committed and on those internal controls that are necessary to profitable performance. One of the most necessary tools sometimes lacking in quality control circles today is a good set of quality control estimating standards. Companies using gradually descending ratios soon find themselves in trouble.

Intimate knowledge of changing quality requirements is directly related to the most fundamental and necessary planning function for which quality planning is responsible: the preparation and maintenance of the quality procedures manual. This manual is and to establish the policies and procedures for the work that the quality control function is responsible for performing. Because it can have the greatest effect on the cost of the quality control function the manual must be kept constantly in tune with the changing requirements of a dynamic business environment. It should be used as a baseline for normal inputs to proposals and for major quality control system changes when the business picture so demands.

The importance of the quality manual to the business of quality control dictates that the first procedure to be written be one that governs the control and use of the manual itself and the manner in which it interfaces with other quality control documents and management directives. This particular procedure should establish the generation, description, structure, nomenclature, flow, and implementation of each type of document necessary to the total conduct of the quality control business. In its preparation, one will do well to keep the number of different documents to a realistic minimum; too many directions may have the same detrimental effect on performance that too many cooks have on the broth.

A typical quality manual contains a procedure for each individual function toward which quality control has a responsibility or for which it alone is responsible. An optimum procedure delineates responsibility to a fine degree but carefully avoids excess detail to prevent unnecessary complexity and confusion. The manual also contains a forms section to identify and control each form used by quality control and to provide instructions for its use.

To assure validity for the quality manual, all procedures must be correlated with the manual of company procedures, where such as document exists. Satisfactory performance can never be realized If these two conflict. On the other hand, routine incorporation of quality requirements into all appropriate company procedures enhances the value of a quality control programme. This leaves no doubt where the responsibility for certain requirements lies.

At this point, the manual is ready to be enforced. It should contain everything necessary for the ordinary conduct of all quality business and thus should be used as the basis for the initial training of all quality control personnel. In addition, if enforcement is to be realistic and timely, the manual must allow for quick changes. A procedure change system similar to that used by engineering for drawing changes can serve this purpose. Finally, the manual must allow for the proper authorization of abnormal work, which might include such items as temporary additional tasks involved in specific corrective action; work peculiar to a certain programme but not generally required; and such changing administrative requirements as a revised membership list for the material review board or new overtime limitations. This can best be accomplished through a system of quality control management directives which reference the procedures affected and clearly define the changes. When used in conjunction with the manual, such directives should be the only other document of an administrative type needed to conduct all quality control business.

Controlling the budget constitutes the remaining broad function of running the business of quality control. It involves the establishment and justification of budget requirements as well as the control of expenditures. Justifying manpower, travel, overtime, and other monetary needs for quality control will be easy or difficult in direct proportion to management's understanding or lack of appreciation for the quality control function. It is quality planning's responsibility and a critical one continually to reprogramme budget requirements as necessary and to develop improved justification methods and cost standards. Procedures for the distribution, use and accounting of the budget complete this responsibility.

Quality planning must be dedicated to the reduction of paperwork yet at the same time be trained to take each directive seriously. It should be responsible for reviewing every company or programme document that could have an effect on the quality control programme. From this review, it can identify the need for quality control action and insure that this action is planned and incorporated into the appropriate activity. Quality control of course, does not create requirements; its job is to learn them, then take whatever action is necessary to make sure that quality problems never embarrass the company.

Customer involvement in quality control begins with the business management functions that have been described as the business of quality planning. Quality planning, therefore, provides the pricipal liaison with the customer and has the first opportuninty as well as the obligation-to develop good customer relations. When this close association of quality planning and customer is developed with mutual objectivity, the business of quality can be conducted with a minimum of customer Interference.

As organizations mature in the way in which quality is managed, so the emphasis changes from the control of the process to the design. Designing products and processes in which quality problems are prevented rather than detected is not only more cost effective, but also produces more consistent products and services. The application of quality management tools and techniques to the design of products or processes is generally termed advanced quality planning or quality engineering.

The emphasis in quality engineering is upon designing robust products and processes which are tolerant to inherent variabilities within the manufacturing process and the application of the product or service. These variations to which the design needs to be tolerant are often termed noise. There are three basic forms of noise to which the product or service may be subjected.

(a) outer noise (such as variations in environmental conditions);

(b) inner noise (variation due to deterioration or wear within the product);

(c) between product noise (variation from piece to piece due to imperfections in the manufacturing process).

The robustness of the design is therefore the stability of the product to remain within specification when subject to the inherent noise factors. The signal to noise ratio is a term that is used to describe specifications and the noise factors. Robust design is achieved through a prevention-orientated approach in which both products and processes are designed to be tolerant to the noise variation expected.

The application of advanced quality planning techniques is part of the third stage of quality development in which these prevention-orientated techniques dominate. In order to apply these techniques an organization needs to have clearly defined customer requirements, a clear understanding of material and process variability an established culture of teamworking and a passion for improvement. Such organizations are therefore already mature in terms of their quality.

development and this prevention orientation represents an advanced stage of development.

Elements of Advanced Quality Planning

The prevention-orientated approach to quality management is one in which the emphasis is put upon the product and process design activities rather than product inspection or process control activities. This distinction between *on-line* quality activities (such as acceptance) sampling or statistical process control) and *off-line* quality activities (such as quality f!Jnction deployment or design of experiments) reflects the changing emphasis during the quality development of an organization. Rather than evaluating the product or service after it has been produced, the initial stage of development focuses instead upon controlling the production process and finally the emphasis changes to the design activities with the techniques of advanced quality planning.

One of the key contributors to the techniques of advanced quality planning was Dr. Genichi Taguchi. In terms of the role of quality management in the design process, Taguchi identified three principal aspects of design:

1. System design;

2. Parameter design;

3. Tolerance design.

The system design relates to the technical knowledge and background necessary to specify the complete functional design. This process involves relating the customers' requirements to product functionality; and the key technique for providing system design is quality function deployment as described later.

Parameter design is used to establish the process parameters which need to be used to reduce the sensitivity of the design to noise. The key prevention orientated technique for establishing the optimized settings for process parameters is design of experiments as described later. The objective of parameter desigs is to identify process settings which produce robustness to noise factors and increases the signal to noise ratio.

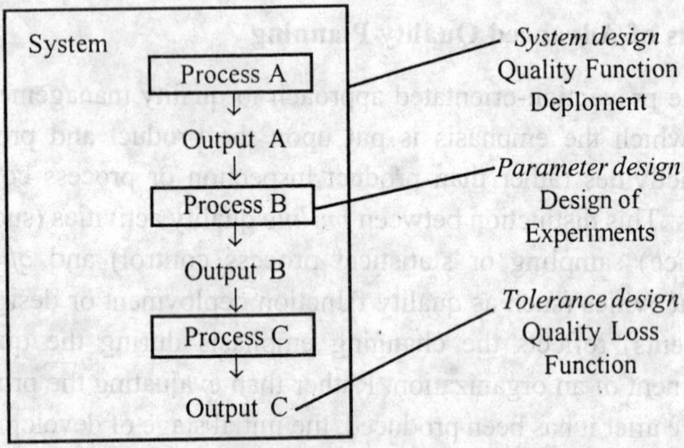

Fig. 1. System, parameter and tolerance design

Tolerance design optimizes the allowable range for the product or process settings by identifying the balance between the costs of conformances and the costs of non-conformance. Traditionally, establishing the tolerances in the design of products or processes is done by some form of technical convention and does not attempt to optimize the settings. Quality loss function is the primary advanced quality planning technique for establishing tolerance design.

The relationship between system, parameter and tolerance design is illustrated in Figure 1.

Benefits of Advanced Quality Planning

The application of the techniques of advanced quality planning represent an investment in prevention which in turn reduces the overall cost of quality. The cost benefits from the application of quality management techniques to the design of the product or service arise from:

(a) reduced costs of non-conformances due to more robust designs which are more in line with the customer's requirements and more tolerant of noise factors;

(b) reduced need for modifications to the product or process specifications which are generally increasingly costly as the product or service moves from the design stage to the manufacturing stage to the application by the customer stage.

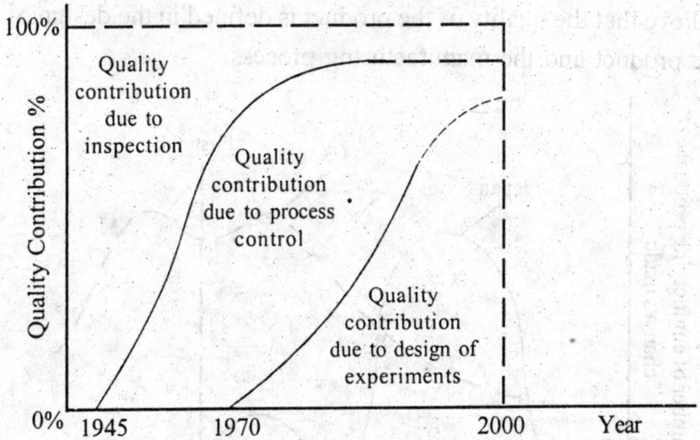

Fig. 2. The changing contribution to quality development of quality management techniques in Japan.

The diminishing returns from devoting increasing organizational effort to inspection and verification activities encourages companies to become improvement orientated to reduce process variation and to solve the basic problems which cause defects. Eventually improvements in products and processes which are not robustly designed also exhibit diminishing returns and the organization needs to place more emphasis upon the initial design of the product or process by adopting a prevention-orientated approach through the application of advanced quality management tools. The evolution of this process in terms of the changing emphasis in the way quality development is managed is illustrated by the experiences of Japanese manufacturers shown in Figure 2.

Once manufacturing variability is minimized and the quality system is effectively implemented then the major area of quality development opportunity available for most organizations is improved product and process design. Typically for mature companies, where the processes are in control and the systems and procedures well established, then the quality of the product or service is determined largely by the design process (rather than the manufacturing process). Many manufacturers of electronic equipment or motor cars now believe that the quality of the product is defined in the design of both the product and the manufacturing process.

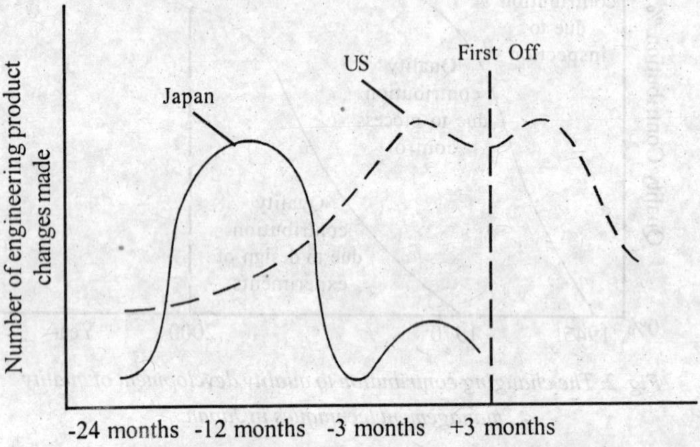

Fig. 3. Comparison of enginering design changes between Japanese and US companies.

The benefits associated with better designs which require fewer subsequent modifications is illustrated in the comparison between Japanese and US manufacturers during the 1980s shown in Figure 3.

Having to make changes to a new product (for example, a new soap powder) after the product has been marketed and launched is not only technically expensive (in terms of the changes to process specifications) but is even more costly in terms of the impact in the market place.

System Design and Customer Requirements

One of the most demanding organizational quality challenges is to design products or services which actually meet the requirements of the customer. The problem often encountered is that the requirements of the customer are very often expressed in a format and a language very different from the product or process specifications used by the designer. For example, the customer-important characteristics of a biscuit (texture, appearance, taste, etc.) are very often not quite the same as the product specification (weight, moisture content, colour). Similarly the customer's requirement from a life insurance policy (reliability, ease of claiming for next of kin, etc.) are expressed in different terms to the specification of the insurance policy (actuarial rates, maturity benefits, etc.). The obstraction needed from a system designer to convert customer requirements (often expressed in subjective; qualitative terms) into product performance (usually defined objectively in quantitative terms) is considerable. The primary quality management technique to assist in this process and make the translation of customer requirements more systematic is quality function deployment (QFD).

The basic objective of OFD is to systematically relate the requirements of the customer (termed the 'voice of the customer, to the features of the product (termed the 'counterpart characteristics'), QFD relates these characteristics through a set of matrices which build to form the 'house of quality' so called because of the structure of the way in which the relationships are represented. Having established the relationship between the product characteristics and the customer's requirements, the OFD technique then evaluates the relative importance of the requirements, compares performance with (potential) competitors' performance and then deploys the important requirements down to the sub-components and to the manufacturing processes. Overall OFD generates four different diagrams or matrices as illustrated in Figure 4.

The first of these matrices is termed the planning matrix which relates the voice of the customer to the specific counterpart characteristics.

The second of the matrices is the deployment matrix which decomposes the product characteristic requirements down to the requirement of the major components. This is a mechanism for ensuring the customer's requirements are deployed down to the characteristics of the components of the product and are reflected in the component design.

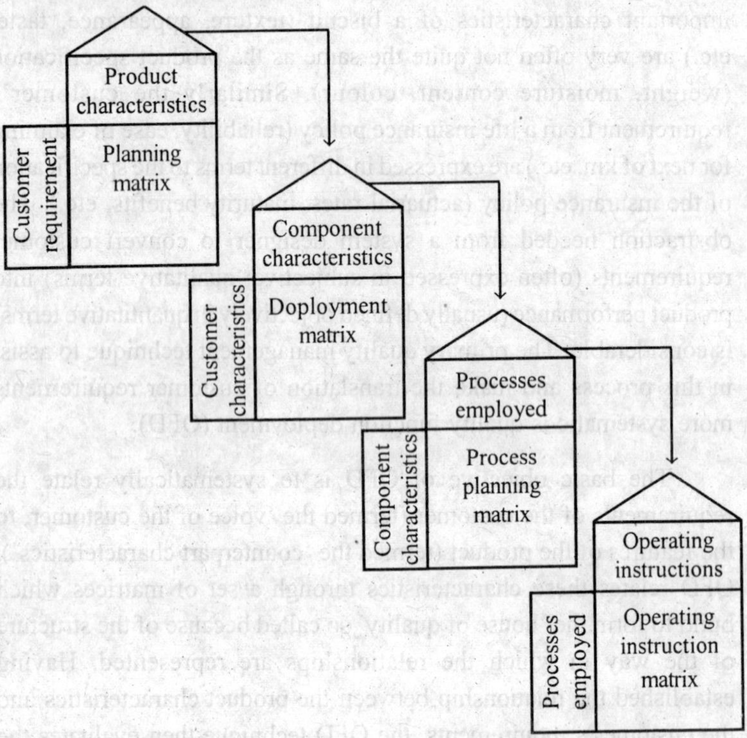

Fig. 4. The four matrices documented in quality function deployment.

The third of the matrices is termed the process planning and quality control chart. It identifies the critical control points which ensure that the product and sub-component characteristics are controlled during the manufacturing process. Control points represent those aspects of the process which need to be checked to ensure the correlations between the product of component characteristics and the customer requirements are maintained.

Finally the operating instructions matrix further deploys the critical product and component parameters down to the operating instructions used by process operators.

This overall approach of integrating customer requirements to the product characteristics process controls and operating procedures represents a rigorous methodology for product systems design.

Definition of Quality Loss Function

The approach to quality promoted by Taguchi based upon quality of a product being considered as: 'the (minimum) loss imparted by the product to the society from the time the product is shipped'. From this definition Taguchi represented the quality loss as a quadratic function—that is the loss varies with the square of the deviation of the quality characteristic, as illustrated in Figure 5.

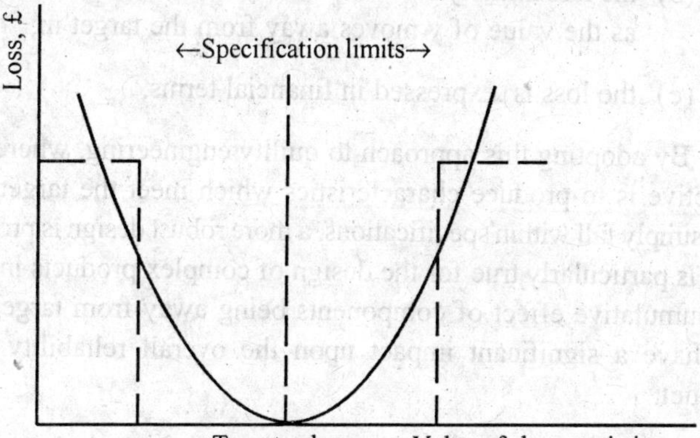

Fig. 5. The quality loss function.

The quality loss function is therefore given by:

$$L(y) = K\,(y - m)^2$$

Where L(y) = the monetary loss per unit of product when the quality characteristic is equal to the value y,

y = the value of the characteristic (for example, length, concentration, voltage, etc.)

m = the target value of the characteristic y;

k = the proportionality constant which depends upon the financial significance of the product to society.

The expression for loss implies a continuous function whereby the loss increases as soon as the value of the characteristic varies from the target. This approach is to be contrasted with the traditional view of quality in which the cost of non-conformance is only incurred once the product characteristic falls outside the specification limits.

The features resulting from the quality loss function being considered as a quadratic expression are:

(a) the loss is minimized when y = m;

(b) the loss initially increases slowly but increases more rapidly as the value of y moves away from the target m;

(c) the loss is .expressed in financial terms.

By adopting this approach to quility engineering, whereby the objective is to produce characteristics which meet the target rather than simply fall within specifications, a more robust design is produced. This is particularly true for the design of complex products in which the cumulative effect of components being away from target value can have a significant impact upon the overall reliability of the product.

The quality loss function also enables tolerance design to be undertaken from the viewpoint of the overall loss to society rather tolerances being selected simply on the basis of material or process capability.

Quality Characteristics

The first stage in quality engineering involves identifying the chararcteristics of the product or service which are to be measured. Taguchi classifies these quality characteristics as either:

(a) measurable (variable) characteristics which are definable according to some continuous scale;

(b) attribute characteristics which are measured according to some form of acceptable/unacceptable criteria which are often subjective; or

(c) dynamic characteristics which are the properties of a 'system' and are determined on the basis of the relationship between the input to the system and the resulting output.

The measurable characteristics can be further classified in terms of the target value for the quality loss function. Three classifications are used:

(a) nominal the best - in which the characteristics has a specific target value (for exampre, dimensions, purity or density);

(b) smaller-the better-where the target for the characteristic is ultimately zero (for example, wear, deterioration or impurities);

(c) larger-the-better - where the target is ultimately infinity (for example, strength, useful life or efficiencies).

For the nominal- the best characteristic the quility loss function is minimized when the characteristic y approaches the target value and is given by:

$$L(y) = d(y - m)^2 \text{ Nominal-the-best}$$

For the seler-the-better characteristic the quality loss function is minimized when the characteristic y approaches zero and is given by:

$$L(y) = Ky^2 \text{ srnaller-the-better}$$

Finally, for the larger-the-better characteristic the quality loss function is minimized when the chacteristic y approaches infinity and is given by:

$$L\ (y) = k = \left(\frac{1}{y}\right)^2 \text{ Larger-the-better}$$

A comparison of the three types of measurable characteristic is shown in figure 6.

The quality loss functions described above do, however, relate to the loss associated with only one unit. In most practical cases more than one unit is produced and for the nominal-the-best characteristic the quality loss function becomes:

$$L(y) = k\,\frac{(y_1 - m)^2 + (y_2 - m)^2 + (y_3 - m) + \ldots (y_n - m)^2}{n}$$

$$= k\left[\frac{1}{n}\sum_{i=1}^{n}(y_1 - m)^2\right]$$

$$= k\left[\left[\frac{1}{n}\sum_{i=1}^{n}\left(y_1 - \bar{y}\right)^2\right] + \left(\bar{y} - m\right)^2\right]$$

$$= k\left[\sigma^2 + \left(\bar{y} - m\right)^2\right]$$

here:

$$\sigma^2 = \frac{1}{n}\sum_{i=1}^{n}\left(y_i - \bar{y}\right)^2$$

The σ^2 describes the consistency of the batch and the $(y - m)^2$ term is a measure of the accuracy.

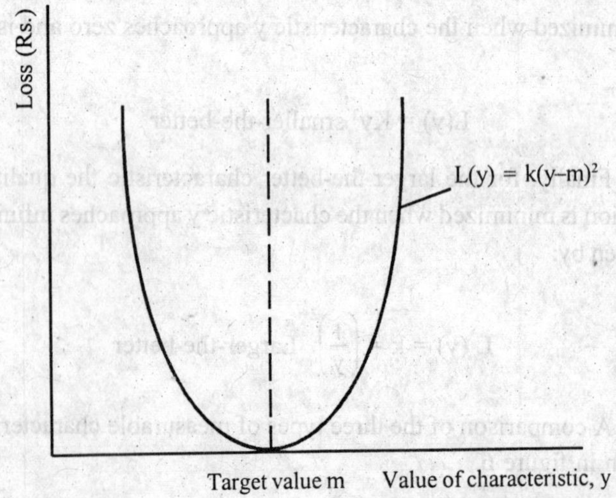

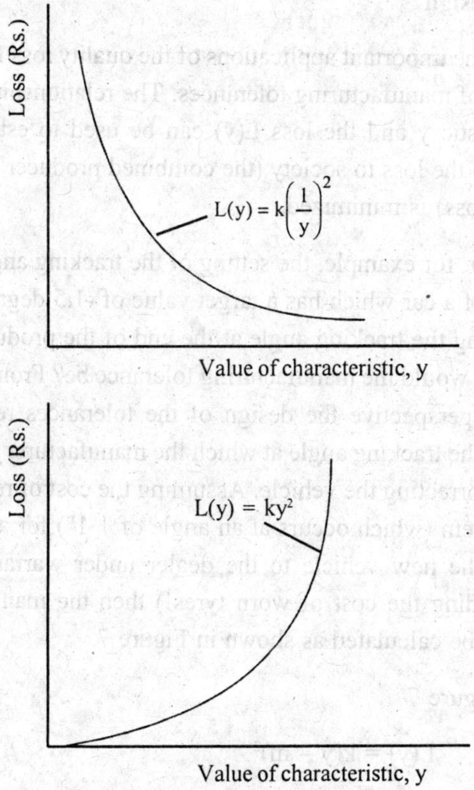

Fig. 6. A comparison of the three types of measurable characteristics.

The loss associated with a particular process can therefore be reduced by either improving the consistency (reduced variability) or by improving the accuracy (adjusting the mean to the target).

Similarly the quality loss function for more than one unit can be expressed for the smaller-the-better characteristic as:

$$L(y) = \sigma^2 + y^2$$

and for the larger the better characteristic as:

$$L(y) = \frac{1}{n}\sum_{i-1}^{n}\frac{1}{y_1^2}$$

Tolerance Design

One of the important applications of the quality loss function is in the design of manufacturing tolerances. The relationship between the characteristic y and the loss L(y) can be used to establish the point at which the loss to society (the combined producer's loss and consumer's (loss) is minimized.

Consider, for example, the setting of the tracking angle for the front wheels of a car which has a target value of -1.5 degrees. If the cost of resetting the tracking angle at the end of the production line Rs. 800, What would the manufacturing tolerance be? From a quality loss function perspective the design of the tolerances requires an evaluation of the tracking angle at which the manufacturer justifiably spends 8.00 correcting the vehicle. Assuming the cost of rectifying a tracking problem (which occurs at an angle of + 1°) for a customer who returns the new vehicle to the dealer under warranty is As. 140.00 (including the cost of worn tyres!) then the manufacturing tolerance can be calculated as shown in Figure 7.

From Figure 7

$$L(y) = k(y - m)^2$$

for $y = 1°$, $L = \text{Rs. } 140$, $m = -1.5°$

hence $$k = \frac{140}{(25)^2} = 22.4 \text{ Rs. }/°$$

The manufacturing tolerance can therefore be found by calculating the value of tracking angle (y) which corrsponds to a loss of Rs. 8.00 Hence:

$$L(y) = \text{Rs. } 8 = k(y - m)^2$$

$$\therefore \pm\sqrt{\frac{8}{22.4}} + m = y$$

hence $$y = -15° \pm 0.6°$$

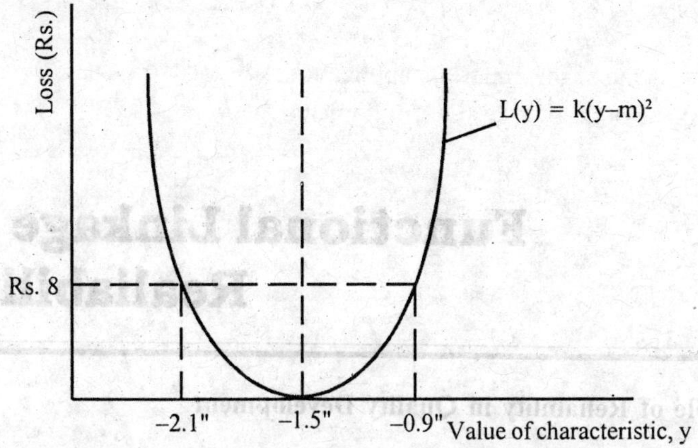

Fig. 7. Tolerance design using the quality loss function.

The manufacturing tolerance is therefore plus or minus 0.6 degrees. If the vehicle is manufactured with the tracking outsiae these limits then the manufacturer should the tracking angle otherwise the loss to society is not optimized.

This approach to tolerance design attempts to integrate both the manufacturer's and the customer's quality cost requirements.

❐

4

Functional Linkage of Realiability

Role of Reliability in Quality Development

The reliability of a product or service is synonymous with the concept of 'Quality' in the mind of the customer. Reliability is perceived to be the quality performance of the product or service over time, and in many sectors of industry and commerce reliability is considered the most important attribute. For example:

(a) in safety-critical applications

(b) in military applications

(c) in transport applications.

The concept of maintaining product or service quality over time is very much part of the development of an organization in the way in which quality is managed.

In the early stages of development, where the focus is upon the implementation of effective systems, the critical activity is the defining of performance requirements and establishing procedures and methods to meet these requirements. As organizations mature, improvements are made to both the product and processes to enhance reliability and reduce the causes of failure. Finally as a prevention orientation dominates the reliability is incorporated into the basic design and the product focus is for failure proofing and the process emphasis is upon preventative maintenance.

The application of the tools and techniques of reliability management in the quality development process is shown in Fig 1.

Within manufacturing, the management of reliability focuses upon both:

(a) product reliability in terms of the performance in the marketplace and the perceptions of the customer;

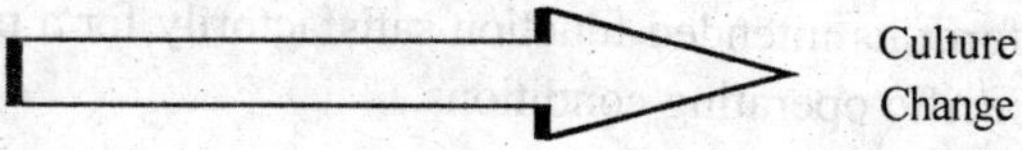

Stage I Develop a Systems Orientation	Stage II Develop on Improvement Orientation	Stage III Develop on Prevention Orientation
Actions		
– Definitions of performance requirements	– Measurement of reliability	– Design reliability through FMEA
– Corrective actions and servicing	– Product and process reliability analysis	– Systems predictability and availability
	– Component and systems reliability improvement	– Total preventative maintenance.

Fig. 1. Application of reliability management to the quality development process

(b) process reliability in terms of the availability of the manufacturing process and the consistency of production;

The business pressures to improve each of these elements are:

(c) product liability and the requirements of manufacturers to produce products which are safe in service and meet the growing national and international product liability legislation;

(d) manufacturing performance and process repeatability largely being determined by production reliability and availability, particularly in the process industries.

Certainly the techniques and concepts of reliability management are now an integral part of business development through quality.

Basic Elements of Reliability

The key concepts in the management of reliability can be understood from the following definitions:

Reliability. This is the probability that a product (or system) will perform its intended function satisfactorily for a period of time under specific operating conditions.

Probability. The analysis of reliability involves the determination and manipulation of probabilistic values.

Functionality. The operation of the product or system needs to be defined in terms of the requirements of the customer or the design specification.

Time. The stated reliability is quoted at a specific point in time and represents the cumulative probability to that point in time.

Operating Conditions. The environmental conditions under which the product or system operates is clearly a critical factor in the reliability and needs to be defined and adhered to.

Two of these elements are concerned with measurement, namely probability and time, whilst the other two, functionality and operating conditions are concerned with specification. Most of the analytical techniques associated with reliability management are therefore concerned with the relationship between probability and time. Reliability from the definition above is the probability that the component or system will still be functioning at the end of the stated time period and is therefore a survival function. Commonly used is the corresponding failure function and very often the performance associated with component or system reliability are descriptions of failure probability.

Reliability Management and Costs

From a quality management perspective, the main organizational areas for the application of reliability techniques are:

(a) **design management** promoting failure mode analysis and the development of robust product designs;

(b) **maintenance management** ensuring the availability of processes and the ability to conform to planned arrangements and to minimize disruptive costs;

(c) **logistics management** to ensure the availability of products on time and to predict the requirements for spares and services provision;

(d) **marketing management** to evaluate the performance of products in the marketplace and in particular to assess the performance of new products or services.

The generalized techniques described below can be used in each of these areas of the organization and are increasingly applied to the planning activities within companies.

Evaluating the costs associated with product or process reliability is also an important contribution to quality development. The maturing company evaluates the mechanisms for the conversion of failure costs (product failures, equipment breakdown) to prevention costs (reliability and failure analysis). The process cost model can be used to evaluate the relationship between the cost of conformance (reliability) and the cost of non-conformance (failure).

In terms of the typical cost analysis for capital equipment the life-cycle costs (LCG) are often calculated where:

Life-cycle costs = I + K (O + M + S) – R

where: I = initial cost's of equipment;

K = life-cycle constant;

O = operating costs per annum;

M = maintenance costs per annum;

S = standing costs per annum;

R = residual value of equipment.

This more 'total view' of the cost of equipment shows the dependency upon the reliability of the equipment through the cost of maintenance. By taking a simplistic view based upon the initial price of the equipment (1), the life-cycle profit (Life-cycle costs-life-cycle revenues) is optimized by minimizing the total LCC and not simply by taking the option which affords the lowest initial or operating costs.

Failure Characteristics

As described above the definition of reliability is based upon the relationship between the failure probability and time. All of the characteristics used to describe and measure reliability are based upon this probability—time relationship.

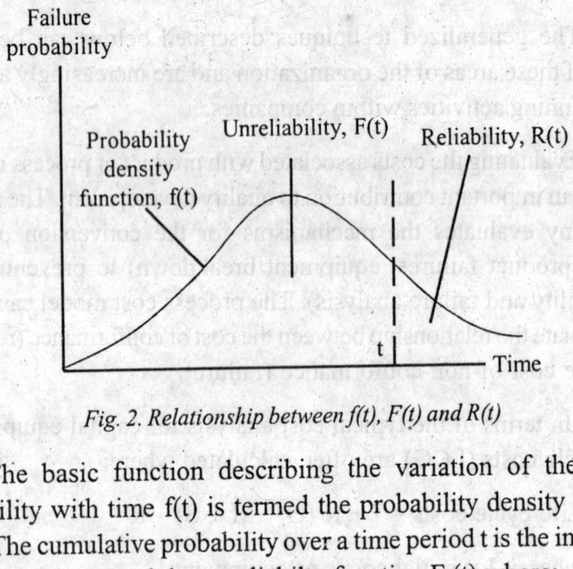

Fig. 2. Relationship between f(t), F(t) and R(t)

The basic function describing the variation of the failure probability with time f(t) is termed the probability density function (pdf). The cumulative probability over a time period t is the integral of the pdf and is termed the unreliabilty function F (t) where:

$$F(t) = \int_0^{\infty} f(t).dt$$

Given that failure and survival (reliability) are complementary and mutually exclusive, then the reliability function R (t) is therefore:

$$R(t) = 1 - F(t)$$

The relationship between the probability density function, the unreliability function and the reliability function is illustrated in Figure 3.

The general forms of the curves for each of these functions is shown in Fig 4 which illustrates the three important stages in the reliability life- cycle, namely;

(a) **AB—early life failure**, sometimes referred to as 'infant mortality', where the product or system fails prematurely due normally to a design or raw material failure. This aspect of reliability is normally the focus for the first stage of quality development and is through the implementation of a quality systems approach.

(b) **BC—constant failure**, sometimes referred to as 'random failure', where the failure rate is approximately constant. This is often prescribed as the normal working life of the product or system and the reduction in the failure rate is generally brought about during the secopd stage of quality development where the focus is upon continuous improvement.

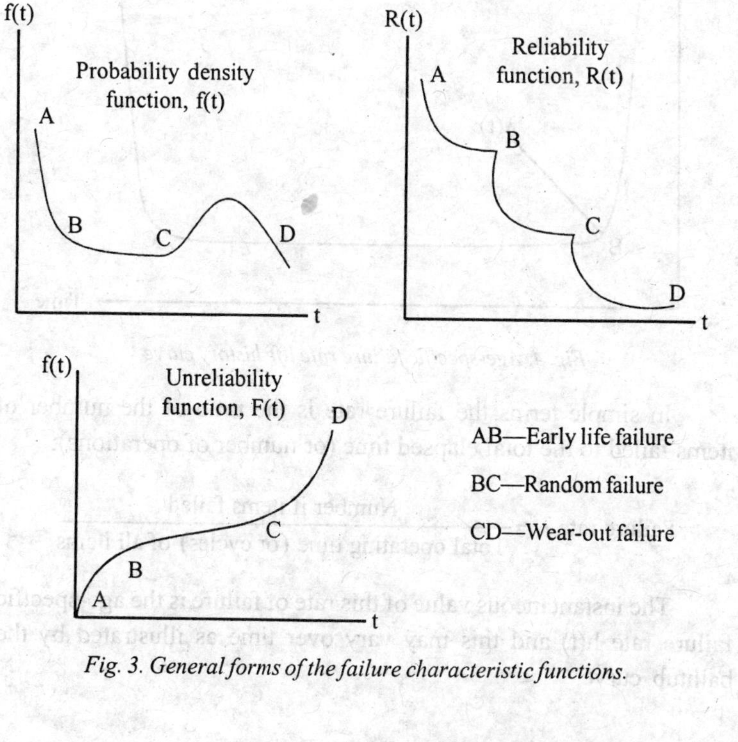

Fig. 3. General forms of the failure characteristic functions.

(c) **CD—wear-out failure**, sometimes referred to as 'old-age failure,' which represents an increasing failure rate due to components or systems failing through incurring wear beyond the design or 'intended life. This final aspect of reliability is extended during the final stage of quality development during which there is an investments in a prevention orientation.

Another important characteristic function of reliability is the age specific failure rate, h(i). This is perhaps the most commonly known distnbution as the shape of the curve is the classical 'bathtub' whereby the initially high failure rate falls to remain constant during the working life of the product only to increase again due to the cumulative ageing of the product, as shown in Fig. 4.

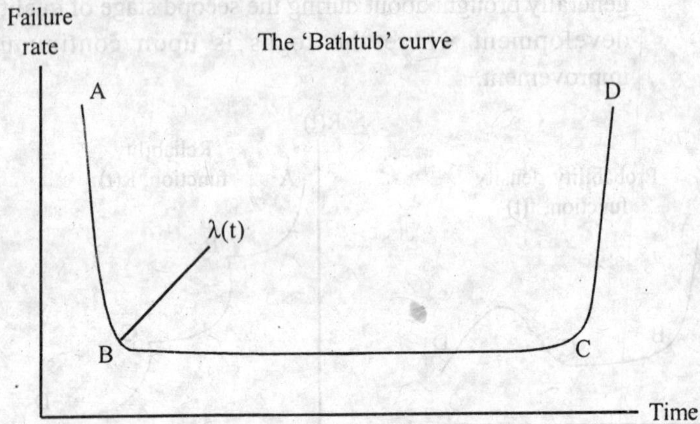

Fig. 4. Age-specific failure rate life history curve

In simple terms the failure rate is the ratio of the number of items failed to the total elapsed time (or number of operations):

$$\text{Failure rate } \lambda = \frac{\text{Number if items failed}}{\text{Total operating time (or cycles) of all items}}$$

The instantaneous value of this rate of failure is the age-specific failure rate h(t) and this may vary over time as illustrated by the bathtub curve.

This bathtub distribution intuitively mirrors the failure performance of many manufactured products. The motor car for example, often exhibits unreliability when brand new as the vehicle undergoes 'teething' problems not detected at the pre-delivery inspection. A period of use for the motor car then exists (typically around 80,000 Km for modern cars) in which the reliability is fairly constant and subject only to the random failure of components. Finally the motor vehicle becomes unreliable as major steering, engine or transmission components begin to cumulatively fail.

When considering the maintenance or servicing of products or systems the two most commonly used characteristics of reliability are the mean time to failure (MTTF) or, where components are repaired, the mean time between failures (MTBF).

Again, in its most simple terms, the mean time to failure represents the average time to failure for all the items tested. Where the failure rate is constant then the MTTF is the ratio of the total elapsed time (or number of operations) to the number of items failing, in other words the inverse of the failure rate:

$$MTTF = \frac{1}{\lambda}$$

In terms of the variation of the failure probability with time (the probability density function, f (t) a more comprehensive expression for the MTTF is given by:

$$MTTF = \int_0^\infty t.f(t).dt$$

Within maintenance management the concept of mean time between failures (MTBF) is more generally used as this is clearly factor in determining the planned maintenance periodicity and the number of spare parts required. The problem in practice, however, in determining the correct value of MTBF is that the timing depends upon the nature of the repair which can be either:

(a) **maximized repair** whereby the component or system is effectively made as good as new and therefore assumes the failure rate of a new item; or

(b) **minimized repair** whereby the component or system is brought to the same condition in terms of failure rate as the item was in just prior to the failure.

Clearly if the simple constant failure rate model is adopted (as it is in many industrial preventative maintenance programmer) then the nature of the repair is not a significant factor and the MTBF is given by:

$$MTBF = MTTF = \frac{1}{\lambda}$$

where the failure rate, h, is a constant.

Where the probability density function for a repaired unit $f_r(t)$ can be determined then the MTBF for the maintained component or system can be established from:

$$MTBF = \int_0^\infty tf_r.dt$$

In servicing industries such as computer equipment repair or electric motor repair, very often there is sufficient data available to determine the failure characteristics of the repaired product and as a result warranty periods and spare part stocks are adjusted accordingly.

Failure Distributions

In order to determine the useful reliability characteristics such as failure rate, MTTF and MTBF, there is therefore a need to be able to 'model' the failure probability with time, the probability density function, f(t).

From the appearance of the generalized curves shown and one's own intuitive understanding that different items fail in different ways, it is clearly a great challenge in the management and analysis of reliability to obtain an appropriate expression for f (t).

A number of different formulae (or distributions) have been adopted to model the way in which items fail over time and the three most common types are:

(a) **exponential distribution** which is appropriate for modelling the failure characteristics where the failure rate is constant, *i.e.* region BC of the bathtub curve whereby failure is random;

(b) **normal distribution** whicn is appropriate in situations where the probability of failure is distributed about a mean value and the failure rate increases with time;

(c) **Weibull distribution** which uses a sealing constant which can be varied to reflect the reliability characteristic in each of the main regions of the bathtub curve, AB early life failure, BC random failure, CD wear-out failure.

The exponential distribution is probably the most widely used function to describe failure probability with time. This popularity is due to the combined benefits of simplicity and applicability. The probability density function is described using the exponential distribution as follow:

$$f(t) = \lambda.e^{-\lambda.t}$$

The failure function is therefore given by:

$$f(t) = \int_0^t f(t).dt = 1 - e^{-\lambda.t}$$

and hence the reliability function takes the simple form:

$$R(t) = 1 - F(t) = e^{-\lambda.t}$$

The assumption here is of course that the failure rate is constant and therefore is only applicable to the period during which failures are random, covered by the region BC on the bathtub curve.

As this represents the normal working life of the product or system the exponential distribution is applicable to the type of failure most commonly under consideration.

As stated above the MTTF can be derived when the failure rate is constant as follows:

$$\text{MTTF} = \int_0^{\infty} t.f(t).dt = \int_0^{\infty} t.\lambda.c^{-\lambda.t}.dt = \frac{1}{\lambda}$$

An important corollary of this is seen when the reliability of the product or system is calculated at the MTTF:

$$R(\text{MTTF}) = e^{-\lambda.t} = c^{-\lambda.\frac{1}{\lambda}} = c^{-1} = 0.368$$

which means that only 36.8% of the items are expected to survive at the MITF and therefore the maintenance period is normally set well within the MITF.

The normal distribution is perhaps the least used of the functions although as expected it is an appropriate model for 'natural' components or systems. The normal distribution is appropriate where the failure of items is symmetrically distributed about the mean value and the failure rate increases with time. This model accurately depicts the normal wear-out failure of components or systems reaching old age or at the end of the design life. Neither premature failure nor random failure is appropriately described using the normal distribution.

The Weibull distribution is particularly important in the modelling of reliability due to the ability to describe each of the three main stages of the bathtub curve. The general form of the probability density function using the Weibull function is as follows:

$$f(t) = \frac{\beta}{\alpha}.\left[\frac{t - t_0}{\alpha}\right]^{\beta-1}.e^{-\left[\frac{t-t_0}{\alpha}\right]^{\beta}}$$

and hence the failure function:

$$f(t) = 1 - e^{-\left[\frac{t-t_0}{\alpha}\right]^{\beta}}$$

and therefore the reliability function becomes:

$$R(t) = e^{-\left[\frac{t-t_0}{\alpha}\right]^{\beta}}$$

Where α = scaling constant;

β = shaping constant;

t_0 = locating constant.

The Weibull distribution is capable of modelling early life, random and wear-out through the selection of appropriate values for the shaping constant, β. The special cases are as follows:

$\beta = 1$ represents the region BC, random failure;

$\beta < 1$ represents the region AB, early life failure;

$\beta > 1$ represents the region CD, wear out failure.

This flexibility of the Weibull distribution has a number of practical benefits in terms of its application to reliability management. For example, failure data on a new product can be evaluated using the Weibull distribution to determine the reliability performance of the product and indicate from the value of β whether the product is failing prematurely, randomly or due to ageing beyond the design life. Appropriate corrective actions in terms of the quality development tools and techniques to employ can then be specified based upon the value of β. Similarly if the value of β is known for a particular system, then the maintenance period can be determined using the Weibull distribution to ensure a specified level of system reliability. This flexibility has resulted in the growing popularity of the Weibull distribution as an approach to modelling reliability.

A comparison of the exponential, normal and Weibull probability density functions is shown in fig 5. The corresponding failure rate curves are shown in fig 6. together with the Weibull distribution to replicate the bathtub curve through the variation of the value of β.

Reliability Analysis

The simplest of the distributions used to describe the probability density function is the exponential function. The associated ease of use is, however, the main benefit in adopting this approach to the modelling of reliability.

As the failure rate is assumed constant using the exponential distribution then λ can be determined from experimental data by simply taking the ratio of the number of items failed to the total operating time (or number of cycles) as described abov. With the failure rate known, the reliability of a component or system at a particular point in time can be determined as shown in the example below:

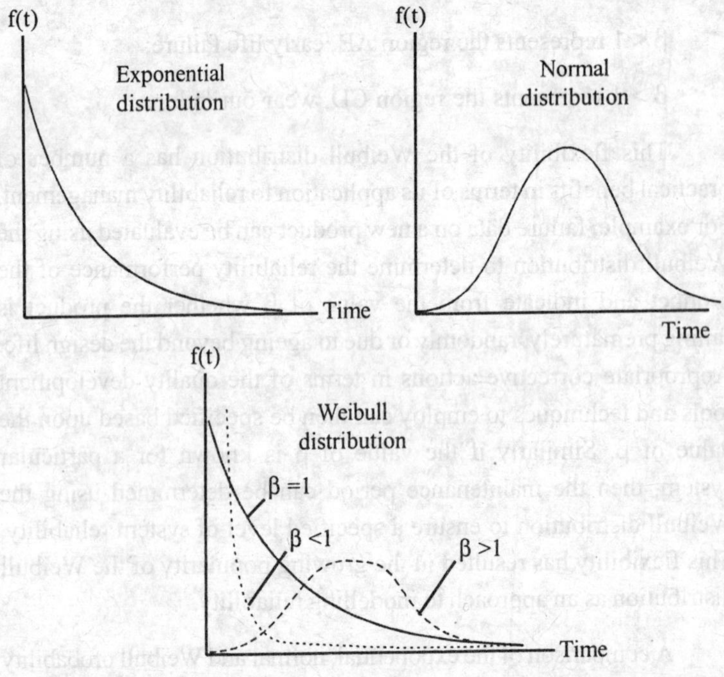

Fig. 5. Frequency distributions for exponential, normal and Weibull functions.

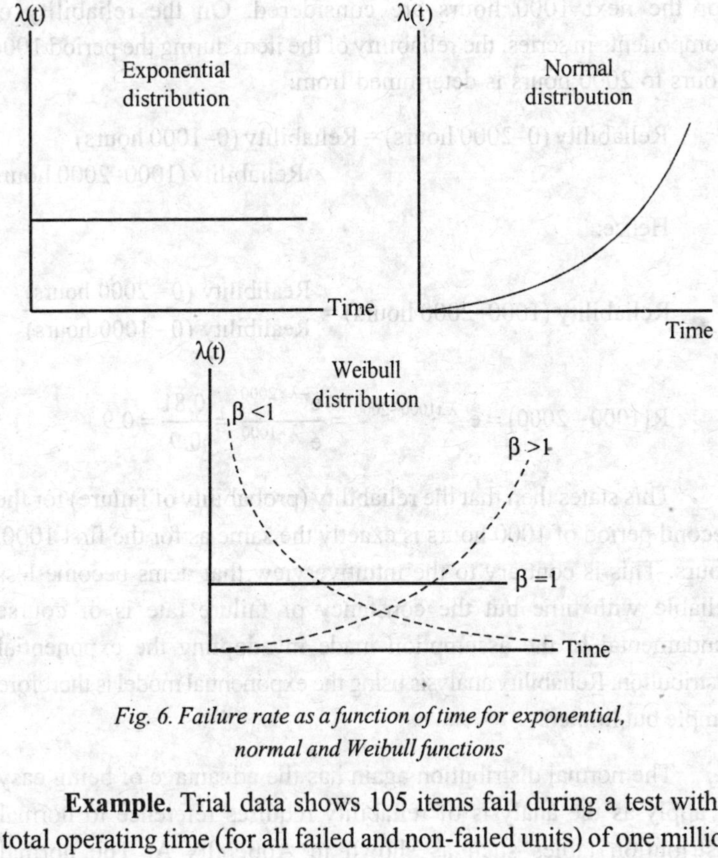

Fig. 6. Failure rate as a function of time for exponential, normal and Weibull functions

Example. Trial data shows 105 items fail during a test with a total operating time (for all failed and non-failed units) of one million hours. Hence:

$$\text{Failure rate, } \lambda = \frac{105}{10^6} = 1.05 \times 10^{-4}$$

What is the reliability of the item after 1000 hours?

$$\text{Reliability, R (1000)} = e^{-\lambda . t} = e^{-1.05 \times 10^{-4} \times 1000} = 0.9$$

Therefore an item has a 90% chance of surviving to 1000 hours.

As can be seen, this form of reliability analysis is relatively straightforward although the limitations emerge when the reliability for the next 1000 hours are considered. On the reliability of components in series, the reliability of the item during the period 1000 hours to 2000 hours is determined from:

Reliability (0–2000 hours) = Reliability (0–1000 hours)
× Reliability (1000–2000 hours

Hence:

$$\text{Reliability (1000–2000 hours)} = \frac{\text{Realibility }(0-2000\text{ hours})}{\text{Realibility }(0-1000\text{ hours})}$$

$$R(1000-2000) = e^{-\lambda.t1000-2000} = \frac{e^{-\lambda\times 2000}}{e^{-\lambda\times 1000}} = \frac{0.81}{0.9} = 0.9$$

This states then that the reliability (probability of failure) for the second period of 1000 hours is exactly the same as for the first 1000, hours. This is contrary to the intuitive view that items become less reliable with time but the constancy of failure rate is of course fundamental to the assumption made in adopting the exponential distribution. Reliability analysis using the exponential model is therefore simple but limited.

The normal distribution again has the advantage of being easy to apply as the analysis of reliability requires reference to normal distribution tables such as shown in Appendix A. The normal distribution is appropriate for the analysis of reliability during the wear-out phase of the bathtub curve. The unreliability function is given by determining the area under the curve from the normal distribution table. The reliability is therefore the remaining area under the normal distribution curve as illustrated abave in Fig.

Reliability analysis using the Weibull distribution involves the graphical determination of the Weibull parameters which can then be used in the expression for the reliability function. The graphical technique to determine the Weibull parameters makes use of special log-log xlog paper (Chartwell graph paper ref.. 6572). The Chartwell system uses:

$$R(t) = e^{-\left[\frac{t-t_0}{\eta-t_0}\right]^{\beta}}$$

Where η is the characteristic life and $\eta - t_0 = \alpha$ the Weibull scaling constant.

Using the log-log × log paper produces:

$$\ln\left[\ln\left(\frac{1}{R(t)}\right)\right] = \beta \ln\left[\frac{t-t_0}{\eta-t_0}\right]$$

and therefore by plotting on the Chartwell paper the cumulative percentage failure against time (or cycles) to failure this will give a straight line (providing $t_0 = 0$) which can be used to estimate the shaping constant β. This constant effectively 'tunes' the Weibull distribution to model the appropriate phase of the bathtub curve.

The Application and Classification of Systems Reliability

The reliability analysis techniques described previously relate to the process of determining the probability of failure for a single entity which could be modelled using some form of failure distribution. In most practical situations, however, it is more common that the product or process under consideration comprises a number of separate entities combined to form a system.

To analyse and determine the reliability of components combined together to form systems requires the manipulation of probabilities. To analyse the combined reliability of a group of entities by using the individual probability density functions becomes extremely unwieldy even for the simplest of systems. The analysis of systems is normally undertaken using the reliability function, that is the probability of survival at a specified time.

The other basic assumption in the analysis of the reliability of systems is the concept of independence. It is assumed that the elements of a system fail independently and therefore the failure of any single item has no bearing upon the ongoing reliability of the surviving items. Cleariy this assumption is inappropriate in situations where the failure of one item influences (often reduces) the reliability of other elements of the system. One approach to this limitation is to adopt a dual or multi-reliability model for the components of the system whereby the reliability probability can be amended (perhaps more than once) as other items within the system fail.

The formal analysis of systems comprising a number of components combined together requires the classification of certain system 'building blocks'. The basic system classifications for the analysis of reliability are as follows:

(a) **series** systems where the overall reliability requires all the components within the system to survive;

(b) **parallel** systems where the overall reliability requires any one of the components within the system to survive;

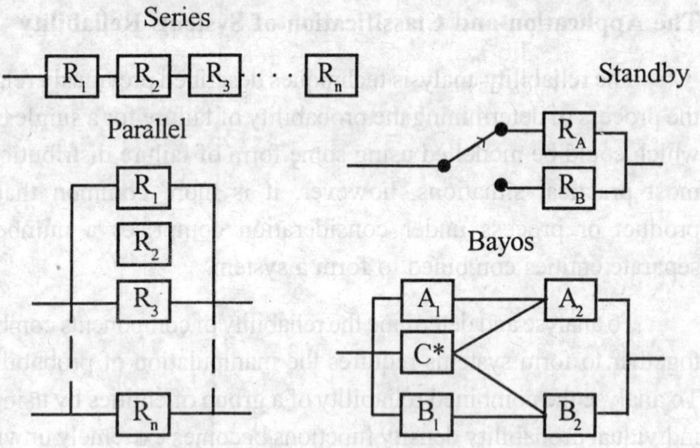

Fig. 7. Systems and arrangement for series, parallel, standby and Bayes elements

(c) **standby** systems where the system failure requires both the primary and standby elements to sequentially fail;

(d) Bayes systems in which components exist and influence the reliabilty of the overall system without being able to be classed as either series, parallel or standby.

The basic arrangement of each of these systems building blocks is shown in Fig.

Systems Reliability Analysis

To analyse the effect of combining reliabilities it is important to understand two basic elements of probability theory:

If A and B are two independent events with probabilities of occurrence of P(A) and P(B) then the probability that both events will occur is:

$$P(AB) = P(A). P(B)$$

In other words the system reliability is the product of the individual probabilities.

If events A and B are complementary and mutually exclusive then:

$$P(A) + P(B) = 1$$

The reliability therefore of a system which comprises components arranged in series as shown above in Figure. 7 is given by:

$$R(S) = R_1 \times R_2 \times R_3 \times ...... \times R_n$$

For a system which requires all the component elements to survive, the reliability is the product of the individual reliabilities. As the individual reliabilities are generally less than 1 then the reliability of the system is less than the reliability of any individual component when configured in series.

When components are arranged in parallel to form a system then the system failure occurs only when all of the individual components fail. The failure of the system arranged in parallel is therefore given by:

$$F(s) = F_1 \times F_2 \times F_3 \times .... \times F_n$$

Now as a failure and survival are complementary and mutually exclusive then if the failure functions are replaced with one minus the reliability function the expression for parallel systems becomes:

$$(1 - R(s)) = (1 - R_1) \times (1 - R_2) \times (1 - R_3) \times ..... \times (1 - R_n)$$

or, where the components all have the same reliability R:

$$R(s) = 1 - (1 - R)^n$$

Unlike with components arranged in series, where components are arranged in parallel the overall systems reliability is generally greater than the reliability of the individual components.

In certain applications, however, it is neither possible nor desirable to improve the reliability of the system by arranging components in parallel. For example, the electrical characteristics of a system change when components are arranged in parallel or alternatively the energy consumption of a system may be increased if a second power source is operated in parallel. For these reasons use is often made of component arranged in standby in which a standby components is arranged in parallel but only brought into operation if the primary component fails, as illustrated above in Fig.

In such standby configurations, the probability that the system will survive is the probability of either component. A surviving or component A failing and component B surviving. The system reliability for components arranged in standby is therefore given by:

$$R(s) = R(A) + F(A) \times R(B)$$
$$= R(A) + (1 - R(A)) \times R(B) \text{ (standby)}$$

Most practical systems are a combination of series, parallel and standby arrangements as shown in Fig.

The approach to analysing such combined systems involves the reduction of series configurations to a single element and the reduction of any parallel or standby configurations to a single reliability. Through the process illustrated in Figure 8 even the most complex systems can be reduced to a simple series c. parallel arrangement.

There are certain types of system configurations, however, which cannot be reduced to either series, parallel or standby systems. One of the most common examples of such a configuration is in systems in which a component has been installed in paralled with either of two other components as illustrated in Figure 9.

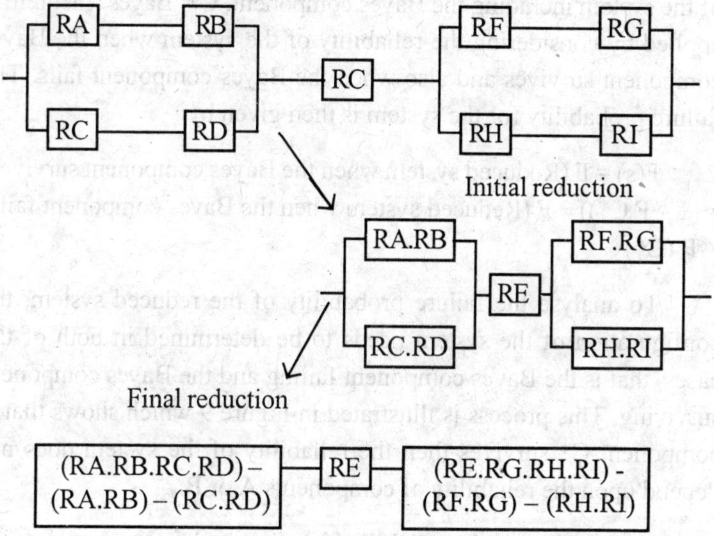

Fig. 8. Combined Systems Reliability Analysis

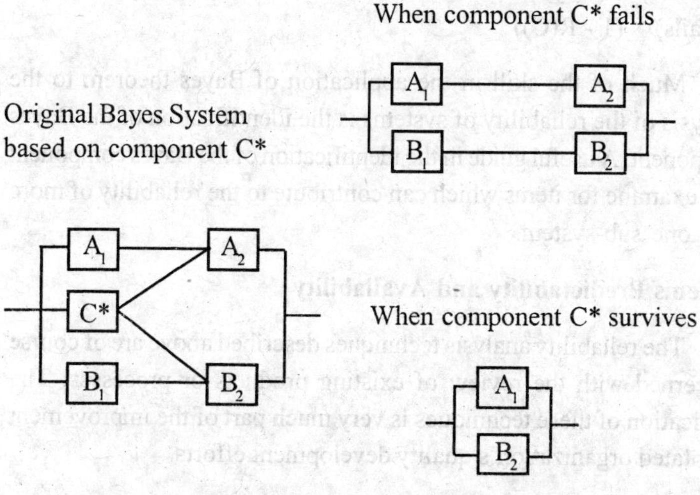

Fig. 9. The Bayes Component Analysis

This reasonably common approach to improving the system design reliability requires the use of Bayes' theorem for the analysis of the system including the Bayes component, C*. Bayes' theorem is applied by considering the reliability of the system when the Bayes component survives and also when the Bayes component fails. The failure probability for the system is then given by:

F(s) = F (Reduced system when the Bayes component survives) × (1 – F C*)) ≠ F (Reduced system when the Bayes component fails) × F (C*)

To analyse the failure probability of the reduced system, the configuration of the system needs to be determined in both of the cases, that is the Bayes component failing and the Bayes component surviving. This process is illustrated in Figure 9 which shows that if component C* survives then the reliability of the system does not depend upon the reliability of components A or B.

By substituting the reliability function in the above expression for the Bayes configuration the system reliability becomes:

R(s) = R (system when C* survives) × R(C)+ R (system when C* fails) × (1 - R(C))

Much of the skill in the application of Bayes theorem to the analysis of the reliability of systems is the identification of the Bayes component. A useful guide in the identification of the Bayes component is to examine for items which can contribute to the reliability of more than one sub-system.

Systems Predictability and Availability

The reliability analysis techniques described above are of course concerned with the review of existing products or processes. The application of these techniques is very much part of the improvement orientated organization's quality development efforts.

A prevention-orientated approach, however, demands that greater emphasis be given to the concept of reliability at the product or process design stage. To evaluate the potential reliability of a product or process at the design stage requires the application of predictive techniques, the two most common of which are:

(a) failure mode and effects analysis;

(b) fault tree analysis.

Failure Mode and Effects Analysis (FMEA)

In terms of the application of FMEA to reliability management, the design FMEA is used to asses potential failures of the product due to component or sub-system unreliability. The design FMEA is normally undertaken by a team selected from the marketing, production, sales and service functions in addition to the design team. The objective is to review the product design and to establish the following:

(a) What are the main functional elements of the design?

(b) What are the potential failures?

(c) What are the effects of the failure?

(d) What are the main causes of failure?

(e) What are the controls used to prevent failure?

From this analysis an assessment is made of the failure potential of the design and this is expressed as the risk priority number (RPN). The reliability of the component or the sub-system (as determined using the exponential, normal or Weibull distributions) is used to calculate the 'occurrence' value. Where the value of the RPN is high (typically greater than 90) this indicates the need for design corrective action to prevent the lilelihood of reliability problems.

In terms of the process FMEA this can be used by maintenance managers to identify processes with high failure risks and therefore to focus maintenance corrective actions and preventative maintenance programmes.

The second predictive technique, fault tree analysis (FTA), is a valuable method for understanding the relationships between elements within a system and how a particular mode of failure depends upon other failure events. The value in undertaking FTA is that it can often assist in the prediction of major failures due to the failure of minor components or sub-systems. Detection mechanisms can be implemented for the minor failures to prevent the occurrence of the generally more expensive major failure.

Such detection mechanisms are more apparent once the system has been systematically analysed using FTA. The process of generating an FTA involves determining the logical connectivity between events using 'and' and 'or' type logic. For example, the failure of an engine system can be predicted from the failure of an elemental component such as the lubrication sub-system as shown in Fig.

The predicted reliability performance of a product or process is generally measured in terms of the availability. This measure is particularly important in the maintenance of systems and is usually expressed as either the operational availability (A_0) which is expressed in terms of the mean time between maintenance (MTBM) and the mean downtime (MDT) as given by:

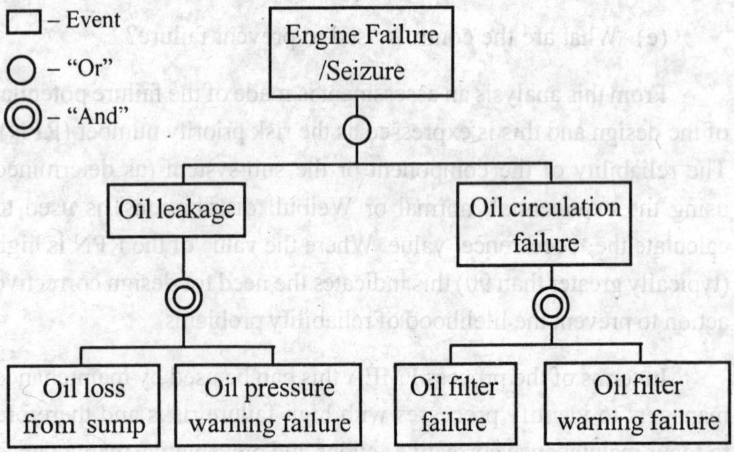

Fig. 10. Fault Tree Analysis

$$A_0 = \frac{\text{MTBM}}{\text{MTBM} + \text{MDT}}$$

or alternatively for the design of processes or products, the inherent availability (A_1) is used in terms of the mean time between failure (MTBF) and the mean time to repair (MTTR) as given by:

$$A_1 = \frac{\text{MTBF}}{\text{MTBF} + \text{MTTR}}$$

The inherent availability does not assume any preventative maintenance downtime (as this cannot be predicted at the design stage) and is therefore a design prediction of the compromise relationship between reliabality and maintainability.

❐

5

Quality Management Process

A successful total quality programme must be based on certain basic principles. Now we will consider in detail how to approach its implementation. Underlying the whole approach are six fundamental requirements based on the concept that people are at the heart of a successful programme. These are:

(a) top management commitment

(b) attitude change

(c) continuous improvement

(d) strengthened supervision

(e) extensive training

(f) recognition of performance.

Top management should continuously reinforce a total quality programme by what they do. Whether in management meeting company magazines or newsletters, they should ensure their complete commitment to the approach. Despite the fact that key influences on the quality movement have emphasized the importance of management commitment since the late 1950s, the disturbing thing is we still do not seem in general to have made the breakthrough in Western management. In Japan, and increasingly in the Pacific basin, no member of management can have any doubts about the need for his or her complete commitment to the total quality process. British shortcomings in this respect can often be explained through short-term perspectives by management, pressures to achieve short-term results and concern about costs.

We have to recognize that changing management attitudes is the key to success within an organization and that must start at the very top. In one major seafood organization at the start of a total quality programme, the site director (who has a main board director) told his middle management that there could be no doubt of the importance of quality in maintaining the organization's leading position in the market place and that the purpose of the total quality programme was to ensure it. The future success of the organization was dependent on his commitment and their commitment. He personally demonstrated his commitment by being highly visible in the total quality programme and thus created an environment where management knew that their performance was measured directly in their commitment and support for the programme.

To show commitment top management should make sure that everybody within the organization from top to bottom is clear about the long-term goals—this affects management style, the quality of communications, indeed everything that is done within an organization. Total quality requires a complete change in the attitude culture prevailing within organizations. The remarkable turnaround stories of Jaguar Cars and British Airways are examples where the organizations moved decisively away from a general view that delays, mistakes, defective materials were "just part of life". Another interesting example is SAS, the Scandinavian airline, which some years ago was losing money and drifting hopelessly in the marketplace. With a new chief executive, Jan Carlzon, the airline embarked on a major programme based on an identified market niche: the business market. The airline carried out extensive surveys of businessman, asking what were the main factors that persuaded them to travel on a particular airline. The airline was thus able to make significant operational changes which in turn created an environments.

During the introduction of quality programmes in many different organizations and industries, the issue of attitudes has always emerged early in the process. Ask the production employees what their biggest problem is and they will almost invariably say that the machine or equipment is always breaking down. The engineers do not know how to maintain the equipment properly, they are never available and they seem to take a long time to repair breakdowns. Ask the maintenance employees what their biggest problem is and they well tell you the production workers: they never look after the equipment, they drive the equipment too hard and beyond specifications, and they will never call us out until a breakdown occurs.

Within a major seafood organisation we were able to break down some of these barriers by creating much closer links between a specific engineer and a production area, so there was a mutual interest in keeping the machines going. Similar problems existed in the steel industry between production departments. Quality problems within rolling mills would almost invariably be blamed on the steel-making department, who allegedly did not produce the hot metal to specifications. Similarly you could guarantee that within the steel plant the major problems would always be referred to the blast furnace.

Some of the problems of attitude were well illustrated by the managing director of Matsushita Communication Industrial Company, Hajima Karatsu, who was summarizing the differences between what the Japanese have achieved in adopting Deming's approach and Western management: In Western business the super-elite give full play to their originality, but workers at the lower level are simply made to do standardized work on the basis of manuals. Originally quality control was designed to restrict the occurrence of inferior products within a certain tolerance range. In Japan, however, it has been changed into a movement for total elimination of inferior products through creative cooperation by all quarters concerned. When inferior goods are produced Japanese workers consider it a shame and even weep. Total quality control has revived an old spirit of crafts manship at modern factories.

Linked to attitude change is the create a climate of continuous improvement. Organizations need to ensure that they have real evidence at all times, through the use of statistical process control and control charts and many other simple techniques, that they understand what is happening in a particular process. This moves the culture of the organization away from checking whether a particular product or process is working effectively after the event to ensuring that one understands and identifies any quality problems early in the process and seeks continuously to improve performance. It also requires all levels to understand their responsibility for this quality process. The most notable example that come across in recent years was within one of the Canon Cameras factories in Japan. It became apparent as the factory that there was no obvious inspection process. Some 10 years earlier they had inspectors at all the major points on the assembly line checking the work had been completed. They had slowly created an environment whereby employees and supervisors felt responsible for the quality of their areas until they reached a point where they had suffcient confidence in the process and the only formal inspection process was sample inspecting of finished cameras at the end of the production line.

Traditionally the issues of quality and inspection have been confined to manufacturing processes within organizations but for long-term success the attitude of continuous improvement should apply to all levels from top management downwards and to all parts of the process, including the offices, sales force and finance department. Whenever we go into an organization to discuss a total quality programme, we often met with amazement, particularly in manufacturing organizations, when we suggest to top (or even middle) management that the programme should involve not only the 'shop floor' workers but also the 'white collar' employee.

As a small example, a secretarial quality circle group within one organization can be away from the direct manufacturing processes. As a small example, a secretarial quality circle group within one organization identified savings of two person years if members of staff providing material for typing (either audio or written) presented this material properly, without repeated redrafting. This represented a saving of some 9% of the total secretarial workforce. Quality improvement should always be at the forefront of every thing that is done, continuously reinforced and developed by management through the systems, processes and organizations which make such improvements possible.

Within the steel industry in Japan it is interesting that since the introduction of quality improvement programme some 25 years ago, many different emphasis have been placed on different aspects of the process. In the sixties the emphasis was very much on quality of product. As the oil crises hit Japan, the emphasis changed in the early seventies to energy conservation—a major issue in the steel industry, which is a very heavy user of energy and can be badly affected by large increases in energy costs. In the late seventies and early eighties the emphasis changed again to cost and productivity; certainly by the mid eighties, when we visited the Nippon steel works, everybody was wearing CAP badges.

At a more trivial level, a major chemical works in the North West of England set up project terms for a quality improvement programme who required specialist advice from a number of central departments. These project terms soon ground to a halt because the central departments did not consider attendance at appropriate meetings to be a priority and achieved by creating an environment where the organization culture allows and encourages support between different areas.

Any total quality programme is unlikely to be completely successful all of the time. Management must recognize that achieving breakthrough requires constant support and positive feedback to everyone involved. The Japanese are particularly successful at creating this environment. At Canon Cameras, there was lists of names indicating some sort of performance level. It is surprised at this thinking it might be some sort of bonus system, but found it was a record of suggestions made by employees within a particular department. Any suggestion, however small was recorded on the chart and at the most suggestions. While the specific approach might not be appropriate to the UK environment the underlying message was clear enough: every step needs to be taken to encourage individuals within an organization to be part of the improvement process and to look for opportunities to make changes. Within large parts of British industry supervision traditionally has been seen as the 'authority' within a particular department responsible for telling the workforce what to do and taking appropriate disciplinary action if they did not comply.

The successful introduction of total quality gives a key role to supervision in ensuring that the quality message is carried down to grass-roots level. In The Road to Nissan, Peter Wickens shows the way forward: In order to enhance the responsibility and role of production supervision it is essential to give back many of the responsibilities that have been taken away over the years. Nissan supervisors are responsible for making the decisions on who will work for them they have full responsibility for quality, housekeeping they layout their work area and material arrives blindside where they want it to come.

If the key success lies with supervision, then it is important to ensure that the selection, training and motivation of supervision allows for the development of the skills which enable them to became a dynamic force for improving performance. Top management needs to provide opportunities and the investment in training to ensure the quality of supervision improves. The success of a total quality programme depends on supervision (and indeed everybody!) being given the tools, skills and ability to manage the process. Too often top management confuses briefing with providing development and training. In the initial stages of any total quality programmes that have found resistance to taking supervisors away from their jobs for any length of time on the grounds that they are too busy; 'just tell them what they need to know is often heard. Attitude change can only be achieved through a much longer-term perspective.

One of the major successes of the Japanese approach has been the very extensive training programmes that have been used in the total quality programmes. It is interesting to note that Professor Ishikawa, often known as the 'father of quality circles' recognized in 1963 that once the extensive training of supervisors had taken place, the next logical step was to involve the stop floor. Thus were born quality circles. We first considered how best to get grass-roots workers to understand and practise QC (Quality control). The ideal was to educate all people working at factories throughout the country but this was asking too much.

Motivation theory and practice emphasize strongly the importance of recognizing performance and achievement. This applies in any total quality programme, the question is how it is best achieved. The traditional suggestion scheme approach, whereby there is the link between the reward and suggestion, generally does not work in a total quality programme if only because it creates a further layer of bureaucracy in evaluating each proposal. In Japan recognition is generally given through prizes and competitions for either the most or the 'best' proposals and projects. On a more spectacular basis, Sony selects the 'best' quality circle projects that have been carried out in all the major countries where Sony has a presence. The quality circle leaders and members meet once a year for a major quality circle convention in Tokyo, where a further competition takes place to establish the outstanding project for the year. The emphasis is very much on recognition of contribution and achievement with no direct monetary reward. This approach creates a momentum for the total quality programme and encourages individuals and groups to seek continuous improvement. Interestingly, the competition approach is not welcomed in all organizations: certainly in one North-Eastern-based manufacturing plant there was considerable resistance to such an approach, despite the fact that there was a successful total quality programme running.

Management Process

When it comes to the description, design and control of a general industrial or business process, the classic approaches of process engineering and process control are useful but inadequate and limited, because they are based on the concept of closed technological processes. Because managing quality pertains to the conformance of the work product to requirements, it essentially implies a way of managing the business process. Although this fact has been recognized recently by leading industrial and business organizations in actuality very little is available to management in terms of structured disciplines or theoretical foundations for planning and organizing business process management.

One of the most basic errors committed by management is to confuse process with organization. Quality management must concentrate on the process, not on organization. A fundamental characteristic of a process is that it comprises a series of related activities which result in a work product, which in turn must conform to stated requirements. As will be seen later, such activities usually cut across organizations and even functional boundaries. The success of managing the process and controlling its output and consequently controlling quality will depend on management's ability to define and separate the components of the process from other organizational, political, and functional considerations and influences and to allow them to operate as a whole by removing barriers to process flow.

Process Design

Every process—technological or administrative, complex or simple must be designed around three fundamental concepts.

(1) The basic feedback loop, also known as the "command and control" concept. This means that to achieve satisfactory results—that is, conformance to requirements-those responsible for managing the process must always be in a position to *(a)* know what is to be done and *(b)* know what is being done and take corrective action if and when necessary (control). Many processes, mostly administrative and political, break down because those responsible are not in a position to take such action for lock of authority—legal, political or otherwise.

Without the basic feedback loop, no set of components, however well chosen and ordered, and no sophisticated management system will ensure effective operation and, as a result, conformance to requirements.

(2) Independence of purpose, coupled with a clearly defined relationship to other processes, and organizational and functional entities within the business. Such relationships are usually ensured through a properly implemented management system, which establishes the scope and relative position of a given process within the overall business environment.

The basic characteristics of an independent process include:

(a) The process must be in control and capable of producing defect-free output: Which means it must be effective. Process effectiveness is ensured through continuing quality improvement.

Process effectiveness sometimes includes further desirable or prescribed attributes dependent on the work product required and the environment in which the process is implemented:

(i) **Repeatability.** The process must be able to perform its operations activities in a specified, successive number of times, in the same place.

(ii) Some processes must also be reproducible, which means the duplication or replication of the same set of process components and their inter-relationships in another place at the same or another time.

Sometimes the need for process portability also exists-the need to transfer the same process, along with its components to another place for repeated or continued operations.

(b) **The Process must be Efficient.** It has to operate at optimum cost. Process efficiency is ensured through process optimization.

A process should always be designed for continued quality improvement as well as process optimization.

(c) **The Process must be Adaptable.** There has to be an effective and economical way of changing it over time as a result of corrections necessitated by variations in output, or by changing requirements. This means that changes to the process should be applicable without adverse impact on its effectiveness or efficiency. Process adaptability is ensured through appropriate design and process optimization.

The importance of process adaptability was recently pointed out by a senior Defence Department official, who equated the success of highly complex technological processes with the capability to absorb change and be, self-corrective: "Finally, I came to realize that the "common denominator was to be found in the programmes that had failed or come in second best. An example was the German atomic bomb programme of World War II, a programme that was so highly structured and formal that it was unable to correct itself. By contrast, the Manhattan Project was dynamic, contentious, full of scientific give and take, and therefore capable of speedily correcting its own' errors."

(3) Clear and complete definition of components People, procedures, information, equipment, materials, and energy. Procedures include the description of interrelationships of these components and of the activities they are expected to perform.

The definition of the process components must include:

(a) Inputs (materials, energy, information, and so on)

(b) Procedures (problem analysis, error elimination, corrective actions, process changes)

(c) Requirements (statement of customer/recipient needs and expectations). Specifications (description of output)

(d) Organization (People, responsibilities, information flow)

(e) Process hierarchy (subprocesses or activities)

(f) Measurement system

(g) Feedback (control points)

Incorporation of all three concepts is necessary for food process design and satisfactory operation. Whether the process is controlled by sophisticated methods, such as statistical techniques, or by simple visual observation and manual intervention these three design concepts will determine its ultimate success or failure.

The term process design as used in this text refers to the activities of planning the work process in order to achieve quality objectives. There is no such thing as process design in the abstract; the related planning is done to meet known objectives. The end result of this planning cycle is the process plan: a list of activities to be done, identification of the components needed to do them, a schedule, and other "elements of design" as appropriate. Design is complete when all components of the process are in place and in a state of readiness for implementation.

Major Process Planning

Certain processes can be carried out by a few individuals in a department. Others require participation from multiple company departments or functions. For example, the order entry process requires varying degrees of participation from marketing, information systems, manufacturing, and service. For best results it is important to delineate in terms of process components—the scope of every process which management intends to control as a separate entity. In the final analysis, a process thus defined can comprise a small number of business activities or the entire business itself. In the case of major industrial undertakings, such as the design and production of a new and complex product, process definition and delineation become critical, as it would be risky to rely on traditional departmental planning. In some companies, the success of the enterprise may depend on the results attained in several major processes. For such key processes, companies create special management mechanisms to provide tailor-made process planning and management. As will be seen later, the process management mechanism usually comprises:

(a) A process owner

(b) A committee or team of managers guiding and controlling the process and advising the owner.

(c) A process office to carry out the details of planning, measurements, reporting, feedback, and so on. In some cases, the process office is responsible for more than planning and coordination; it may also control funding as well as exercise "task-oriented control" over such line functions as product development or manufacturing. In such cases, personnel from the traditional organization are assigned to the process for the duration.

Making the process succeed requires that there be agreement among top management as to the assignment of responsibilities, authority, and accountability. This also requires that the activities comprising the process be subdivided into subprocesses small enough to be clearly identifiable and manageable. The vast majority of industrial and business processes are constructed around one of three basic forms. Obviously, these forms affect the extent of process design and planning as well as the choice of who does it.

(a) Departmental Process. This process form receives its inputs and produces its output within an single, self-contained organization, usually a department. Wellknown examples include programming departments in information systems organization, the tool room in a manufacturing facility, word processing centers, and libraries. In many cases, formal planning for such departmental processes is carried out by a member of the department or its manager. In very small departments, planning may be assigned to individual workers.

(b) Three Process. Widely used in manufacturing and electronic industries which build railroad equipment, heavy machinery, automobiles, household appliances, and electronic products. The base of the tree comprises vendors or in-house functions producing parts and components. These in turn are turned into sub-assemblies by still other functions and departments. Final assembly of the product completes the process. The tree process requires planning of two different kinds: traditional departmental and interdepartmental (or process level). In complex processes, it becomes mandatory to use the process design staff to coordinate interdepartmental planning activities.

(c) **Serial Process.** This process form may again comprise numerous vendors and in-house departments. However, all activities proceed sequentially through the participating functions and departments, each representing an operation which ultimately contributes to the final process result. This process form is found in the majority of "process industries," such as petroleum refineries, chemical plants, and the like.

Process Effectiveness

Of the three basic characteristics of an independent process, effectiveness is the most critical because it, above all, ensures conformance to requirements. The process owner should be able to assess in advance whether the process will be able to turn out defect-free products—that is, whether it will be effective. There are several ways of ensuring this: from direct measurements on the process, from product conformance to specifications from data on product usage or from process capability studies. Each of these methods has advantages and disadvantages as we discuss now.

(a) **Prediction from Direct Process Measurements.** One advantage is immediacy, that is, measurements are made without waiting for the work product to be available for processing; another is that defects in process facilities are detected, along with some causes. The disadvantage is that the process tested is not "under load." A typical example is the manufacture of machine tools, where machines are tested prior to shipment by placing various measuring devices in selected places and positions on the machine.

(b) **Prediction from Successful Usage.** The advantage of this is that actual use being the ultimate proof, it carries weight mostly with business management. Disadvantages include failure to provide quantitative performance measurements and the fact that usage feedback is not transferable to follow-on products still in design.

(c) **Prediction from Product Conformance to Specifications.** Its advantage is that it is still widely accepted in machine manufacturing as the traditional method. Disadvantages include failure to quantify capability with respect to the process variables involved and limited predictability in terms of ability to transfer available process knowledge to new product design.

(d) **Prediction Through Measuring Process Capability.** This is the most recent development in process management, and it is the basis of quality management through process improvement. Its advantage is the availability of quantitative data which can be used to predict the effectiveness of future designs. Its disadvantage is the added initial effort and resources needed for measurements, data analysis, and process capability assessment.

Process capability is determined by the total variation that comes from common causes—in other words, the minimum variation that can be achieved after all special causes of variation have been removed. Thus, process capability represents the performance of the process itself, as demonstrated when it is in a state of stability. Capability is often thought of in terms of the proportion of output that will be within stated limits.

As long as the process remains stable, it will continue to produce the same proportion of out-of specification products. Management action upon the process to reduce the variation from common causes is required to improve process capability—the ability to consistently meet specifications. This is known as process improvement. In short, the process must first be stabilized by identifying and removing special causes of variation. Only then will its performance become predictable and its capability to meet specifications assessable and improvable. This is the theoretical basis for the concept of continuing quality improvement.

The designer's greatest contribution to process effectiveness and, therefore, to product quality is most likely the concept of designing the process to be defect free. Where this type of design is economically feasible, it provides excellent solution to some very difficult process management problems:

(a) Elimination of defects resulting from special causes, especially from inadvertent or wilful human error such as a result of inattention, or indifference. A defect-free process, by definition is also a process in control.

(b) Redundancy, including multiple approvals, checking procedures and audit reviews in administrative processes, multiple code identification to prevent product mix-ups.

(c) Bypassing complex problem analyses and error-cause detection efforts by providing a solution even though the cause of variation remains unknown. Some of the more usual forms of making the process defect free are.

(d) Fail-safe mechanisms, which can consist of interlocking sequences, alarms and cutoffs, foolproof fixtures, tamper-free packaging and the like.

(e) Countdowns, which are prearranged sensing and information procedures parallel to the operation of the process to check operational steps against the prescribed sequence of events.

Process Requirements

Any business operation can be characterized as a set of interrelated processes. In a large business enterprise, examples of such processes are:

(a) Order entry

(b) Billing

(c) Accounting

(d) Distribution

(e) Backlog management

(f) Procurement/Purchasing

(g) Product design

(h) Production control

(i) Materials management

(j) Product introduction

(k) Product service and maintenance

(l) Parts management

Each of these processes, in turn, is made up of sub-processes: for instance, in the case of billing, there is purchase billing, service billing, rental billing, and the like. Beyond the basic external statement describing required process output, process design must also include the following process requirements:

(a) **Total Process Requirements.** In addition to user requirements, which shape the end product of the process, internal requirements may include such business requirements as productivity, and adherence to personnel policies and practices, legal guidelines, as well as prevailing standards for safety, security, etc.

(b) **Work Activity Requirements and Specifications.** For each activity, its input, component tasks, output, and conformance criteria, as well as input-output linkages to other activities. These, in turn, require specification of the control activities, such as measurements, defect elimination cycle, and possible corrective actions. Work activity specifications include activity procedures, which are the guidelines and operating instructions for people and change control procedures in case work activities have to be modified to meet conformance requirements. Procedures for change control assure adequate review and approval of proposed changes prior to implementation, communicate proposed changes and their implementation plan to those affected, force accountability, and provide a record of change.

Process controls, especially the defect elimination cycle, are the underlying elements of process design. Their purpose is to enable process management to operate and change the process, if necessary, so that requirements will be met. Process design may be generalised into such concepts as "standard design". Several different enterprises have arrived at the concept of achieving better quality control through standardized design of subprocess or even entire business processes.

Design for Worker Self-control

In some processes, especially simple administrative and business situations, the end user requirement becomes the basis for both management's and worker's knowledge of what is to be done. This is especially true when workers are in direct contact with end users, for example, in such traditional trades as the electrician or plumber. In larger enterprises and more complex industrial or business processes, work product specifications are widely used as a substitute for knowledge of end user requirements. In such cases management must have the means to assess and control the conformance of specifications to end user requirements.

Also, other essential precautions must be observed, such as providing clear and consistent information through the various information sources reaching the workers; priority information; explanations of purpose supporting the specifications; standards in support of, or to enhance, specifications; and last but not least, adequate training for workers, including special training for specific conditions, for example, safety, contingency plans, emergencies, and so on. In many situations it is not even practical to provide product specifications to the workers. Identifiable characteristics may not appear within the particular subprocess, as the actual product may take shape only in a later operation. There may be no provisions for measuring the product until its final assembly. In such processes, workers involved in earlystage activities are provided with process criteria or variable. Workers in certain stages of a process need knowledge of what is happening in the process and what they are specifically doing. Only from such knowledge can it be determined whether or not a variation exists and corrective action is needed. Such knowledge is derived from multiple sources, such as personal observation, measurements inherent in the process, measurements by the operator, or measurement by supervisors or inspectors.

The Work Process

An essential component of any industrial or business process is the human element: its people. In general terms, any process including humans is termed a social process, which includes all political, industrial, and business endeavours which require involvement, intervention, or supervision by humans and which are not purely technological or fully automated.

Process Theory

General system theory classifies living organisms as open systems; by extension, any process that includes humans must also be classified as an open system—inherently capable of improvement and adaptation. The modern industrial or business process is the result of the disciplined design and implementation, as well as the continuing enhancement of a complete range of activities performed by the interrelated components of the process. Their object is to assure quality to the user and optimum process performance to the enterprise. Just as the overall process can be viewed as a single open system, the many activities that must be brought together in proper relationship to provide the single major function of getting a quality work product to the end user can be regarded as sub-systems.

The overall process, then, is an integrated system, and the objectives of management are to *(1)* create within the process the most effective work pattern of people, equipment, materials, and information to ensure conformance to user requirements; and *(2)* optimize it in terms of efficiency and productivity at a minimum cost of quality. The system theoretical approach simply provides the conceptual framework for design implementation and process change: In system theoretical terms, a process is defined as a system put into operation to produce an output of higher value than that of the sum of its inputs.

Characteristics of organization whether of a living organism or a social process, include the concepts of growth, differentiation, hierarchical order, dominance, control, and competitiveness. Such notions do not appear in conventional physics or in closed systems, to which conventional physics apply. However, system theory with the inclusion of open systems is well capable of dealing with these matters. There are, however, many aspects of organizations which do not easily lend themselves to quantitative interpretation or description.

An open system may "actively" tend toward a state of higher organization; that is, it may pass from a lower to a higher state of order, as a result of conditions in or actions upon the system. The notion of continuing quality improvement is based on this principle. A feedback mechanism can "reactively" reach a higher state of organization as a result of learning that is information fed into the system from external sources. Feedback systems are a significant, but special class of self regulating systems capable of adaptation: they are "open" to incoming information, but "closed" to the exchange of matter and energy. A typical example is the defect elimihation cycle in quality management, which is essentially a basic feedback loop. For purposes of process management theory, such feedback mechanisms, as "secondary regulators" are considered as embedded in the overall process, which is dynamic and can be considered as the "primary regulator".

There is dynamic interaction among the process components as well as the work activities in addition to the exchange of information, matter, and energy with the outside environment which allows us to view the overall process as an open system. For purposes of manageability and efficiency of individual work activities, the associated control mechanisms are organized into feedback loops, within which dynamic interaction no longer occurs, causal trains, such as the relationship between and sequence of tasks, are linear and unidirectional.

Process control theory has traditionally focused on technological or production processes. However, the concept is eminently applicable, through the process management approach to business and industrial processes as well for example, purchasing, product assembly, orders and movements, people management, and the like. In the casually evolved quality management approaches that were characteristic of the past, the quality responsibility of management was equally casual. But experience indicates that the modern, structured business processes are so broad that they will downgrade and disintegrate unless from their inception they are managed on a systematic basis that is equally broad to ensure that any given process will produce the intended results. Furthermore, the basic characteristics of the business process, which transcend established organizational and functional limits, make it necessary that the basic responsibility for the implementation of processes must rest in the hands of company general management rather than in the hands of its functional units.

The management approach which characterized industrial operations for more than the first half of this century was based on what might be called improvement through specialized division of effort. This philosophy in turn led to the development of a wide variety of individual technical and managerial specialities. Indeed, specialization has brought significant advances to industrial development, especially during and immediately after World War II. It has been recognized since, however, that carried beyond a certain point, the theory of division of effort creates more problems than it solves, including narrowness of perspective, bureaucracy, duplication diffusion of responsibility, and extremely complex confusing lines of communication—hence the revived interest in integration of effort through prudent process management. Because of the scope of process integration, which extends from initial requirements definition to assurance of actual end user satisfaction, the process can be thought of as "horizontal" in an organizational sense. This is in sharp contrast to the assignment of responsibilities in traditional quality control approaches, where quality control is assigned by function and can be thought of as organizationally vertical. The organizational approach for total process management involves two parallel steps:

(1) Definition and establishment of the process.

(2) Addition of the horizontal organizational concept of process management achieved from a general management viewpoint through process ownership.

The key aspects of establishing process ownership are:

(a) **Selection.** The process owner must preferably be the line or functional manager with the most resources invested and the highest related workload. This person is most affected by non-conformance and also has the highest leverage on the overall process.

(b) **Organization.** Here a "quasi-line structure" is created to manage and control the key sub-processes which normally cut across traditional business organization and functions.

(c) **Responsibilities.** The process owner, among other things, is firstly responsible for quality improvement through.

(a) Process design, documentation, and quantifiable process improvement goals. In designing the process its components are defined and assembled, bearing in mind that factors affecting quality can be divided into two major groupings: *(1)* technological; including equipment, materials, energy, procedures, standards, and the like; and *(2)* human; including workers, supervisors, managers, and other personnel. Of these factors the human is of greater importance in quality management by far.

Hierarchy of Process Components

Process component	**Organizational entity**
Process	Multiple departments or functions
Sub-process	Department or function
Activity	Project team or task force
Task	Small team or individual

(b) Process control: Defect detection and corrective action.

(c) Process improvement by means of *(1)* definition of user requirements and specifications; *(2)* analysis of process capability measurements; and *(3)* corrective action on the process.

(d) Reporting of progress in formal periodic reviews.

The process owner, within these responsibilities, sees to the establishment of a measurement system, control procedures, feedback on corrective actions, certification of process performance, and changes to the process for continued quality improvement. He or she also ensures that appropriate process management tools are made available, personnel are trained, and the necessary material and financial resources are committed. The allocation of resources, both financial and human, changes as process management matures over time. Resources previously put in place for classic quality control tasks such as inspection, quality control, and rework gradually diminish and partially give place to those devoted to process planning, defect prevention and process control.

There exist several management tools for the structured and disciplined definition and analysis of a process. Among these are business systems planning primarily an information-flow modelling tool; department activity analysis a non-quantitative technique for establishing management priorities in departmental processes; structured analysis a portrayal methodology with limited problem analysis capability; and the process analysis technique, a tool for the analysis and improvement of time-dependent interfunctional processes. Of the management responsibilities in this area, processes certification and the rating criteria on which it is based deserve special attention. As the process moves through its stages toward maturity, it is the process owner's responsibility to assess and report on the overall performance of the process and certify it to top company management. Process optimization, which is the second major responsibility of the process owner, deals with maintaining and improving both the productivity and the efficiency of the process.

Process adaptation, the process owner's third key responsibility, is the continuing modification of the current process to ensure its continued effectiveness and efficiency in the face of new requirements or other environmental and business changes anticipated in the future. Basic to process adoptation is the ability to anticipate and evaluate future user requirements and to identify specific process or sub-process constraints and deficiencies in the light of these. The process adaptation or change plan would include means of eliminating or circumventing the constraints and deficiencies, as well as a schedule for implementing changes before overall business performance is impacted by the lack of them.

❒

6

Functional Linkage of Quality System Standards

In order to fully appreciate the extremely important business developments in relation to quality system standards, one first has to understand the meaning of the term 'quality'. A number of informative definitions have emerged:

(a) the features and characteristics of a product or service which bear upon its ability to satisfy a stated or implied need' (ISO 8402);

(b) conformance to specification';

(c) 'fitness 'for purpose';

(d) 'meeting customers' requirements, and exceeding their expectations';

(e) 'doing things right first time'.

If one looks carefully, all the above definitions essentially lead to one thing and it is, "To provide company operating systems which promote conformance to specifications."

In order to achieve above objective, following are essentially required.

(a) specifications (or requirements) need to be clearly defined;

(b) a 'systems' approach is required involving all aspects of the business;

(c) responsibilities, processes, methods and materials all need to be prescribed.

It is from this holistic view of quality which developed during the late 1970 that the concept of a Quality System began to gain widespread industrial acceptance. The limitations of product standards, the move towards a quality assurance rather than quality control philosophy and the ever increasing pressure to provide better and better quality products and services led to the adoption of the concept of a quality system which could be defined as, "The organizational structure, responsibilities, procedures, processes and resources for implementing quality management."

The emergence of this 'Systems based' approach to the management of Quality led to the need for a generalized standard for assessing such quality systems which provided:

(a) a general framework or agenda for assessing a company's quality system;

(b) a structure which is applicable to all organizations from manufacturing to service from large to small;

(c) an independently verifiable, internationally accepted systems checklist.

In terms of what constituted a quality system the approach adopted has been that this covers all business functions with the exception of finance (the argument here being that financial systems have alternative, often, legal audit requirements). The main elements of a quality system are shown in Fig 1.

Whilst the main sector for the implementation of quality systems has been manufacturing industry, the concept can also be applied to service companies, in which case the term 'manufacturing' is taken to mean transaction processing.

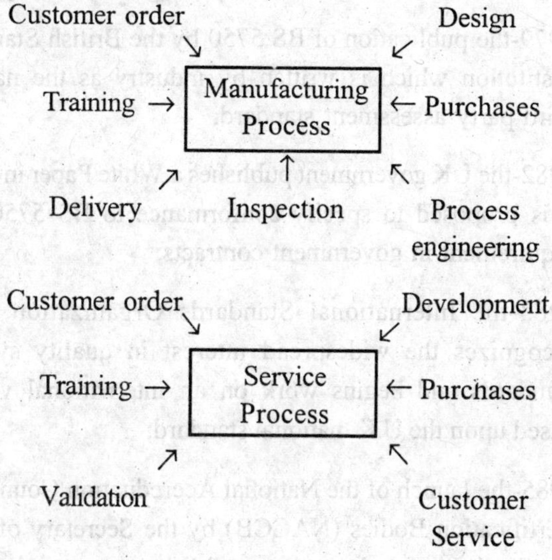

Fig. 1. Typical elements of a quality system.

Development of Quality System Standards

The late 1970s saw increasing international pressure for improvements in the management of quality and in particular forstandards for assessing the way in which quality was managed within a supplier company. These pressures included:

(a) increased international competition, particularly from Japanese manufacturers;

(b) the proliferation of multiple assessments whereby supplier companies would be assessed by many different customers;

(c) increasing product liability concerns and the limitations of product if standards in providing supplier protection.

The developments particularly in the UK during this period were typical of international trends in the adoption of quality system standards:

(a) 1974-the publication of BS 5173 Guide to the Operation and Evaluation of Quality Systems;

(b) 1979-the publication of BS 5750 by the British Standards Institution which is written by industry as the national third-party assessment standard;

(c) 1982-the UK government publishes a White Paper in which it is proposed to specify conformance to BS 5750 as a requirement in government contracts;

(d) 1983-the International Standards Organization (ISO) recognizes the widespread interest in quality systems standards and begins work on an international version based upon the U.K. national standard;

(e) 1985-the launch of the National Accreditation Council for Certification Bodies (NACCB) by the Secretary of State for Trade and Industry to establish competencies, and impartiality for bodies providing certification to BS 5750;

(f) 1987-the Consumer Protection Act provides an incentive to businesses to ensure the quality of their products or services in order to limit liability.

All these developments and plans culminated in the publication in 1987 of a range of common national and international quality system standards entitled Quality Systems—Model for quality Assurance,

(a) 1992-the European Community moves towards a common trading market which highlights the need for a Community-wide supplier assessment standard;

(b) 1994-revision of international quality system standards.

These standards, which were identical in content, included:

(c) BS 5750: 1987 Parts 0, 1, 2 and 3 (from 1994 entitled BS EN ISO 9000 series):

(d) ISO 49000 Series 9001, 9002, 9003. and 9004;

(e) EN 29000 Series 29001, 29002, 29003, 29004.

(f) IS 14000 Series 14001, 14002, 14003 and 14004.

Although these standards are issued an updated by the appropriate standards organizations (British Standards Institution, International Standards Organization, European Committee for Standardization Bureau of Indian Standards), the accreditation to the standard can be awarded by anyone of a number of organisations. These include bodies approved by the NACCB, for example:

(a) British Standards Institution, Lloyds, SGS Yarsleys, etc., and national standards bodies, for example:

(b) Singapore -Institute for Standards and Industrial Research, Standards and Industrial Research Institute of Malaysia DNV, Indian Register of Shipping etc.

The national—and indeed international—accreditation to IS 14000/855759 ISO 9000/EN 29000 has become a very standardized process and there exists only marginal differences between the methodologies adopted by the different certification bodies. The great strength of these standards has been their universal acceptance and application using a common format; together they represent the single most important international development in quality management since the Second World War.

Types of Quality System Standards

Quality system standards specify a set of minimum quality assurance requirements and are primarily used for:

(a) guiding supplier companies who are introducing quality assurance and helping in the structure of the quality system design;

(b) providing-a basis for assessing or evaluating a supplier's (or potential supplier's) quality system;

(c) establishing a contractual basis for quality system requirements.

Quality system standards are to be contrasted therefore with product standards which define the product requirements for a particular item or group of items (for example, electrical devices, safaty equipment, etc.). Quality system standards are concerned with the way in which the company is organized and operate and are independent of the product or service provided. Basically there are two types of standard.

Industry-ralated Standards are used by (usually large) purchasing bodies for example the defence, aerospace or nuclear industries. A typical example of an industry-based standard is the Ford Motor Company's Q101 Worldwide Supplier quality System Standard is as follows:

(1) Planning for Quality

(i) Definition of responsibilities

(ii) Formalized methods for quality planning

(iii) Review of quality plan changes

Total marks planning = 30

(2) Statistical Methods

(i) Use of SPC on significant parameters

(ii) Use of preliminary statistical studies

(iii) Use of process control charts

(iv) Application of continuous improvement

(v) Control of incoming products and services

Total marks statistics = 50

(3) General Quality Assurance

(i) Defined audit functions and responsibilities

(ii) Documented policy and procedures

(iii) Documented work instructions

(iv) Measuring and test equipment

(v) Test equipment maintenance and calibration

(vi) Control of inspection status

(vii) Quality records

(viii) Reaction to customer concerns

Total marks general = 80

(4) In-process and Outgoing

(i) Defined inspection methods

(ii) Documented rework and scrap procedures

(iii) Handling, storage and packaging procedures

(iv) Housekeeping issues

Total marks process = 40

Total marks for all 20 elements = 200

The basis of the Q101 is an assessment of each of the 20 elements. These are each marked out of a potential score of ten with a minimum total score of 140 required with no individual element scoring less than five marks.

Another widely adopted industry-specific quality system standard is the AQAP series used by the defence industries:

(a) AQAP 1-3 NATO Requirements for an Industrial Quality Control System;

(b) AQAP 4-2 NATO Inspection System Requirements for Industry;

(c) AQAP 9-2NATO Basic Inspection Requirements for Industry.

General Standards are those published by national standards bodies for general throughout industry and commerce. In recent years there has been an international convergence of these standards, as illustrated by the comparison of national quality system standards shown in Table 1.

Table 1. Comparison of National Quality System Standards

National standards body	*ISO 9001-Design Manufacture and Test*	*ISO 9002- Manufacture and Test*	*ISO 9003- Test*
United Kingdom	BS 5750: Part 1	BS 5750: Part 2	BS5750: Part 3
Australia	As 3901	CSAZ 299.2.45	CSAZ299.4.85
Canada	CSAZ 299.1-85	CSAZ299.2-85	CSAZ299.4-85
India	IS 14001	IS 14002	IS 14003
Ireland	IS 300:Part	IS 300:Part 2	IS 300:Part 3
Singapore	SS 308:Part 1	SS 308:Part 2	SS 308:Part 3
Europe	EN 29001	EN 29002	EN 29003
USA	ANS1/ASQCQ91	ANSI/ASQCQ92	ANSI/ASQCQ93

The main advantages for business in the publication of these quality system standards are as follows:

(a) They provide a common framework for assessing the management of quality and this removes the variability of traditional customer assessments.

(b) They provide for an international 'currency' in terms of the evaluation of a company's quality management which is important in export markets.

(c) They provide an internal focus for quality development which, because it is externally assessed, assists in the management of change process.

The main disadvantages of these universally applied quality system evaluation standards are, however, as follows:

(a) They represent a 'minimum' standard and therefore do not provide for long-term competitive advantage.

(b) They are mainly directed towards manufacturing or manufacturing engineering industries and therefore require interpretation for other business sectors.

(c) They are written in general terms and therefore open to interpretation.

The Benefits of ISO 9000 Accreditation

The international quality system standard ISO 9000 has been widely applied across a range of manufacturing industries from engineering to textiles, from chemicals to food, and increasingly in non-manufacturing sectors including banks, insurance companies, hotels and colleges of further education. The benefits of gaining accreditation to ISO 9000 can be summarized as follow:

* National and international recognition of the quality systems employed at the company is increasingly seen as an essential prerequisite to international trade. Many countries viewed the developments in ISO 9000 in the late 1980s as part of a 'Fortress Europe' policy to prevent imports to the European Community. The Standard has, however, been adopted throughout the world as the basis for good management practice for quality assurance.

In many sectors of industry it has become a minimum supplier requirement so that companies which do not possess ISO 9000 accreditation are not even asked to tender. The international chemicals group ICI has over 100 group companies approved to ISO 9000. In a recent survey (Figure 2) most companies implementing ISO 9000 had experienced an increase in turnover due to the opening of new markets and improvements in companies quality profile.

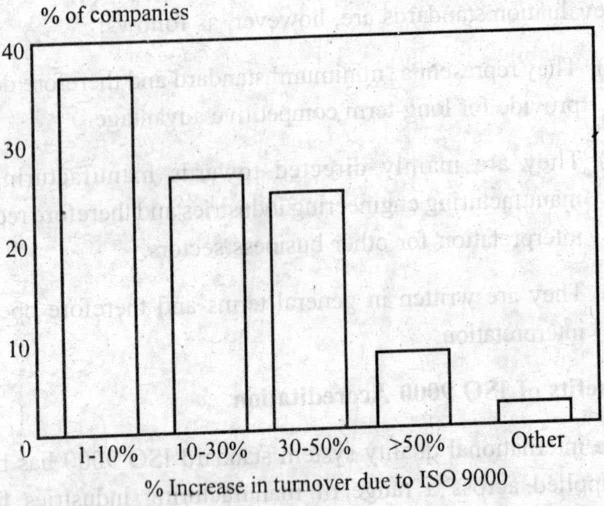

Fig. 2. Percentage increase in turnover to ISO 9000

* As more and more organizations have adopted ISO 9000 as the supplier standard this has reduced the need for multiple assessment. This provides national benefit in terms of reducing the overall expenditure on quality assessments and also reduces the number of assessments which have to be hosted by individual companies. Individual companies can also be as certain as the assessor as to what the agenda for assessment will be. The requirement of the ISO 9000 standard for an approved company to in turn have assessed its own suppliers has led to a 'mushrooming' effect whereby companies that have gained accreditation begin to impose ISO 9000 on their suppliers.

(a) ISO 9000 represents the basis for most companies' quality development by providing a foundation for future quality improvements. The Standard lends itself to implementation even before the organizational culture change necessary for total quality management is in place.

(b) Many companies have become more and more concerned with the potentially very damaging implications of product liability litigation. The enormous cost of industrial health and safety tragedies has led insurance agents to seek assurances as to the way in which client companies manage product quality. ISO 9000 systems are seen to provide documented evidence of conformance to contractual specifications and therefore lawyers and insurers have increasingly pressed for clients working in safety-critical areas to be ISO 9000 approved.

(c) ISO 9000 has increasingly become the basis of a range of product and process standards. Product approval in India now requires the manufacturer to have ISO 9000/IS 14000/ BS 5750/ EN 29000 accreditation, and in areas such as hazard and critical control point (HACCP) analysis in the food industry ISO 9000 is seen as an enabling system.

(d) On a personal level, individual employees are seeing a number of benefits in working for ISO 9000 approved organizations. These include the availability of well-defined methods and procedures which help the induction of new employees and a readily treasurable appreciation of quality system requirements. This applies to all types of employees, from designers to production engineers, from purchasing managers to clerical staff, as well as the more obvious quality specialists.

Many of the commentators on quality management, particularly those in the USA and Japan, have expressed concern that the European-dominated ISO 9000 approach does not deliver 'worldclass' manufacturing performance and 'gurus' such as Juran have suggested that quality system standards will not deliver continuous quality improvement. The point that is often missed, however, is that ISO 9000 has its major impact on organizations who are at an early stage of quality development and in particular the Standard has had a significant affect on small to medium sized companies who are not necessarily seeking world-class status. Indeed, for companies who are very mature in their management of quality then ISO 9000 may not offer significant developmental benefits.

The Scope and Interpretation of ISO 9000

The quality system standard ISO 9000 specifies three basic levels of system.

(a) **Level 1** (ISO 9001, EN 29001, IS 14001) applies, where the contract specifically requires design effort and the product or service requirements are principally stated in performance terms.

(b) **Level 2** (ISO 9002, EN 29002, IS 14002) applies where the specified requirements for the product or service are stated in terms of an established design or specification (which may be generated by the customer).

(c) **Level 3** (ISO 9003, EN 29003, IS 14003) applies where conformance to specified requirements can be adequately established by final inspection and testing of the finished product or service.

The ISO 9000 series therefore be seen as an 'encompassing' standard whereby all of the requirements of Level 3 are included in Level 2 and all the requirements of Levels 2 and 3 are included in Level 1:

Level 1	*Level 2*	*Level 3*
Design	—	—
Manufacture	Manufacture	—
Test	Test	Test

Sections in each part of the Standard are virtually the same so that the main differences between the levels therefore relate to the presence or absence of certain sections of the Standard. Table 2 provides a comparison of the parts of the Standard to illustrate the difference in scope.

The scope of the Standard, in terms of which of the elements are present and to what extent, determines how the Standard should be applied to any particular company. Typically a quality system designed to meet the requirements of Part 1 of the Standard will be in, excess of 30% larger than a Part 2 application despite there being - only one (5%) additional element.

Table 2. Cross Reference of Quality System Elements

Clause of ISO 9004	*Description of quality system element*	*ISO 9001*	*ISO 9002*	*ISO 9003*
1	*2*	*3*	*4*	*5*
4	Management Responsibility	4.1	4.1*	4.1*
5	Quality System	42	4.2	4.2*
7	Contract Review	4.3	4.3	4.3
8	Design Control	4.4	N/A	N/A
17	Document Centrol	4.5	4.5	4.5
9	Purchasing	4.6	4.6	N/A
–	Purchaser Supplier Product	4.7	4.7	4.7
11.2	Product-Identiftcation and Traceability	4.8	4.8	4.8*
10	Procss Control	4.9	4.9	N/A
12	Inspection and Testing	4.10	4.10	4.10*
13	Inspection Measuring and Test Equipment	4.11	4.11	4.11
11.7	Inspection and Test Status	4.12	4.12	4.12
14	Control of Non-Conforming Product	4.13	4.13	4.13*

Contd.

1	*2*	*3*	*4*	*5*
15	Corrective Action	4.14	4.14	4.14*
16	Handling, Storage, Packaging and Delivery	4.15	4.15	4.15*
17.3	Quality Records	4.16	4.16	4.16
5.4	Internal Quality Audits	4.17	4.17	4.17*
18	Training	4.18	4.18	4.18*
16.2	Servicing	4.19	4.19	N/A
20	Statistical Techniques	4.20	4.20	4.20*

Key * : Requirements less stringent than ISO 9001 or ISO 9002.

N/A : Element not present.

Note. The 1994 revision of ISO adopts a common nllmbering system for clauses in each of the three parts (*e.g.* in part 2, Design is referenced as 4.4 and described as not applicable) and in addition Part 2 was extended to 19 sections to include Servicing.

❐

7

Conceptual Approach to Source of Quality

The theories are narrow, idiosyncratic and highly particular to explain superior quality performance. They single out specific individuals or equipment, unique to the firm and deem them the primary contributors to quality. Occasionally, however, common explanations appear. Over time, these theories gain string support; today many of them are routinely and often unthinkingly cited by managers as the sources of superior quality. In the room air conditioning industry for example, managers at several firms were quick to claim that "we build in quality, we don't inspect it in". Other companies were equally insistent that their quality advantage came from "conservative engineering" or from a purchasing department that was "tough on vendors". Such claims are almost impossible to verify, because they involve broad generalisations.

Common explanations could easily mask distinctive practices and behaviours. Moreover, companies normally lack the data required to construct sound theories about the sources of quality. Their evidence is usually anecdotal and piecemeal, a series of highly visible examples from such evidence. The same is true of most academic research on the subject, but for different reasons. Few scholars have taken the time to examine prevailing controlled, comparative samples-have been rare. Rather, prescription has been the norm, and the primary tools have been statistical methods and mathematical proofs. But since researchers have spent little time examining actual quality levels or quality variations among firms, what works in practice has remained in doubt. By focusing on a single American industry and isolating specific practices and behaviours that are associated with superior quality performance, they avoid the problems listed above.

Moreover, it can only identify patterns of behaviour. With a sample of eleven manufacturing plants, independent variation among the several hundred possible contributors to quality is certain to be limited, and the impact of may single variable is almost impossible to determine. To aid in interpreting the results, plants have been grouped into four categories of quality performance: best, better, fair and poor. Two plants fell in the best category, and three in each of the other categories. Several measures were used to ensure consistency, companies did not always employ identical practices in recording information about quality. To organise the discussion, explanation for superior quality have also been grouped into categories, moving generally from early to later stages in the production chain.

Design Process

Surprisingly, the basic steps in the design process were quite similar at all plants in the industry, whatever their level of quality performance. New products typically progressed through four stages: concept development, engineering prototypes, pilot runs, and production units. Along the way, signoffs were obtained from marketing, quality control, manufacturing, purchasing, and service. At both the best and worst quality performers, were subject to the same engineering tests. In part, the similarity reflects the influence of trade associations, such as the American Refrigeration institute and the association, of Home Appliance Manufacturers, whose test standards were recognised throughout the industry. But even when managers claimed uniqueness, pointing to tests more rigorous than the norm, identical procedures were observed at competitors. For example, plants in several quality categories claimed that their reliability was enhanced by testing new products at temperatures above recommended standards.

The same was true of another often-repeated claim about the design process. Several plants reported that their defect rates were low because "our engineers sit down with manufacturing beforehand

and strive for manufacturability". Yet at virtually every plant, manufacturing's earliest involvement in the design process came at the same point: after prototypes had been constructed. Pilot runs were equally universal. At only one plant which boasted the highest defect rate in the industry was resistance reported. There, engineers claimed that manufacturing managers, under pressure to control costs, sometimes resisted pilot runs to avoid being charged for the set-up of new tooling. Because they were so widely shared, such practices as pilot runs and tests at high ambient temperatures cannot explain variations in quality performance. They were common denominators, not differentiators Managers in this industry were therefore mistaken in their belief that these practices distinguished good quality from bad. In one area, however the use of reliability engineering pronounced differences were found among plants. Despite the long history of these techniquê and their proven record in enhancing reliability, only the best and better quality performers showed any inclination to use them. At these plants, failure made and effects analysis, which assesses likely failure for new products. The other reliability techniques described were employed to lesser degrees. At only one plant, however, was there a comprehensive attempt to manage product reliability, and it was associated with one of the best quality records in the industry. At this plant, all stages of the design process included explicit discussions of reliability. For both new products and major product revisions, marketing was required to state quantitative reliability goals up front. The objective of the process was clear. According to the company's reliability and quality policy, managers were expected to "usê reliability and quality standards above the average of what constitutes good industry practice".

A large quality engineering staff was then empowered to conduct FMEAs, hazard and safety checks, and other formal assessments of reliability product performance was predicted using such measures as first year failure rates, mean time between failures, and mean time between maintenance. Eventuary, the results of these analyses were summarised in a management visualisation document; its purpose was to advise top management of potential product risks that might result in "the loss of product availability, loss of company reputation, or the incurrence of warranty expenses that may exceed planned reserve levels."

Signoffs on this document were require before pilot runs could begin; it was updated again before initiating full production. Finally, equipment and components were qualified to ensure that they were capable of meeting reliability requirements. Test procedures were stipulated, and choice was made between in-house testing and field trials. Because of its technical complexity, the choice process was directed by a special committee, the Programme Qualification Board, comprising experts from product engineering, development engineering, reliability engineering, quality control, service engineering, and marketing. Such a comprehensive approach to reliability was unique in the industry. Its link to subsequent quality performance-particularly to lower service call rates should be obvious. In fact, several other manufacturers also recognised up-front engineering and design as key contributors to superior quality, but they emphasised a very different approach: conservative engineering.

Conservative Engineering

In theory, conservative engineering is straight-forward. It requires that products be designed with ample safety margins. Components might be used below designated stress levels; units might be tested in conditions more demanding than normal operation; or exceptionally durable parts might be specified for critical sub-systems. In each case, the underlying motivation remains the same: to avoid problems, especially those that are unanticipated. Designers can seldom predict all conceivable failures. Among engineers this is known as the "ignorance factor". Because of it, large safety margins are frequently built unto products to compensate for "unknown stresses that might occur, variability in the strength of the materials used, variability due to workmanship". Conservative engineering, then, rests on well-established principles.

Several manufacturers claimed to be practicing conservative engineering, but when pressed, many had difficulty citing specific actions or behaviours as evidence. One chief engineer was blunt. After noting that his plant tore down and analysed only three to four competitive models per year, he admitted: "We like to think we're conservative in engineering, but we really don't know by comparison with the industry". At best, managers were able to cite two or three practices that they felt were indicative of conservative engineering. One, the testing of new models under especially stressful conditions, such as high ambient temperatures, has already been discussed; it was found at plants of both high and low quality performance.

Another, involving average compression ratios compression ratio in the first place. A dramatic example was provided by two plants that claimed the same numerical compression ratio for their product lines. One regarded the figure as average for the industry, while the other insisted it was low. A final practice that mangers associated with conservative engineering was choice of components. For marketing and cost reasons, designers frequently used different parts to perform the same function; occasionally they justified their choices by citing superior reliability or ruggedness. This was true of both thermostats and fan motors.

Bimetallic thermostats were generally considered simpler and less prone to breakage. Sealed fan motors were normally viewed as better protected and more reliable. But were these assumptions correct? One can get a rough idea by breaking out first-year service call rates by component, and then searching for differences in failure rates by types of parts. Lower failure rates should be associated with more reliable parts. But in this case, no statistically significant differences were found. Bulb and bimetallic thermostats had comparable failure rates, as did open and sealed fan motors.

Design choices, of course, involve more than components and test methods. Features, sizes, energy efficiencies, and the amount of customisation across models must also be considered. These decisions might be linked to a company's overall quality performance in a number of ways. For example, some models are inherently complex, and company that chooses to manufacture them exclusively might have an unusually high failure rate. Proliferating features might lead to the same result. Occasionally, variety alone might cause quality problems because of the difficulties it creates for manufacturing.

In terms of two critical variables that managers thought were related to quality performance-energy efficiency and Btu capacity-the answer is no. Models with energy efficiency ratings above the industry average were found at all levels of quality performance. Nor did results change when EERs were averaged by plant. Even then high overall EER scores were reported by plants in the best and worst quality categories. The same was true of btu capacity, which measures an air conditioner's cooling power and also serves as a proxy for size.

Most indicated that 30 to 40 percent of their sales came from models of less than 9,000 Btu have lower than average service call rates. While there was some evidence linking the poorest quality performers with the very highest Btu units suggesting that in terms of size and capacity, they had the widest range of offerings the differences were small and the production volumes insignificant.

A number of other measures might be used to examine product variety. The most commonly cited was the total number of models produced, for in most cases the large the number of models, the greater the variety. Some models, however, are closely related so much so that shifting from one to another causes hardly any description in manufacturing or design. In such cases, a better measure of variety is the number of chassis sizes produced. Each chassis size represents a distinct model family, a collection of units built around shared characteristics.

Using these criteria, the best quality performers were offering narrower product lines and less variety than their competitors. They manufactured an average of three chassis sizes and fifty-six models; by contrast, plants with the poorest quality offered eight chassis sizes and eightynine models. "When measured by the number of chassis sizes, these differences were statically significant across all quality categories. But the relationship was not significant when variety was measured by differences in the number of models-largely because of high variations within categories-even though the best and better plants generally offered narrower product lines than the fair and poor plants. These relationships make good sense.

A simple, narrow product line has the advantage of focus. In both design and manufacturing, each model receives ample attention. Fewer parts must be handled, fewer blueprints developed, fewer assembly operations mastered, and fewer disruptions overcome. Purchasing, production control, and work force management are greatly simplified, and higher productivity is the frequent result. Overall, the evidence in this chapter has been mixed. While superior quality was associated with narrow product lines and careful reliability engineering, few other relationships were found. Neither conservative engineering nor sophisticated test procedures had much explanatory power. High EERs and a broad range of Btu capacities were equally common at plants of widely varying quality performance.

Vendor Selection

Plants in this industry reported that most supply relationships were cordial and long-standing. A typical relationship was estimated at twelve years. In the same spirit, few vendors were dropped for quality reasons—a median of less than three per year. Such stability is easily explained. In this industry, neither products nor components have changed appreciably in recent years. A mature technology is involved, and also a mature supplier base. Choices are quite limited, especially for major components; according to industry sources, there were three primary suppliers of compressors, three of thermostats, six of fan motors, and one of switches. With the exception of compressors, where the Japanese have emerged recently as a new source of supply, pairings between manufacturers and vendors were expected to continue for many years.

For these reasons, traditional approaches to vendor selection were of limited value in explaining quality variation in the industry. Most changes of suppliers involved secondary components; even then they were few in number, Nevertheless, plants' policies in this area were still examined to see if approaches differed by categories of quality performance. No significant differences were found. Practices were either common to all plants, absent at most, or visible at both ends of the quality spectrum. For example, all plants involved members of the engineering department in vendor selection, but hardly any required visits to all potential suppliers before they were accepted as vendors. At both the best and worst quality performers, members of the quality department were actively involved in vendor selection. Overall, there was little or no evidence in the industry of an association between a plant's quality performance and its approaches to vendor selection.

Vendor Management

Approaches to vendor management on the other hand were clearly linked to categories of quality performance. Vendor management refers to the ongoing process of monitoring suppliers, responding to quality problems and improving incoming parts and materials. In each of these areas the best and better quality performers were employing practices quite different from their competitors. All of the best and better plants, for example, had formal programmes to prevent degradation of supplier quality. Typically, the programmes involved some type of "hit list" or "Ten Most Wanted List", identifying problem vendors on the basis of high incoming rejection rates. Most list were compiled annually and served as the basis for remedial action.

Vendors on the list were first contacted by the purchasing department and their shipment history was reviewed; frequently, members of the engineering and quality departments were then called upon to assist in problem-solving. Rapid improvement was expected, backed by an implicit threat: Too many years on the hit list, and business would be lost. To underline the connection, shipments from problem vendors were monitored especially carefully. No such practices were found at plants with fair or poor quality. Remedial programmes were ad hoc, if they existed at all. Even when problem vendors were identified, follow-up was partial and ineffective. Recurrent problems were the norm. In part, such behaviour reflects low expectations and an unwillingness to confront vendors.

For example, the quality control manager at the plant reporting the highest incoming rejection rate in the industry noted that in his three and a half years at the plant he could recall "only ten instances perhaps of leaning on vendors; and only one was changed after trying everything we could". Such accepting attitudes go a long way toward explaining vendor quality performance. A common tenet among managers is that "you get what you expect". But attitudes are only part of the story. A number of specific practices were also observed at the best and better quality performers but not other plants. These practice all revolved around the role of the purchasing department and the extent of its involvement in quality management.

Historically, U.S. companies have assigned a narrow role to purchasing departments. Technical skills have often been weak. As one manufacturing manager observed his purchasing agents were qualified to little but "shop for sources". Technical assessments of vendors have usually been assigned to members of the engineering and quality control departments. In the room air conditioning industry, that was the typical pattern at fair and poor quality performers. But at the best and better plants, purchasing agents took a more active role. Many had been trained in quality analysis and other technical skills, often in courses by their companies.

Thus, at these plants members of the purchasing department received regular reports on field failure rates; no such data came to purchasing agents at lesser quality performers. Using these reports, quantitative goals were set for vendor quality another practice lacking at lesser performers. Three of the best and better plants had gone even farther, creating special purchasing positions devoted to quality management. The individuals in these position, were responsible for monitoring suppliers and taking the lead in initiating improvement programmes. Perhaps the clearest indication of purchasing's role at superior performs was its involvement in new product development. At the best and better plants, members of the purchasing department were expected to attend design reviews and to keep suppliers in formed of new demands.

Expectations of vendors were low even at the most successful performers. Few managers thought that incoming quality could be greatly improved. At one of the better plants, the quality control manager observed that his goal was simply to keep incoming rejections below 2 percent—a number he had "dreamed up because in his experience it was the best that American manufacturers could do. Yet in the same industry, drawing from a similar set of suppliers, one plant had achieved an incoming rejection rate of 0.82 percent. Five years earlier the rate had been nearly three times higher. Forty-five percent of incoming parts and materials were now sent directly to the assembly line without receiving inspection and the number of receiving inspectors had fallen by a third.

At this plant, improvements in supplier quality were pursued aggressively. Programmes were proactive as well as remedial and the *status quo* was never accepted as "the best out vendors can do". For example, letters were sent from the plant's vice president for procurement to the presidents and chief executive officers of all suppliers, informing them of the need to improve their quality and announcing several new assistance programmes. Buyers were trained in such technical areas as design review, failure mode and effects analysis, and cost of quality calculations. With these tools in hand, they were trying to help suppliers design quality into their manufacturing systems instead of relying on end-of-the-line inspections. Suppliers were also held accountable for results. Each had to meet a number of quantitative goals, including cost per lot, permissible number of defects, and quality audit problems die to defective parts. To ensure proper oversight, the receiving plant's purchasing manager was evaluated each year on nearly identical measures: the number of unacceptable suppliers, incoming lot rejections, stock and assembly line rejections, and the percentage of quality audit problems and field failures due to defective parts.

The experience of this plant is revealing, for it shows that supplier quality can be improved even without intensive inspection. Most other plants in the industry, however, were less advanced and reported fewer direct contacts with vendors. For that reason, their receiving inspection practices played a more central role in explaining variations in quality performance. Receiving inspection involves the review of incoming parts and materials before they are combined into sub-assemblies and final products.

Reviews can be cursory or careful: at one extreme, they may provide for detailed oversight; at the other, their looseness may encourage permissiveness and lax standards. Assessing the degree of oversight is essential when comparing companies' approaches to receiving inspections in this analysis, the degree of oversight has been measured by two simple variables: the incoming inspection plan and a list of the criteria used to test incoming parts and materials. Because of its high cost, few plants today rely on 100 percent inspection. Rather, small samples of incoming goods are checked, usually on a lot-by-lot basis; should defects be found, inspection then expands to a larger number of items. This is a time honoured practice. Yet despite the long history, in this industry only the best and better quality performers were sampling according to accepted statistical techniques. Most were using some variant of Military Standard 105D, a well-known sampling plan. By contrast, the fair and poor plants were using unscientific, *ad hoc* approaches. In some cases, only the first item in a lot was checked; in others; the number of items to be checked was without any clear rational. Round numbers-for example, "check half a dozen" were common. Even more disturbing, at several plants production pressures were so great that entire lots were sometimes diverted around receiving inspection and sent directly to the assembly line.

At one plant, production schedules and orders from suppliers were poorly synchronised, leaving little slack; at another plant, receiving inspection was grossly understaffed with two workers responsible for reviewing 14,000 incoming shipments per year; at a third plant, the receiver at the shipping dock had long worked for the materials control department rather than the quality department, so his overriding loyalty was to keeping the assembly line moving. Whatever their roots, these practices had a similar impact: They shifted the discovery of defective parts and materials to later stages of the production process.

Approaches to sampling, then, were closely related to plants overall quality performance. They provide an obvious clue to the rigor of receiving inspection. By contrast, another measure of supplier oversight, the criteria used for testing incoming parts and materials, had little explanatory power. Plants at all levels of quality claimed to be conducting both functional and dimensional tests. All plants, for example, checked parts for conformance to blueprints and specifications; most also tested some aspects of performance. Comparable tests were cited for major components such as compressors, fan motors, and thermostats. Overall, incoming test procedures were little differentiated. Nevertheless, in a small number of cases improvements in quality could be traced directly to changes in test procedures. One of the better plants, for example, had resolved its problems with capacitors by insisting that they be checked electronically on arrival in the receiving laboratory. It had also curbed fan problems by introducing dynamic testing of fan blades. Improvements in vendor performance had quickly followed, and for the simplest of reasons: Faulty parts were now immediately visible'. As the plant's quality control manager noted: "Once the vendors found out they were being measured, they got better".

Unlike design practices, then, approaches to vendor management were clearly linked to levels of quality performance. Superior performers monitored incomings shipments through statistical sampling plans, identified problem vendors, insisted on remedial action, set quantitative goals for supplier quality and allowed purchasing departments to play an active role in product design and vendor evaluation. Such activities were lacking or attenuated at plants with lower quality. There, vendor monitoring was ad hoc or non-existent, receiving inspection was frequently bypassed, feedback to vendors was limited and unsystematic, and purchasing departments lacked the technical skills to do much than shop for sources.

Production and Work Force Management

Once designs have been set and components purchased, production at the factory can begin. A variety of processes are normally involved. For convenience they can be grouped into two broad categories: sub-assembly and final assembly operations. The former includes the fabrication and brazing of coils and the wiring of control panels; the latter involves the attachment of parts and the combining of sub-assemblies into working units. In this industry, neither stage is particularly complex. The technology has been stable for many years and products are standardised and mature. One would therefore expect to see great commonality among plants in both subassembly and final assembly operations. And, in fact, most plants had divided tasks similarly between the two stages. Sub-assembly activities normally took place off the assembly line and were worker-paced, while final assembly operations invariably employed a moving line set to operate at a predetermined speed.

Despite these similarities, manufacturing processes were not identical. Factories employed different layouts and used equipment of different vintages. Manufacturing tasks varied in sequence and duration. Assembly lines were sometimes short and sometimes ling; companies differed as well in their reliance on feeder lines. All these variables can be combined into a single, overarching category: process design, or the choice of methods, equipment, and approaches to manufacturing. Process design is not the only basis for manufacturing differences. In this industry, plants also differed in how they chose to operate their production processes. Some tried to keep the level of output smooth and unverying over the course of the year, while others allowed pronounced peaks and valleys. Capacity utilisation was tight at some plants but loose at others. Changeovers, second shifts, engineering change orders, and other disruptive influences were present to greater or lesser degrees. And managers had distinctly different ideas about work force training and supervision. Most plants in the industry employed comparable production processes. Technologies were basic and unsophisticated: the brazing of tubing, the handwiring of electrical connections, and the use of simple tools to mount mechanical parts.

There was only one significant exception, but it was found at one of the best plants in the industry. At this plant, managers observed that "the factory was designed around the product". A plastic molding technology had been specially developed for the air conditioner's casing and base pan; the resulting one-piece construction sharply reduced the number of required parts and attachments.

Simple assembly errors were eliminated by having screw holes prealigned. Most tubing was sealed by epoxy joints cured in an oven rather than by brazing; the resulting leak rates were only one-tenth of competitors'. Modern equipment was in place throughout the factory, including company-designed test equipment and a decoupled assembly line that allowed earlier and later stages of final assembly to be paced at different speeds. The connection between such advanced manufacturing processes and overall quality performance is obvious. Superior technology limits the opportunity for errors, simplifies the product, substitutes more reliable methods for those that are less certain, and builds flexibility into assembly-line management. Yet, despite these advantages, no other plant in the industry had committed comparable resources to the development of new techniques.

Most plants were using processes that had changed little in the past five years, and most had settled on a surprisingly similar sequence of operations. Choosing an assembly sequence for these reasons is hardly unusual. Industrial engineering criteria normally govern such decisions. But process flows are likely to affect quality as well as productivity. For example, parts that are attached earlier may be mounted more securely because workers find themselves less hampered by other components that are in the way. For the same reason, inspections may be easier when sub-systems are completed and tested before moving on the next stage of assembly. Errors may be reduced by ensuring that critical tasks like wiring are performed before units have become clogged with other parts. The connection between production sequences and quality performance can be tested empirically. At two plants, fans and associated parts were attached earlier; and at two plants, compressors were mounted much earlier in the process; at three plants, fans and associated parts were attached earlier; and at two plants, compressors were mounted much later.

Since first-year service call rates were collected at the level of individual components, failure rates can be compared to see if different production sequences were associated with differences in component reliability. The results of the analysis were mixed. Early attachment of fans made little difference in the incidence of service calls due to fans and associated parts. But the time at which such major components as fan motors and compressors were mounted was far more significant. The two plants that attached fan motors early had the lowest fan motor failure rates in the industry, and the two that attached compressors late had the highest compressor failure rates in the industry.

Of course, production sequencing is only one element of process design. Other elements that might affect quality performance include the age of plant and equipment, layout, and the configuration and speed of assembly lines. In this industry, age of facilities was not a significant factor. Of the best quality performers, one had the newest plant in the industry and the other the second oldest. The poorest quality performers included the oldest plant in the industry as well as the second newest. In terms of layout, virtually all companies had constructed feeder lines for building subassemblies; they were invariably worker-paced or else moving lines run at extremely slow speeds. Most final assembly lines were arranged in a semicircular or twisting flow; there was no obvious connection, however, between line configuration and such variables as ease of assembly or the spacing of workers along the line.

The best quality performers generally had short assembly lines and long cycle time. They therefore imposed only a limited division of labour. But the same was true of the poorest performers, who not only ran their assembly lines slower than other groups in the industry but also used relatively short lines. There was also high variance within quality categories, and the results for intermediate quality performers were without obvious pattern. Few firm conclusions can be drawn from such data. In three areas, however-each linked in some way to the intensity with which facilities were used differences among plants were more systematic, although not always statistically significant.

Superior quality performers left less space between workers on the line, had lower capacity utilisation rates, and ran production with less variation across the year. The first of these findings fits well with the literature on just-in-time production methods, which argues that eliminating the buffers between manufacturing processes leads to improvements in both quality and productivity. The other findings reflect the pressure put on production facilities and the amount of change introduced into manufacturing. In most cases, greater variation and pressure were associated with lower quality.

A limited set of process characteristics varied directly with overall performance. Most plants employed comparable technologies and equipment. Assembly-line length, layout, and speed were poorly related to quality. Production sequencing, however, was linked to component failure rates. Investments in major process changes were important as well for the only plant in the industry that had invested heavily in new production methods had defect and field failure rates among the lowest observed.

Confusion and change virtually an iron among production managers that change is the enemy of quality. In their eyes, variability and confusion go hand in hand. Shifts in skills and requirements impose new demands; they make control difficult and consistent output hard to obtain. New products, employees, and manufacturing methods often disrupt established operations and reduce quality. Change—especially when it is unanticipated or discontinuous—is frequently at the heart of the problem.

Manufacturing disruptions take a variety of forms. Most, however, can be grouped into three categories: changes include absenteeism, turnover, layoffs, overtime, and bumping anything, in fact, that alters the level of employee experience of reduces skills because of fatigue or lost knowledge. Production changes are closely related. They involve disruptions of manufacturing know-how or product familiarity that result from such production decisions as run length and the frequency of changeovers. Finally, product changes include the rate of new product introductions, the frequency of engineering change orders, and related variables tied to the stability of designs. Surprisingly, there was little relationship between overall quality performance and most traditional measures of labour force stability. Absenteeism, turnover, average overtime, new hires as a percentage of direct labour, and layoffs as a percentage of direct labour did not vary systematically with levels of quality. The variance within quality categories was large. And the same was true of the tenure of managers and supervisors. Longterm relationships were observed at both the best and the poorest plants.

These findings are difficult to explain, for labour force changes were cited frequently as a leading cause of quality problems. At one of the better plants, for example the director of quality claimed that "manpower moves the single biggest deterrent to quality" that he faced. In other industries, excessive overtime has been linked with reduced quality. Labour force changes might well have an important impact on quality even though they did not discriminate among plants in different quality categories.

The same was clearly true of bumping. Bumping occurs when several of a company's factories, all in a tight geographical area, are covered by the same union and seniority ladder. Layoffs at one location then trigger multiple job changes; workers will be "bumped" from one factory to another as the least senior people are removed from the system. Of course, bumping also occurs within factories as layoffs trigger job changes. But in this industry, managers claimed that bumping within factories had little impact on quality. By contrast, managers of plants at all quality problems, and one whose impact persisted for days. Two reasons were usually given: changing cycle times and the skill required for key jobs. In most cases, workers were bumped from operations with slow assembly speeds to operations that were run much faster. For example, one company was forced to move workers from its commercial refrigeration plants, with cycle times of 20-25 minutes, to its room air conditioner plant, with cycle times of 40-45 seconds. Workers who had previously regarded themselves as craftsmen were suddenly assigned to narrow, tightly defined tasks. The results were predictable: a high degree of "emotional upset" and mushrooming quality problems. By contrast, the one company reporting little difficulty with bumping was able to transfer workers between plants with comparable cycle times: 32-37 minutes at the high-seniority plant and .26-33 minutes at the room air conditioner plant. Bumping problems were also associated with changes in key jobs. Because these jobs went unprotected, untrained employees could be bumped into positions that were critical to subsequent quality performance. The impact was usually an immediate increase in defect rates until the new skills were mattered.

Bumping had a pronounced impact on other aspects of performance as well. At one plant, line speeds were slowed so much after bumping that two and one-half days of volume were lost. Another plant estimated that defect rates increased 25-50 percent after bumping and stayed at that level for three to four days. Most plants also reported a short-term increase in the number of inspectors and supervisors required to manage the assembly line. Thus, bumping provides a classic example of productivity and quality moving hand in hand. The same is true of manufacturing experience. Greater output brings increased product familiarity, refined methods, and new skills and techniques; these, in turn, are expected to improve efficiency and lower costs. A large literature has grown up around these principles and the associated mathematics-learning curves, experience curves, and progress functions. Surprisingly little, however, has been written about the relationship between manufacturing experience and quality.

Yet managers often see a clear connection industry, for example, changeovers were cited frequently as a source of quality problems. Changeovers occur when a company shifts from taking one model to making another and must "change over" the assembly line so that necessary parts, equipment, and staffing are available and in position. In the process, learning is frequently disrupted and the benefits of experience are lost. Not all changeovers, however, have the same impact. Some are readily accommodated, with few adjustments; other require sharp changes in assembly line operation. Managers claimed to have few problems with changeover within model families, because the sizing of products remained roughly the same and changes in job requirements were few.

A different size product was usually involved; with it came changes in line balancing, new mixes of task and skill, different welding and wiring configurations and different parts requirements. All of these imposed new demands on the production system and disrupted past learning. Managers reported that defect rates remained abnormally high for several hours after these changeovers. Estimates ranged from a 3-5 percent increase in defect rates to a 50 percent increase when especially complex unit were involved. A 10-15 percent increase was cited most frequently. Moreover, such problems were equally common at superior and inferior performers, since there was no statistically significant difference in the frequency of changeover at plants in different quality categories. A closely related measure of production experience is run length—the number of units produced each time a model is manufactured. Few plants meet their annual quantities through one production run. Rather, they build models in smaller volumes and separate lots at different times of the year. The precise size and timing of the runs is a scheduling decision, which all plants in the industry said was governed by sales and inventory targets. Quality seldom entered into the equation. Yet at the same time, several managers pointed to a connection between runn length and defect rates. Long runs, they noted, provided a stable environment—the opportunity to mater required skill through repetition. As techniques improved, defect rates normally fill, up to a point.

Differences in average run length were enormously important; they alone explained more than 30 percent of the variance in defect rates among plants in the industry. Even better results were obtained when the analysis was limited to a single plant. One producer provided data on leak rates and run lengths for three different models that it manufactured. Depending on the model, differences in run length explained a remarkable 50 to 70 percent of the variance in leak rates. From a quality standpoint, the worst manufacturing environment is one with bumping, short runs, and frequent changeovers. Each changeover is likely to cause defects to rise abnormally for a brief period. Because changing work assignments and short runs mean that workers never reap the full benefits of experience, defect rates will fall only a small amount between changeovers. The net result will be persistently high defect rates. It is no coincidence that the room air conditioning plant with the highest defect rate had frequent bumping and both the shortest average run length and the largest number of changeovers in the industry.

On the product side, engineering change orders are the counterparts of bumping, changeovers, and short-run lengths. They too introduce new elements into manufacturing––in this case, modifications in design often without suitable training or explanation. At one plant, for example, ECOs were never circulated to the quality department for prior comment or approval. Most other plants also reported problems in introducing ECOs smoothly in to manufacturing. The disruptive potential of such changes is obvious. But even though the best quality plants processed far fewer ECOs than the poorest plants-forty-two per year, as opposed to 131 the differences across quality categories were not statistically significant. The primary reason was high variance within one quality category. Plants with fair quality reported both the largest and smallest number of ECOs in the industry.

In some cases conventional wisdom has been undercut; in other cases it has been soundly supported. Overall, the following conclusions emerge: Design practices differed little at plants of varying quality performance, with one notable exception: Only the best and better quality plants used reliability engineering; The best and better quality plants generally offered narrower product lines than their competitors; Approaches to vendor selection differed at plants at plants of varying quality performance; The best and better quality plants all had formal programmes to prevent degradation of supplier quality; the fair and poor plants did not; Receiving inspection procedures were based on statistical methods at the best and better quality plants but were ad hoc or ignored at fair and poor plants.

Managing Quality

Today's quality professionals bear little resemblance to their turn-of-the-century predecessors. They are managers, not inspectors; planners, not controllers; sensitive to markets as well as to manufacturing. Competitive pressures have broadened their perspective and forced them to link quality with other business needs. The result is a discipline that now attracts the interest of managers at all levels. The discipline's center of gravity, in fact, has been shifting steadily toward greater and greater emphasis on management. Quality is no longer an isolated, independent function, dominated by technical experts. At a growing number of companies, it has entered the corporate mainstream, becoming an activity as worthy of attention as marketing or finance.

Strategic quality management is thus the capstone of a trend that began more than a century ago. In its original incarnation, quality was the responsibility of the manufacturing department; today it has emerged from the factory and has entered the boardroom. The accompanying shift in perspective is crucial to understanding modern thinking about quality. A succinct summary of the new view appears in a report prepared for the 1983 White House Conference on productivity:

Managing the quality dimension of an organization is not generically different from any other aspect of management. It involves the formulation of strategies, setting goals and objectives, developing action plans, implementing plans, and using control system for monitoring feedback and taking corrective action.

At the outset it might be helpful to define our understanding of 'management' and therefore refer the reader to two existing definitions of the word. Both are task-focused and point to the central role of the people, the human resources in an institution to achieve the tasks.

So 'management' is 'the process of securing decisions about what activities the organisation will undertake and mobilising the human and material resources to undertake them'; or it is, 'achieving goals by, with and through people and managers and all those responsible for the world of other adults'. In this context 'management development' can be defined as, 'the process whereby the management function of an organisation is performed with increasing effectiveness'.

There is clearly an imperative to improve strategies for management development at all levels in the education service. For example, Her Majesty's Inspectors reporting on school and college inspections during the period 1982/86 wrote that, 'one of the most significant determinants of a good school was high-quality leadership and good management'.

This was followed by a statement from the Senior Chief Inspector reporting on the state of England's education service and quoted in the Times Educational Supplement in 1990. He said, '...the management of schools leaves much to be desired. In only about a third of those inspected was senior management judged to be particularly effective'.[...] Therefore, the need for more coherent and effective strategies for school management development has never been more urgent.

Strategic Planning for Management Development

The effective delivery of management development must begin with strategic planning at several levels in the education service.

Schools. There is now much good practice available in terms of the effective planning and delivery of staff development and within this broader context for management development at school level. Such good practice must now become normal practice in all schools. The planning should have three main strands. The first is the drawing up of an institutional development plan (IDP) which is informed by an evaluation of the school. The IDP, relatively brief and readable document, will then be available as a basis for all other aspects of school planning such as curriculum development, staffing, budgeting and making decisions about the priorities for staff development. The second is the establishment of a staff development committee which is broadly representative of all groups on the staff and has appropriate delegated authority to plan and deliver a school's programme of staff in-service education and training within the agreed framework of priorities set out in the IDP. The third is a scheme of staff appraisal which is adequately resource and provides information about individual development needs.

Local Network. Local networks can help to prevent school-focused staff development from becoming too inward-looking by providing opportunities to work with colleagues fro, other schools in the area.

Regional and National. Effective planning for management development also requires a broader perspective at regional and national levels to help avoid too much 're-invention of wheels' and also to address strategic issues of more than local importance like the accreditation of programmes of management development and the preparation for headship.

Other Agencies. Several other agencies will continue to make a significant contribution to management development at all levels,

(1) **Industry.** One of the most encouraging features of school management development over the past few years has been the increased involvement of personnel from industry working on the basis of a partnership with education. A less regular feature of such co-operative arrangements in the movement of personnel from industry into schools or other aspects of the education service.

(2) **Professional Associations.** The teacher associations have also shown an increasing commitment to the professional development of their members and many now offer a wide range of courses and other forms of in-service education and training.

(3) **Higher Education and Independent Providers.** Higher education and a growing number to independent providers will continue to contribute to school management development at all levels. In the future their success or failure in this role will depend much more on the pressures of the marketplace, Schools, consortia and other networks of institutions or individuals will be shopping around for the best and most appropriate opportunities for management development at prices which they can afford.

Succession Planning and Career Development

An overall strategy for management development should embrace the maintenance and development of institutional management structures as well as the personal development of individual managers. From time to time key people will leave an institution for a variety of reasons and, although man individual resignations are unpredictable, local a regional patterns in vacancies are discernible. Succession planning begins with this type of analysis and uses the results to consider the action required to increase the chances of filling vacancies with a minimum loss of overall management performance in an organization.

Large organizations are more able to implement in house systems of succession planning and can fill many vacancies through internal promotion. Schools on the other hand are preventative of small and medium-sized organizations which can do much less to predict succession problems and must usually resort to external appointments to fill their vacancies. This means that they are more vulnerable to market forces over which they have little control. There is a danger that the move towards the local management of schools will compound the problem of fragmentation in the education service and put further limits on the possibility of succession planning at local level.

However, the education service as a whole has usually grown; its own managers. It is therefore quite possible to envisage on approach to succession planning which has a local perspective provided that overall data about teacher supply and conditions is available at national level. Such data could then be supplemented by regional and local knowledge of staffing structures in schools, age structures, wastage rates and recruitment patterns which are potentially available to local education authorities. Armed with this knowledge, LEAs and consortia of schools would then be in a position to adopt a more positive approach to succession planning.

For example, they could take steps to increase the number of qualified application for particular types of vacancy in the locality by joint advertising, training and development programmes. Both the development and the selection of staff could be informed, particularly at senior level, by the use of regional educational assessment centres which would provide a profile of managerial potential. Individual career development is clearly an important concomitant of succession planning. In school staff development and the wider provision of in service education and training must find the right balance between the requirements of the present job, personal professional growth and preparation for promotion. Certainly careers advice and appropriate support in the planning of a personal development programme should be available to all teachers as should opportunities to gain experience of management responsibilities at a higher level.

Assessment for Management Development

Without some assessment of need, the time and money spent on the management development of an individual can be wasted or at least, be of only limited value. Staff appraisal and self-analysis questionnaires may help to inform development needs but both are relatively limited and blunt instruments. There would be greater coherence at all levels of management development if we could approach the assessment of need and then the provision of development, using a micro-surgeon's knife rather than the traditional blunderbuss, firing off development opportunities in the hope that a few will strike individual targets.

There is also much to be gained by raising the profile of personal and generic management competencies as a vital component of development programmes alongside the more traditional tasks-related and job-specific aspects of middle and senior management roles in schools. For example, there are plenty of courses available to learn about curriculum planning, timetabling, budgeting and marketing the school but far fewer opportunities which focus on the development of generic competencies like judgement, decisiveness, leadership and written communication.

The Educational Assessment Centre project, started in September 1990 and based in Oxford, worked with 28 clients from the maintained and independent school sectors in England, Wales and Scotland. It is an important and ambitious attempt to meet both the requirements outlined above by providing senior staff with a detailed diagnostic profile for further professional development based on 12 generic management competencies. The initial aim of the EAC project is to improved the management competencies of further headteachers so that they will be effective managers as well as successful educators. It should be emphasized that the project is applicable to management development in all aspects and phases of the education service.

Assessment centres have been used in both the public and private sectors of employment for over 50 years to inform the process of developing and selecting senior managers. Their use has been restricted to senior levels primarily because assessment centres that productive valid and reliable data are relatively expensive to establish and operate. Establishing an assessment centre in particular occupational setting is a complex and technical process which draws on the expertise psycho gists and professionals. The EAC model being adated for use in the UK has been in operation for a out 15 years in North America and Australia. It has been the subject of two large scale independent research studies and its high quality has now been proven.

It is important to stress that an EAC is a process not a place. However the participants and assessors will obviously assemble at a particular place, usually a hotel or management centre to go through the process. It takes about one and a half days for the participants to complete the exercises observed by the assessors. At this point the participants depart and the assessors then spend a further two to three days in 'consensus'. They go through every aspect of each participant's performance on the exercises in fine detail and agree the performance ratings. Each participant will have been directly observed by five of the assessor team during the completion of the exercises so that there is a broadly based and therefore more objective, overview of performance. At the end of consensus each assessor will write a final report on one participant but will draw on the views of the whole assessor team. The report is structured according to the 12 management competencies with a section of strengths followed by a section of competencies which need improvement and finally some suggestion's for further professional development.

The initial focus for further development is always on the things that a participant can do 'on the job' supplemented by the opportunity to spend some time alongside another senior colleague in a nearby school. This can provide the opportunity to observe someone with a difference style working in a less familiar context. For a deputy head wanting to prepare for headship, this might mean working more regularly with their own head (acting as a 'coach') and spending time alongside another experienced head. To help with this developmental support, the EAC project is providing training for experienced heads in the process-skills of coaching and monitoring. A portfolio of further professional development opportunities is also being prepared. This will include a range of high quality and cost-effective opportunities currently available from providers of management development in both the private and public sectors. They have been analysed according to the 12 competencies so that if, for example, a participant is relatively weak in problem analysis, judgement, organizational ability and leadership then he can be directed to appropriate management development which focuses on that particular cluster of competencies. In so doing, we believe that the EAC process is getting us closer to the 'micro-surgeon's knife' of professional development referred to earlier in the section. It is expected that EAC participants will also draw on other forms of support for their further development like the LEA, higher education, industrial placements and professional associations. Inevitably the EAC process will lead some participants away from headship as the next career move and towards alternatives which would better utilize their particular range of strengths.

❐

8

Quality Costs and Taguchi Loss Function

The fact that quality development is a most essential element for competitiveness is based upon the notion that the costs are outweighed by the business benefits. Two foremost questions in the minds of managers responsible for implementing quality improvement are:

(a) What is the cost of quality management?

(b) What are the returns of quality improvement?

Perhaps the most powerful message that emerged during the 1870's and 1980's in relation to the importance of managing quality effectively was:

"Quality development can simultaneously improve the external economics of a company (in terms of market share/revenue) and the internal economic (in terms of the cost of providing the product or service)."

It is no secret that in business there are only two problems—customers and competitors and therefore the attractiveness to a chief executive of a process that at the same time both improves the satisfaction of customers and reduces costs in comparison with competitors is overwhelming.

If quality is considered as the 'conformance to specifications' then in essence the economics of quality relates to the balance between:

(a) the cost of conformance; and

(b) the cost of non-conformance.

In terms of the overall economics of quality, the message is a simple one:

No product or service is ever cheaper to provide through doing things wrong the first time. Failure is expensive and often manageable sometimes inviting legal complications whereas prevention can be a planned management investment with significant overall cost benefit.

However, to fully understand the 'micro' economic processes within an individual business in terms of how certain quality improvement activities benefit into cost benefits requires careful analysis. Through investing in the cost of conformance, we can reduce the cost of non-conformance and therefore reduce the overall cost of ownership as shown in Figure 1.

It is the positive relationship that exists between the investment in quality improvement and the benefits from operational costs that has prompted commentators such as Crosby to observe that 'Quality is free'.

Typical Quality Costs

It is the magnitude of quality costs that has provided so much of the impetus to the 'quality revolution' in manufacturing and

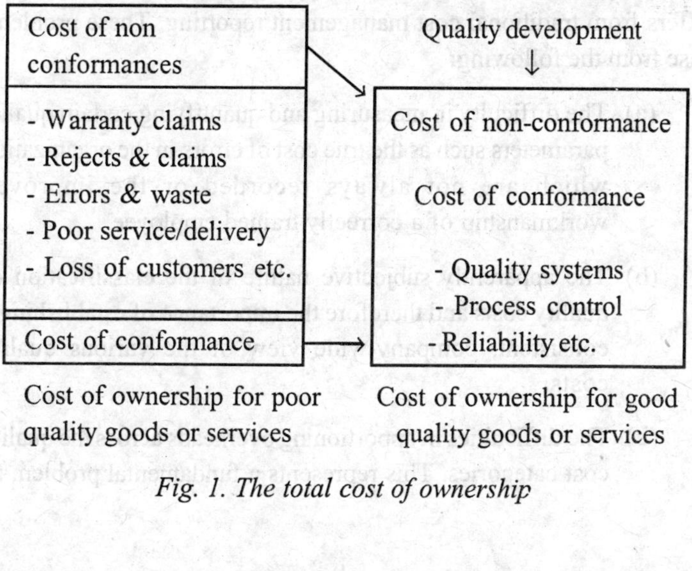

Fig. 1. The total cost of ownership

service companies. Independent surveys from many different countries have shown:

(a) Manufacturing companies typically can spend between 20% and 30% of total sales revenue on the cost of quality;

(b) service companies spend in excess of 50% of their operational costs on the management of quality.

Taking the categories of quality costs (section 3.5) as:

(c) prevention costs;

(d) appraisal costs;

(e) failure costs;

The typical distribution of quality costs through the quality development life-cycle. Represented in this way, the economics of quality is an attractive proposition, particularly in mature markets where the potential for increasing profitability through increased market share is limited.

The Role of Quality Costs in the Quality Development Process

Most organizations experience problems in introducing the concept and the measurement of quality costs, as this approach differs from traditional cost management reporting. These problems arise from the following:

(a) The difficulty in measuring and quantifying certain quality parameters such as the true cost of errors in the organization which are not always recorded or the improved workmanship of a correctly trained employee.

(b) The apparently subjective nature of the classification of quality costs and therefore the importance of establishing a consistent, company-wide view of the various quality costs.

(c) The difficulties in apportioning overheads across the quality cost categories. This represents a fundamental problem as the overhead activities (such as management time spent correcting errors and troubleshooting) are often the key quality costs. The moves towards activity-based systems may improve this particular difficulty.

(d) The technical accounting problems of a cost measurement system which by definition is incomplete (not all costs within an organization are classified as quality costs) and therefore does not produce a 'balanced' account which would permit validation.

Despite these problems, the ongoing measurement of the cost of quality in an important element of quality development. The main benefits in adopting a system for measuring the cost of quality are:

(a) management focus in providing a measure of financial benefit to sceptical senior managers struggling along the demanding road of quality improvement.

(b) project focus in helping to identify which areas of the business should be prioritized in terms of quality improvement activities;

(c) measurement focus in establishing a quantifiable performance measure of the progress made through the more effective management of quality.

The reporting format and frequency are generally, company specific although certain 'standardized' approaches are emerging as discussed in sections 3.4 and 3.5. The key indices normally quoted for the cost of quality are as follows:

(a) Sales Ratio. This is the ratio of the total cost of quality to the net sales value (usually expressed in financial terms and reported to senior management):

$$\frac{\text{Total quality cost}}{\text{Net sales}} \qquad \text{...(1)}$$

(b) **Cost Ratio.** This is the ratio of the total costs of quality to the overall cost ot operation:

$$\frac{\text{Total quality cost}}{\text{Cost of operation}} \quad ...(2)$$

(c) **Unit Ratio.** This is the ratio of the cost of quality per unit produced (manufacturing) or provided (service):

$$\frac{\text{Total quality cost}}{\text{Units produced}} \quad ...(3)$$

(d) **Labour Ratio.** This is the ratio of the cost of quality to the direct cost of labour (usually expressed in hours and reported to line management):

$$\frac{\text{Total quality cost}}{\text{Direct labour costs}} \quad ...(4)$$

The most widely used of these cost quality bases is the sales ratio. This is because this ratio represents both the internal implications of quality management (reduced cost of quality) and the external implication (improved customer service). However, like all simple measures of complex activities, such ratios should be treated with care to ensure that any 'special factors' such as labour automation, product mix changes or transient, market conditions do not distort the measures.

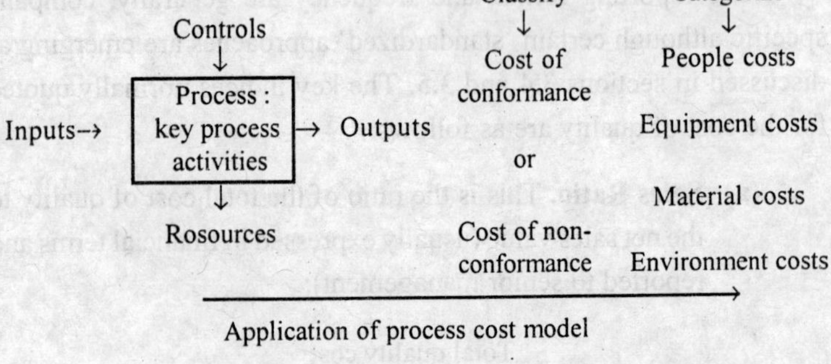

Fig. 2. The process cost of quality model.

Process Cost Models

Two basic approaches to the collection and presentation of the cost of quality have emerged:

(a) prevention, appraisal, failure PAF) costing;

(b) process cost modelling.

The more traditional of the two approaches was the PAF costing model, but increasingly as companies move towards total quality management.

In detetmining the cost of quality for a business process, the basic elements need to be defined as shown in Fig 2.

To identify the cost of quality using the process cost approach the key stages are:

(a) Stage 1. establish the quality improvement team to prepare the process cost model and collect the data.

(b) Stage 2. identify the business processes for which the cost of quality is to be determined.

(c) Stage 3. decompose the business process in terms of the constituent key activities and for each of these activities identify the costs associated with people, equipment, materials or environment.

(d) Stage 4. classify the quality costs in terms of the cost of conformance or the cost of non-conformance.

The costs collected can be either actual costs taken from financial reports or synthesized costs which are derived from elemental data (for example, the number of hours taken to complete an activity x hourly rate). The elements of a typical process model cost of quality report is shown in Fig 3.

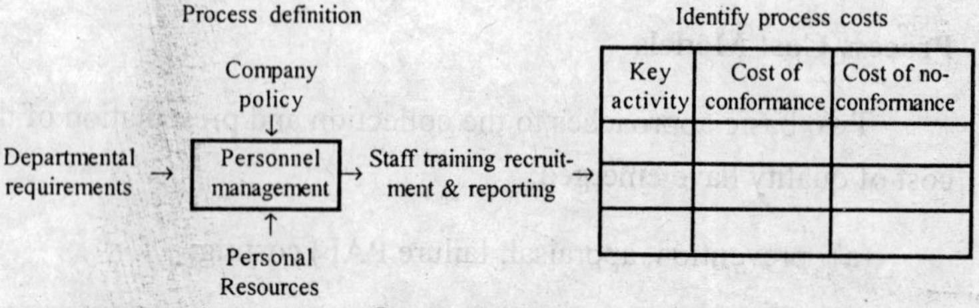

Process cost reprort

Process : Personal			*Process owner : personal manager*		
Process conformance	Cost		Process non-conformance	Cost	
	Actual	Synthesized		Actual	Synthesized
Total process conformance cost:			Toal Process non-conformance cost :		

Fig. 3. The process cost of quality model report.

Prevention, Appraisal and Failure (PAF) Costing

The traditional approach to reporting the cost of quality is to classify the costs as follows:

Prevention Costs are the costs associated with the planning and operation of a quality management system to reduce the failure and appraisal costs.

Typical prevention costs incurred by an organization include:

(a) **development of inspection and test equipment** in terms of the specification of such items and the associated calibration costs, but excluding the capital costs;

(b) **supplier quality assurance**, including development programmes, establishing specifications and supplier assessment;

(c) **training**, including both quality system specific training programmes and the more general staff development activities.

(d) **quality assurance activities** such as quality system design, implementation, audit and review;

Prevention costs primarily relate to the quality assurance activities within the organization.

Appraisal costs are those costs associated with verification activities to ensure conformance to requirements although they exclude those costs associated with re-inspection following the failure of a product or service. Typical appraisal costs include:

(a) **incoming materials/services verification**, including the inspection of pre-contract trials;

(b) **in-process verification**, including all checking of the required parameters to ensure product or process conformance;

(c) **inspection equipment**, including the depreciation costs - of capital equipment, maintenance costs and the cost of consumables used in the inspection activities;

(d) **process control activities**, including the cost of monitoring and evaluating process variation;

(e) **analysing, reviewing, reporting and storing** the appraisal data.

Appraisal costs primarily relate to the quality control activities within the organization.

Internal failure costs are the costs associated with the non-conformance of the product or service prior to the transfer of ownership to the customer. Typical internal failure costs include:

(a) **scrap** of defective product which cannot be reworked, including the material and direct/indirect labour costs associated with the rejected item;

(b) **rework or replacement costs** for product which does not conform to the specified requirements, including the costs associated with the identification of the remedial action and root causes;

(c) **modification downgrading and concessions**, including the effort involved in obtaining agreement to reduce the specification and the loss in sales revenue associated with having to reduce the price;

(d) **re-inspection costs** associated with product having previously failed to meet requirement and having to be reworked.

External Failure costs are those costs associated with non-conformance of the product and which are detected after the transfer of ownership to the customer. Typical external failure costs include:

(a) **rejected/returned product**, including the cost of repairing or replacing the product and the associated handing costs;

(b) **warranty claims and product liability,** which may represent costs significantly in excess of the actual value of the product or service supplied and often include recall costs for equivalent sales to other customers;

(c) **customer dissatisfaction,** including the investigation of complaints, the commercial downgrading of the product or service and the potential loss of future sales.

Internal and external failure costs primarily relate to the ineffectiveness of the way in which quality is managed within the organization.

The main problem in establishing a PRF quality costing system often lies with the judgemental nature of classifying costs as either prevention, appraisal or failure and the different nature of these three concepts. Prevention represents an intention, appraisal represents an activity and failure represents and outcome. For example, a design review is an attempt to prevent errors of specification whereas the activity is one of appraisal and yet the outcome is the detection of internal failures of the designer.

Many companies fail at this classification stage in the implementation of quality costs. However, the real benefits in measuring the cost of quality are derived from analysing the ongoing trend and therefore consistency of interpretation is perhaps more important than accuracy of definition.

The main stages in the implementation of a PAF quality costing system are as follows:

1. Establish senior management support for the philosophy of measuring quality improvement through the report of quality costs.

2. Establish a cost of quality action team comprising staff from a range of functions including finance and quality assurance.

3. Identify the quality costs using the categories described above and collect data on the costs within each of the categories. Often a pilot study in one defined part of the organization is a sensible approach for a company introducing a quarrty cost system for the first time.

4. Introduce awareness training for employees to emphasize the reasons for identifying quality costs and the relationship with programmes for quarrty improvement in reducing the failure costs.

5. Collate and validate the quality cost information to ensure both the accuracy of the data and consistency in the interpretation, and establish procedures for the ongoing preparation and presentation of quality cost reports.

6. Prepare and distribute the quality cost report as a mechanism for focusing and measuring quality improvement and ensuring reaction by the recipients.

Group function:				*Location:*		
Current period				*Year to date*		
Budget	*Actual*	*Var.*	*Quality costs*	*Budget*	*Actual*	*Var.*
			Prevention costs			
			Total prevention costs			
			% of total costs			
			Appraisal costs			
			Total appraisal costs			
			% of total costs			
			Internal failure costs			
			Total internal failure costs			
			% of total costs			
			External failure costs			
			Total external failure costs			
			% of total costs			
			Total cost of quality			

Fig. 4. Typical PAF cost of quality model report.

A typical format for a PAF cost of quality report is shown is Figure 4.

Quality Cost Reporting

Both the process cost approach and the PRF cost approach require the identification and categorization of cost information as illustrated in Figure 5.

Whilst the format of the reports may be different the underlying philosophy remains the same. By focusing upon the cost of conformance data, the process model approach encourages improvements (reductions) in how the organization achieves quality and this is perhaps rather more consistent with an ideology of continuous improvement.

The PAF quality cost reports are traditionally employed primarily to reduce the failure costs. Upon the introduction of a quality cost system, the reporting of the information is normally presented on a relatively frequent basis (typically either monthly or quarterly), although in time annual reporting is perhaps most common.

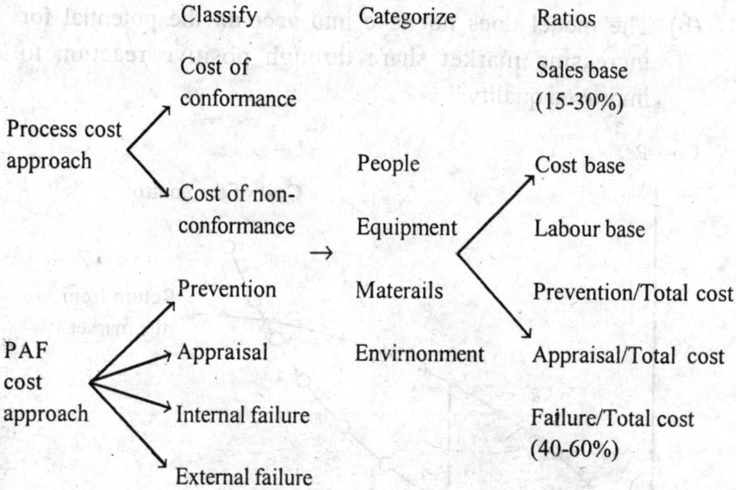

Fig. 5. Approaches to reporting the cost of quality.

The Traditional of the Cost of Quality

One of the main effects of the progress made in recent years in the wide spread and systematic collection and review of quality costs has been to amend management thinking on the relationship between quality and cost. The traditional view of this relationship has focused upon the concept of 'optimization,' whereby at a predefined quality level, the difference between the 'returns' and the 'cost' is maximized. Fundamental to this view is the 'law of dinishing returns'. which indicates that a disproportionate amount of effort is required to further improve the quality of the product or service beyond the stage of general acceptability to the customer. This traditional approach is epitomized by the view of the relationship between the cost of improving the level of quality and the return from the marketplace in terms of how much the customer is willing to pay, as illustrated in 6.

However, when quality management is viewed as a developmental process, this traditional view has two serious flaws:

(a) The model assumes a certain approach to the management of quality, namely quality control rather than quality assurance or total quality management.

(b) The model does not take into account the potential for increasing market share through positive reaction to improved quality.

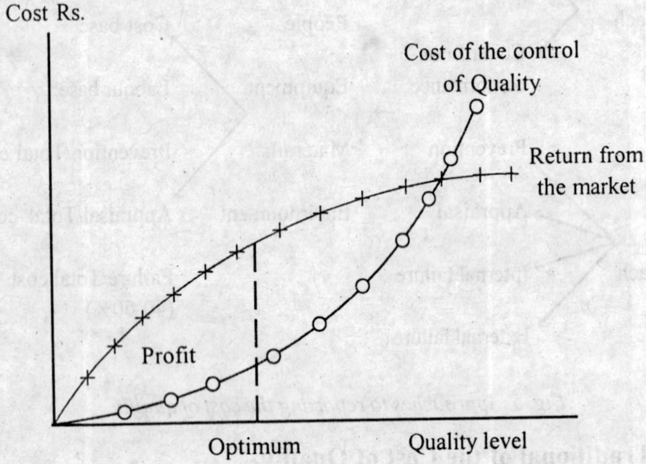

Fig. 6. Traditional view of the relationship between quality and value.

When traditional thinking is applied to the internal costs of managing quality the same misleading relationships emerge, whereby the optimum quality level occurs at the point at which the costs of conformance and non-conformance balance as shown in Fig 7.

Again inherent in the misconception surrounding this view is that quality is controlled through checking/inspecting and the cost continues to rise as epitomized by the phrase 'don't spend too much money on getting the quality right'. It was the fundamental reappraisal, of management thinking on the cost of quality performance models that promoted the international trends in quality development during the 1970 and 1980s.

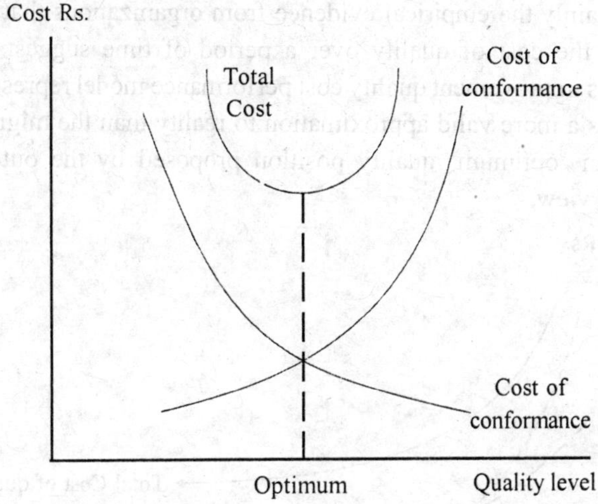

Fig. 7. Traditional view of the internal relationship between the costs of conformance and non-conformance.

The Total Quality-View of the Cost of Quality

One of the most influential corollaries of the quality development process is that mature companies actually spend less on the total cost of quality.

In the terms of the PAF approach to quality costing, the relationship between the investment in prevention activities and the reduction in failure costs suggests that as the quality level improves the cost of achieving it reduces. This represents a powerful inducement for quality development. Similarly, using the process cost model approach the quality improvement process involves a reduction both in the cost of non-conformance (waste and inefficiency issues are often tackled as 'bottom-up' projects involving process operators) and the cost of conformance (generally process management issues requiring 'top-down' involvement).

The investment in improvement and prevention associated with quality development leads to a relationship between cost and quality in which the satisfaction of internal and external customers reduces the overall cost of quality as shown in Fig 8.

Certainly the empirical evidence from organizations that have measured the cost of quality over a period of time suggests that continuous improvement quality cost performance model represented in Fig. 8 is a more valid approximation to reality than the migration towards an 'optimum' quality position proposed by the outdated traditional view.

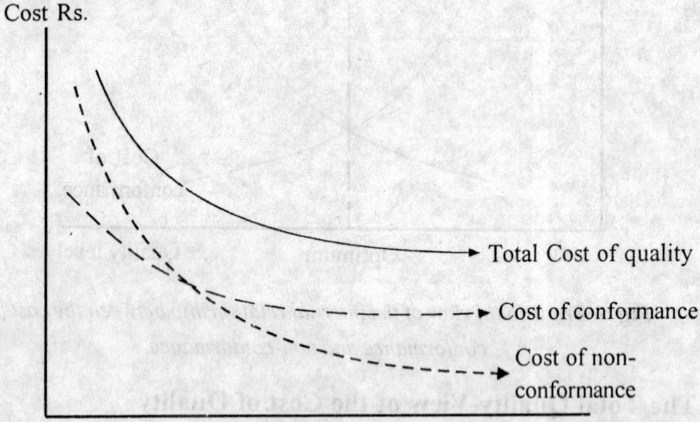

Fig. 8. The total quality relationship between quality cost and quality development.

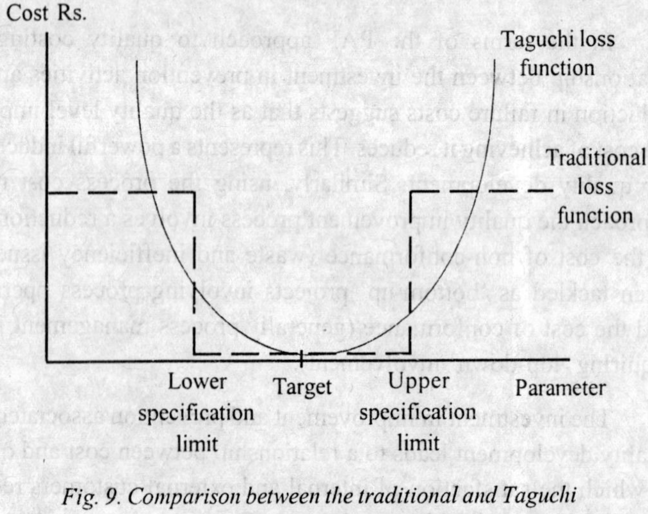

Fig. 9. Comparison between the traditional and Taguchi views of loss due to deviation.

The Taguchi View of the Cost of Quality

A further alternative for the relationship between the performance of cost and quality has been proposed by Taguchi in which quality is defined as: the loss a product causes to society after being shipped. Whilst at first examination this may not appear to be either a very informative definition or indeed consistent with one's intuitive understanding of the meaning of the word 'quality', it does not offer an interesting alternative insight into the way in which quality and cost are related. The traditional view of the cost of non-conformance is that, provided a product or service is supplied within tolerance, then the cost is zero. The cost of non-conformance, by definition, only emerge once the product or service is out of specification limits and therefore the cost model is a discoutinuous step function as illustrated in Figure 9.

The Taguchi view, however, suggests that the cost or loss commences as soon as the product or service deviates from the target (or nominal) value. Further, Taguchi maintains that the relationship is quadratic and that the cost varies with the square of the deviation from the target as shown in Figure 10. The Taguchi loss function is therefore represented by:

$$L(y) = k\,(y - m)^2$$

loss associated with parameter y = A constant k times the square of the difference between the parameter and the target m

Clearly the Taguchi model is a more severe case and plan much greater emphasis upon providing products or services which are as close as possible to the target value and not simply within specification.

These alternative models of the relationship between cost and performance when the product or service lies within specification yet not at the target value begs the question: 'Which view is valid?' Certainly the Taguchi model is appropriate where:

(a) elemental products or services are combined to form a more complex system (for example, the assembly of a motor car, television set or railway timetabling) where the combinational effects of tolerancing can be detrimental;

(b) the cost of quality is to be used to establish the tolerances of the product or service.

The Role of Benchmarking in Quality Development

Another important element in measurement of quality development is the comparative analysis of performance termed benchmarking. Benchmarking can be defined as:

Measuring the performance of processes within your organization, comparing these performance levels with best-in-class companies and, where deficiencies exist, using the information on best practice to improve your organization's own business processes.

The idea of comparing your performance with competitors is clearly not a new concept but has increasingly become a popular quality improvement activity due in part to the following:

(a) There are benefits to be gained from making performance comparisons across a range of business sectors and not simply with your competitors.

(b) Customers are supplied by a wide range of different types of organizations and therefore the standards for customer service may be established by other sectors of commerce or industry.

(c) Lookiny outside your own industry or business sector can lead to 'break-through' thinking and often the implementation of ideas from elsewhere is more readily achieved.

(d) Internally generated improvement objectives or targets. can be unnecessarily limited.

Benchmarking is particularly applicable to service organizations or departments as a mechanism for identifying quality improvements and generally the lessons learnt are very much more transferable.

❐

9

Statistical Process Control

No inspection system was ever designed to check every quality characteristic of every product. Any attempt to do so would he not only economically unfeasible but fooiish and in many instances, physically impossible. And yet some specific knowledge of each quality characteristic's physical status is essential. Without such knowledge, a product could not conceivably be considered ready for delivery to the customer. Therefore, sampling inspection of some sort must be used throughout industry.

Sampling is an attempt to determine for what larger group of characteristics (the population) the statistics for a selected segment (the sample) would be representative and how representative they would be for a given larger group. Sampling by its very nature warns that management risks are involved. In its original role, statistical quality control assessed the value of these risks to determine what sampling plans could be established that would provide the precise degree of protection required or desired by a company. Later it broadened its usefulness to include just about every area of industry where decisions must be based on limited factual information or data.

The ultimate value of statistical quality control goes beyond its application to a particular set of circumstances or problems. Its disclosure of the inherent variation in all things can be employed to better understand the basic need for discipline throughout industry. The use of statistics in industry has grown enormously in recent years; in a purely mathematical sense, the science has become highly complex in many of its applications. No attempt will be made here to delve into purely mathematical applications or derivations of statistical formulas as applied to quality control. Sufficient knowledge to appreciate its management value can be gained from a review of its fundamental usefulness and of certain basic principles involved.

To the nonuser, statistical quality control frequently seems unduly complicated a notion aided and abetted by a jarrgon redolent with such terminology as probabilities, frequency distributions, three sigma control limits, standard deviations, and the like. Once understood, however, this terminology assumes a meaningful role in one's understanding of variation, which, in turn, can sharpen one's mode of thinking. It can help anyone, from machine operator to top executive, make better decisions based on a clearer and broader view of the facts at hand.

The fundamental purpose of statistical quality control is to guard against the manufacture of unacceptable products by utilizing the process of inspection, the analysis of data and action. The quality measured represents the ability of a product to conform to its specifications and is usually termed a "conformance quality." Control is simply the business of assuring conformance. The basic principle of statistical quality control, regardless of volume, is that production should not be allowed to proceed unless there is reasonable assurance that a product of the desired quality will result. The statistical principles and practices applied have as their specific aim the detection of assignable causes of variation where such detection is masked by chance causes. Elimination of assignable causes, one by one, thus achieves greater uniformity, less waste, reduced costs, and assurance of a quality product.

The universal existence of variability must be accepted. Regardless of the amount of care exercised in production, exact dimensions, weight, and other characteristics vary. Production output for a given number of men, or for a given individual, varies from one hour to the next, even though the same physical conditions appear to prevail. Articles in any population that is, the total possible objects, individuals, or things under observation vary among themselves. This would be true even if no real differences existed, because the process of actual measurement introduces apparent differences, or variability. There is no such thing as constancy in nature; all things vary, and the range of variability, whether it be narrow or wide, will not determine whether it is caused by chance alone.

Chance, or random, variability is the natural variation of an operation, whether it is carried on by machine or by hand. Non-random variability is statistically significant and should not be left to chance. Statistical quality control techniques provide criteria which are used to discriminate between random and non-random variability. The determination of whether a particular variation is random or non-random is, therefore, in the classification of a statistical problem. On the other hand, the determination of the assignable cause for a non-random variation, once statistical techniques have disclosed its existence, is not a statistical problem. Such determination requires engineering judgment, experience, and, at times, experimentation. The decision to remove an assignable cause, when discovered, is neither a statistical nor an engineering decision but one of economics or management.

Experience shows that judgment by itself, without the aid of statistics, can be guilty of two kinds of error:

(1) Judgment can seek corrective action when the variation is caused by chance alone.

(2) Judgment can fail to perceive that certain differences should not be left to chance alone but should be investigated. It is impossible to avoid both errors altogether, but statistical techniques can help management achieve a condition of minimum net economic loss. Without the aid of statistics, the loss from these two errors alone is almost certain to assume serious proportions.

Industry needs men who can think statistically, who know when to use a technique, and who know when a technique is valid or not. As one teacher of statistics puts it: "Statistics has come to be regarded by its practitioners, if not by the layman, as a method of making wise decisions in the face of uncertainty."

Any general understanding of the principles underlying statistical techniques must begin with the two principal uses of statistics: first, to provide a language for the description of variability; second, to draw inferences, or conclusions, from a collection of data. When the task is solely one of summarizing a particular body of data already collected and of examining its characteristics, the problem is one of statistical description. But, when the task is to draw conclusions from data on hand about a larger body of data not yet collected, the problem is one of statistical inference. Statistical inference is based on the laws of probability.

The most useful and best-known method of describing patterns of variation for manufactured products is that known as the "frequency distribution." A frequency distribution is simply a graph showing the number of times a particular measurement, or group of measurements, occurred throughout the entire range of recorded measurements. Usually presented in the form of a bar chart 1 it can be developed into a smooth curve. The statistician's judgment can seriously impair the ability of a frequency distribution to reflect a clear picture of product variation. Too many intervals in the data presented will camouflage the desired picture, and too few will blur it. Thus good judgment must be exercised in the selection of intervals to give the picture proper characterization.

Considerable information can be derived from a frequency distribution of any quality characteristic of manufactured products. First of all, such a frequency distribution supplies a useful picture of the way in which that particular characteristic has varied in the past. It helps to establish the principle that some amount of variation must always be expected among manufactured articles. It is also an indication of the general nature and shape that the variation can be expected to take in the future. Finally, it can be used as a starting point for the study and control of a particular variation when-necessary.

Chart 1.
Frequency Distribution

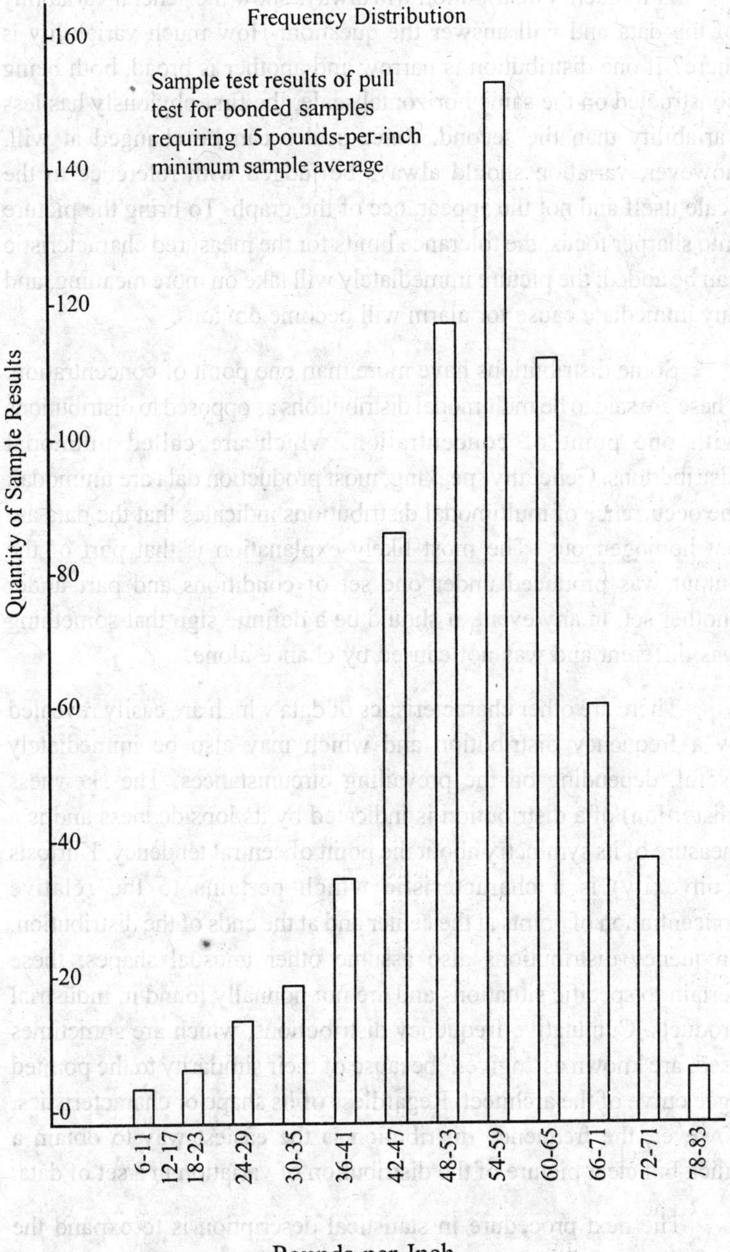

A frequency distribution will always show the general variability of the data and will answer the question: How much variability is there? If one distribution is narrow and another is broad, both being constructed on the same horizontal scale, the first obviously has less variability than the second. Since scales can be changed at will, however, variation should always be judged with reference to the scale itself and not the appearance of the graph. To bring the picture into sharper focus, the tolerance limits for the measured characteristic can be added; the picture immediately will take on more meaning, and any immediate cause for alarm will become obvious.

Some distributions have more than one point of concentration. These are said to be multimodal distributions as opposed to distributions with one point of concentration, which are called unimodal distributions. Generally speaking, most production data are unimodal; the occurrence of multimodal distributions indicates that the data are not homogeneous. The most likely explanation is that part of the output was produced under one set of conditions and part under another set. In any event, it should be a definite sign that something was different and was not caused by chance alone.

There are other characteristics of data which are easily revealed by a frequency distribution and which may also be immediately useful, depending on the prevailing circumstances. The skewness (distortion) of a distribution is indicated by its lopsidedness and is a measure of its symmetry about the point of central tendency. Kurtosis (convexity) is a characteristic which pertains to the relative concentration of points at the center and at the ends of the distribution. Frequency distributions also assume other unusual shapes; these pertain to specific situations and are not nonnally found in industrial products. Cumulative frequency distributions, which are sometimes used, are known as "ogives" because of their similarity to the pointed ogee curve of the architect. Regardless of its shape or characteristics, however, the frequency distribution is the easiest way to obtain a quick but clear picture of the distribution of variation in a set of data.

The next procedure in statistical description is to expand the usefulness of the frequency distribution by providing standard measurements of its most important characteristics its measures of central tendency and dispersion. By providing a mathematical description of its key factors, a given frequency distribution can be compared or fitted to other distributions or pre-established criteria. For example, a distribution that is expected to be normal caused by chance alone can actually be compared mathematically to the normal curve. This represents a major step beyond visual observation.

There are three measures of central tendency for a frequency distribution: the mode, the arithmetic mean, and the median. The mode of a set of data is the value at which the greatest number of cases is concentrated. By definition the point of greatest concentration, the mode is the outstanding measure of central tendency, but it is not commonly used because of the difficulty in handling it mathematically. The median is defined as that value which divides a distribution so that an equal number of items appear on either side of it. It is the value with as many cases above it as there are below.

The arithmetic mean is in such constant, everyday use that almost everyone should be familiar with it. It is more commonly referred to as the "average," or the "mean," and is represented by the symbol $\bar{x}$. Strictly a mathematical measure of central tendency, the arithmetic mean represents the average value for a group of observations. (A number of mathematical short cuts may be taken to compute the data where they are complex.) Where the distribution is unimodal and symmetrical, the mean will occur at the point of heaviest concentration. In discussing the probability of possible results, the mean is often referred to as the "expected value." If the distribution were to be given physical fonn, the mean would be its center of gravity.

Coupled with the measurements of central tendency and completing the mathematical description of a frequency distribution are the measures of general variability, or dispersion. These are the range; the average, or mean, deviation; and the standard deviation. The range, the simplest of the three measures, is the difference between the highest and the lowest value of a set of data. It is represented by the capital letter R. For small samples, it is a relatively sensitive measurement of dispersion. Hence the range is most commonly used in conjunction with the mean when relatively small samples are taken at frequent intervals, as is usually the case when manufacturing processes are being controlled through the use of $\overline{x}$ and R charts.

The average deviation can be obtained by computing from the measurement of central tendency the average of all deviations without regard to the arithmetic sign (absolute values). It can be measured from the mean, the median, or the mode. Computation is easy but would be difficult to handle in subsequent mathematical analysis because absolute values are used. The average deviation has minimum value when measured from the median and hence is generally used as a measure of dispersion whenever the median is used as a measure of central tendency.

The standard deviation, the most widely used measure of general variability is defined as the square root of the average of the squared deviations from the mean. It is a measure of how much the individual observations are scattered about the mean and is represented by the small Greek letter sigma (σ), from which is derived the phrase "three sigma limits." Squaring first and taking the square root later eliminates the difficulty created by the arithmetic signs of the deviations. Because the standard deviation can be used mathematically without any complications, it is the most frequently used measurement of dispersion.

The ultimate value of the measurements of mean and standard deviation for comparative analysis cannot be clearly envisioned until after these measurements have been considered together with the laws of probability. Their importance becomes apparent when their meaning is examined in connection with one of the most important and best known of all distribution formulas, the so-called normal, or Gaussian, distribution. This is the bell-shaped curve where the mean, the median, and the mode are the same. Skewness and kurtosis are zero, and 99.7 percent of all items fall within three sigma limits. The normal curve Chart 2 is used extensively in statistical analysis because it has a direct application to the everyday processes encountered in nature, in production operations, in laboratory research, in market and sales analysis, in accident statistics, and in many more areas.

The normal curve, originally developed by the French-English mathematician Abraham De Moivre and first described in 1733 in a mathematical treatise, was believed by its author to have no practical application beyond the solution of problems encountered in games of chance. Karl Friedrich Gauss, the German mathematician and astronomer, later used it to describe the theory of accidental errors in calculating the orbits of heavenly bodies. This work by Gauss has led to the present-day use of the normal curve in representing the natural, or chance, variation inherent in all things.

Chart 2.
The Normal Curve

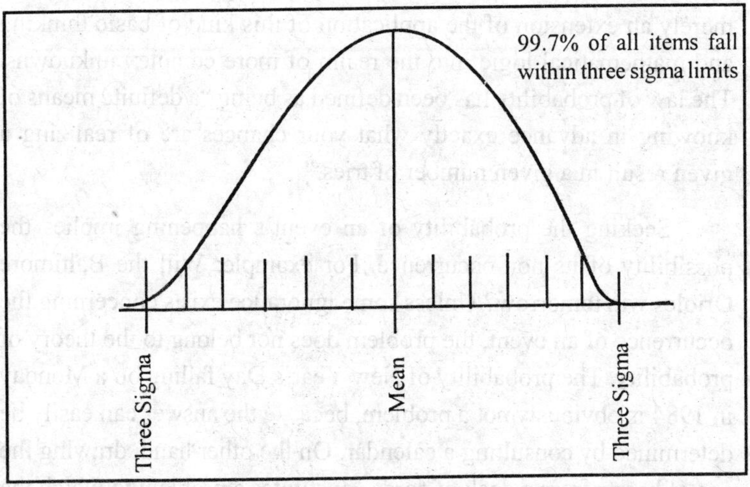

The normal curve is essentially an approximation of an expanded mathematical expression, but it can be illustrated by example as the accumulative result of tossing coins. The following example also illustrates the play of chance in producing a symmetrical distribution. It is not difficult to envision and accept the fact that numerous tossings of two coins will produce the following results: 25 percent heads, 50 percent heads and tails, and 25 percent tails. The plotting of these points is the first step in the development of a normal curve. As the number of coins is increased, the pattern grows. For example, four coins will produce five points to plot: four heads (once in 16 tosses), three heads and one tail (four times in 16), two heads and two tails (six times in 16), one head and three tails (four times in 16), and four tails (once in 16). Continually increasing the number of coins will produce 11 points for 10 coins, 101 points for 100 coins, and so on. As the number of coins becomes infinitely large, the distribution of results will approach as a limit the normal curve of error.

In this discussion of coin tossing, we have already entered the realm of probabilities. Once we accept the premise that the tossing of a coin has an equal chance of ending up either head or tail, we have already accepted the thesis upon which the world of probability is so firmly founded. In essence, the total concept of probabilities is merely an extension of the application of this kind of basic thinking and mathematical logic into the realm of more complex unknowns. The law of probability has been defined as being "a definite means of knowing in advance exactly what your chances are of realizing a given result in a given number of tries."

Seeking the probability of an event's happening implies the possibility of its non-occurrence. For example: Will the Baltimore Orioles win tomorrow? Unless some ignorance exists concerning the occurrence of an event, the problem does not belong to the theory of probability. The probability of New Year's Day falling on a Monday in 1984 is obviously not a problem, because the answer can easily be determined by consulting a calendar. On the other hand, drawing the ace of hearts from a deck of cards constitutes a problem to which the theory of probability provides a definite answer. Granted that the deck is perfect, one card is just as likely to appear as any other; since there are 52 cards in the deck, the chance that the ace of hearts will be drawn is 1/52. The words "just as likely" imply the existence of the ignorance which is essential if a problem is to be suitable for the theory of probability.

If an event can happen in N different ways, all of which are equally likely, and if, among these N ways, r are favourable, the probability (p) of the occurrence of a favourable event will always be r/N for a single trial. For example, the probability of throwing a six on the roll of a die is 1/6, and the probability of drawing a heart from a deck of cards is 1/4. If an event is certain to happen-death and taxes, for example-the probability of its occurrence is one, because all the possible ways are favorable. On the other hand, if an event is certain not to occur, the probability of its occurrence is zero.

The concept of "equally likely" plays a fundamental role in the theory of probability. The need for caution and careful analysis can be illustrated by the following two examples. It would be wrong to assume that the probability of getting two tails with a toss of two coins is 1/3, simply because there are three ways in which the toss could result. There are actually four equally likely ways in which the coins could land, and the probability is 1/4. By the same token, it would be wrong to assume that there are only three ways to get an eight with a roll of the dice, because there are actually five equally likely ways, represented by two combinations of a two and a six, two combinations of a five and a three, and one combination of two fours. Since the total number of equally likely ways in which the dice can fall is 36, the probability of an eight on anyone roll is 5/36.

The preceding examples were easily solved by enumerating all the possible and all the favourable cases. Because such enumerations frequently are extremely laborious, mathematical formulas have been developed to simplify their calculation. For example, there is a relatively simple way to find the number of different combinations that could Occur in any given sample size taken from any given lot size. All explanations of probability, moreover, cite the case with which the prohability can be determined for the selection of any combination of white and black balls from an urn containing known quantities.

Once we have recognized and accepted that the probability of selecting a specific sample from a known universe can be determined, it should be just as easy to recognize the reverse process.That is to say, a sample selected from an unknown universe can be used to determine the probability that it came from a desired universe. This is the way in which most statistical applications are utilized in industry. Whenever sampling is used in this manner, the criteria for the acceptance of a lot must be based on the computed probability that the sample came from a desired lot. The difference between one and the computed probability will represent the management risk associated with the acceptance criteria. In other words, the management risk will be the probability, however small, that a good sample actually came from an undesired lot.

Before the transition from games to problems can be completely accomplished, however, a few additional aspects of probability ought to be understood. These have to do with the dependency of certain events on others and the subsequent effect of this dependency on the computation of probabilities. A set of events is said to be independent when the occurrence of any single event is not influenced by the occurrence of the others. If the occurrence of any single event affects the occurrence of the others, the events are said to be dependent. For example, the drawing of an ace from a deck of cards after one or more aces have already been drawn is a dependent event.

Computing the probability of more than one independent event's occurring merely involves the multiplication of the individual probabilities. This is as easy to understand as a roll of the dice. The probability of rolling "snake eyes" is 1/6 x 1/6, or 1/36. In rolling three dice, the probability of three ones would be 1/6 x 1/6 x 1/6, or 1/216. The obvious multiple combination of probabilities can be verified by actually computing the favourable and the possible combinations of the dice. The method is applicable to any combination of different events, as long as these are independent of each other, and to any number of events.

For dependent events, the probability of two or more events' occurring in succession is also the multiple of the individual probabilities. The difference here is that the occurrence of the first event will always affect the probability for the succeeding event. For example, the probability of drawing a second ace from a deck of cards after one ace has already been drawn will be 3/51. This is based on the fact that 51 cards remain in the deck, among them three aces. The probability of drawing two aces in a row from a deck of cards will then be 4/52 x 3/51, or 1/221. This multiple combination of probabilities can be continued for any number of events in succession.

It is easy to lose one's way in statistics, even in its most fundamental form, if one is not thinking clearly. That is another reason why an understanding of its basic principles is so useful in developing sharper thinking. As a case in point, let's consider the question: What is the probability that a one will appear in three consecutive throws of a single die? The discussion so far should make this a simple problem. The answer: more than 1/6. But how much more?

The solution is really quite simple. The probability of not getting a one in three consecutive throws of a die is the product of the three individual probabilities (5/6 × 5/6 × 5/6), or 125/216. Hence the probability that a one will appear at least once in three throws is the difference between one and the probability that it won't appear (1-12.5'2/6), or 91/216. Another approach to the solution of this problem, hut one which is long and tedious by comparison, is to compute the number of combinations of results that would include a one and number of times up to three and to establish this as the number of favourable events to be compared to the total possible events, or all combinations of three dice.

Further examination of the dependency of one event on another indicates that some events are mutually exclusive; for example, there can only be one winner of a race. Events are defined as being mutually exclusive if the occurrence of one prevents the occurrence of the other. The probability of the occurrence of either the one or the other of two mutually exclusive events is equal to the sum of the individual probabilities. This can be readily seen with the roll of a single die: The probability of rolling either a two or a three is the sum of their individual probabilities, or 1/3. The extension of this thinking to include any number of mutually exclusive events should be fairly obvious.

In using statistics to help solve problems or make better decisions, it is extremely important to understand the relationship of events thoroughly. For any given analysis, the events in question may be independent, dependent, mutually exclusive, or any combination of the three. Statistics cannot make this determination; only clear thinking and a thorough knowledge of the surrounding circumstances can. Once this determination is made, statistics can provide an avenue to the best possible solution. Regardless of its precision, the mathematics of statistics can never improve on the initial judgment of the circumstances; if this judgment is wrong, the results of the statistical analysis will be equally wrong. Herein lies a fallacy that is more often attributed to statistics or to the statistician than to management.

The binomial law is best left for the mathematicians to describe. It can be thought of, however, as a point well within the world of probability. To have journeyed from the tossing of a coin to this point can be considered an accomplishment; an indication of its extent might be gained from reflecting upon the definition previously given for the law of probability—"a definite means of knowing in advance exactly what your chances are of realizing a given result in a given number of tries." From this point on, statistical quality control is merely the application of what we have discussed to specific needs or problems.

When the theory of probability is applied to problems of sampling, it automatically ties together the mathematics of statistical description and the mathematics of probability. Without this common denominator, progress would be impossible. Essentially, the process of application starts with a binomial distribution as representative of a normal, expected, or desired universe. The problem can be represented by a series of samples from an unknown universe; a frequency distribution of the sample results can then be analyzed by the law of probability to determine the exact probability that it came from the desired universe or to determine the parameters for the universe from which it is most likely to have come.

This may be an oversimplification of exactly what happens, but it is a general representation of the type of approach that is possible. Where the sample comprises a significant portion of the universe from which it is drawn, the distribution of sample results can no longer be adequately represented by the binomial distribution.

Here, as with dependent events, the probability of a defective unit may be materially changed as the sample is drawn. The mathematical equivalent of this set of conditions is known as the "hyper-geometric distribution." As previously mentioned, the binomial distribution can be approximated by the normal curve, and this is often done for ease of handling in certain cases. Under other conditions when the probability of success in a single trial is very small and the number of trials is very large there is an even better approximation of the binomial distribution. Known as the "Poisson distribution," it was developed by the 19th century French mathematician Simeon Poisson. In all cases, however, the mathematics can only be as accurate as the initial judgment of the overall circumstances.

The purpose of acceptance sampling plans is to determine a course of action and not to estimate lot quality. Acceptance sampling is applied to a series of lots and is designed to provide a specified degree of quality assurance for the entire series, subject to controlled risk for each individual lot. Inspection can be by at tributes, which merely grade the product as defective or non-defective, or by variables, which involve actual measurement. While not always applicable, variables sampling has definite advantages. By providing specific information about a given quality characteristic, it can provide the same degree of protection with smaller samples and thus is more economical.

All lot-by-lot sampling plans are certain to pass some lots containing defective units, if such units exist. All companies that utilize sampling plans must face this fact. It follows that the selection of a specific plan requires a decision by the user as to the risk he is willing to accept. There is also some risk of rejecting a good lot. If this risk is too high, it may ultimately lead to increased production costs. Both of these offsetting conditions should be carefully considered in establishing specific plans. A properly executed economic trade-off should then result in the acceptance sampling plan which is most suitable for the particular circumstances.

There are almost as many types of sampling plans as there are aspects of statistics. Each has its own operating characteristic curve, which is an indication of its discriminatory power. Selection of individual plans is a job for the statistician; selection of acceptable risks is a job for management. The net result of these decisions controls the level of quality in the products that are passing into the stockrooms as well as any other use being made of sampling. If management's plan follows the practice of screening lots rejected by either the producer or the customer, the net result of sampling can be represented by a curve of average outgoing quality level. Regardless of incoming levels, the peak of this curve will represent the worst condition that can result from the sampling of many lots. This peak is known as the "average outgoing quality limit" (AOQL). If the AOQL is a critical factor, it can be adjusted to any desired level. A control chart is a statistical device which is generally used for the study and control of repetitive processes. The chart may be used to define a goal for a process by serving as an instrument for attaining that goal or as a means of judging whether it has been achieved. The principle of the control chart is similar to that of a sampling plan. Chance variation in a process is the sum of a whole complex of chance causes, none of which is significant enough individually to have a serious effect on the total variation. On the other hand, relatively large variations can be caused by differences in machines, workers, materials, or combinations thereof. When such a situation occurs, the process is said to have been affected by assignable causes. Knowledge of the behaviour of chance variations is the foundation on which control-chart analysis rests. If study of a group of data reveals that its variation conforms to a statistical pattern which might reasonably be produced by chance causes, we can assume that no special assignable causes are present. The conditions which produce this type of variation, accordingly, are said to be under control. But, if the variation in the data does not conform to a chance pattern, we must conclude that one or more assignable causes are present.

The course of variation in a process is readily discernible from the plotting of sample results against time. Regardless of the statistic plotted-fraction defective, mean, or range if its fluctuations follow a normal pattern, there are no assignable causes present. When enough samples have been plotted, the resulting chart can provide the same information as a frequency distribution. If a line is drawn through the average of the sample results and banded by two additional lines equidistant from the mean, the chart becomes a control chart. Normally, the band is constructed to represent three standard deviations from the mean, or three sigma control limits. With reference to the normal curve, this means that 99.7 percent of all chance variations will fall within these limits.

When a control chart is plotted for a significant range of output and time, and all points fall within the control limits without any unusual cycles or runs, the process is said to be in a state of statistical control with respect to the given measurement of quality. Such is usually not the case at the beginning, however, when all departures from the normal pattern must be investigated. As assignable causes are tracked down and individually controlled, a process can be brought into a state of statistical control at the desired level. After control has been satisfactorily attained, future departures from this condition can be quickly detected by maintaining the control chart for current output.

Control charts can be utilized to study and to control fraction defective or defects per unit, as well as any measurable quality characteristic. Variables control charts such as $\bar{x}$ and R charts have the same advantages as variables sampling plans. Like sampling plans, control charts will perform in accordance with an operating characteristic curve, and the same economic trade-offs are required to establish suitable size and frequency of samples. Caution should be exercised to be sure that samples represent subgroups which are as homogeneous as possible; for example, the output of different machines should not be mixed. Control charts can then be as effective as their design.

Sampling plans and control charts are the commonest tools of statistical quality control, but there are numerous other profitable applications of statistics in quality control work. New methods and techniques for specific purposes are being developed daily, and the Use of statistics has become a dynamic and profitable field in industry as a whole. Experience with statistics in detecting unnatural variations and in tracking down assignable causes makes it a natural problem-solving technique. The statistical "design of experiment" allows results to be obtained from experimentation that would otherwise be impossible. Surely, therefore, it will continue to grow and influence industrial decisions.

Many people find it difficult to accept the results of even the simplest statistical analysis without a knowledge of the basic principles of statistics and the soundness of their derivation. This is as true of the inspection supervisor who feels strongly that the only way he can really fulfill his responsibility is to check everything 100 percent as it is of the manager who has more faith in his own intuition than in a bit of mathematical mumho jumbo. The danger here is that, if everyone felt this way, progress and efficiency would be doomed. Fortunately, however, the practical application of statistics has passed such people by; it will continue to march on to even greater successes because it has the power of validity, utility, and value.

❐

10

ISO-9000 Standards and Quality Audits

THE APPLICATION OF ISO 9000

In adopting and applying the requirements of ISO 9000 either to the design or evaluation of a company's quality system, the following considerations need to be made.

(a) What level of activity—1, 2 or 3?

(b) What structure of system should be adopted-functional or project based?

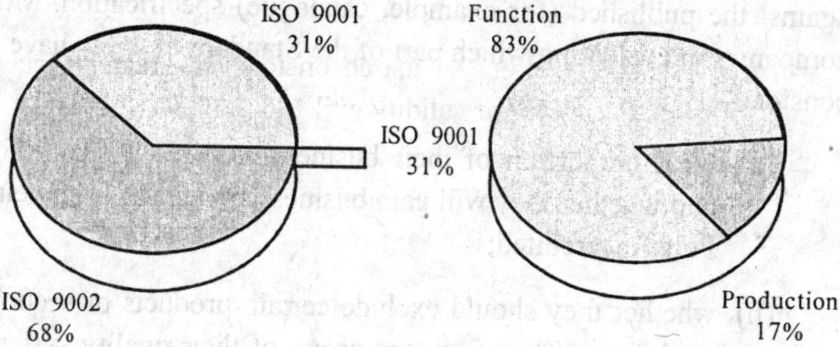

Percentage of companies implementing each of the parts of ISO 9000

Proportion of companies implementing function-based procedures vs product-based quality plans

Figure 1. The application of ISO 9000

A recent survey of the application of ISO 9000 shows that Level 2 of the standard predominates and Level 3 is rarely used, as illustrated in Figure 1. The reason for this distribution of companies is due to the fact that most organizations do not design or develop their products/services on a contract by contract basis (hence Level 2), and other more applicable standards (for example, National Measurement Accreditation Service (NAMAS) can be applied to companies involved primarily in testing.

The same survey also showed that most companies structure their quality systems on a functional basis rather than on a product by product basis, also illustrated in Figure 1. A functional approach means that procedures written for, say, purchasing or inspection apply to all products/services whereby a product-based structure develops quality plans in which procedures are written for particular projects.

In deciding what level of activity to apply, the key distinction, between Levels 1 and 2 is to what extent design plays a key role on a contract-by-contract basis. Clearly all products or services are designed af some stage but the question here is to what extent they are designed for each individual contract. Bearings or an electric kettle are clearly 'designed' products but they are, however, mostly bought against the published (for example, catalogue) specification. Most companies in evaluating which part of the Standard to apply have to consider:

(a) what proportion of their business requires design effort and whether they will gain business advantage from being Part 1 accredited;

(b) whether they should exclude certain products or sections of their business from the scope of their quality systems approval;

(c) In organizational terms, where they should 'bound' their system.

The following examples illustrate the approaches that should be adopted.

Electrical Repair Company Rewinding Electric Motors. Here the service element may indicate Part 1 of the Standard (4.19);

however, this element relates to the (often on-site) surviving and maintenance of product which has been supplied. Part 3 of the Standard is not applicable because, although the oompany does not actually manufacture the motors, the process as described in 4.9 (Part 2) would in this case be the repair process. In addition Part 3 assessment would not control the purchasing of any replacement parts for the motor. Hence the most appropriate level would be ISO 9002.

Motor Parts Manufacturer. Here the company is supplying parts to a major motor car manufacturer, and although there may be a major design element in the parts to be manufactured, this design work is almost certainly undertaken by the customer who would therefore generate the parts specifications that the parts manufacturer would work to. Hence the most appropriate level would be ISC 9002.

Bulk Chemical Producer. Here the product design normally takes the form of an agreed international specification for standard chemicals and therefore the composition and purity are pre-defined. Hence again the most appropriate level would be ISO 9002.

International Electrical/Electronics Products Group. Here the main consideration is where to draw the boundary around the compans, which may have many different subsidiaries, for the purposes of accreditation. In this situation one might assume that the group will need to have some form of all-embracing quality system covering every single group company and almost certainly to the most comprehensive part of the standard. The reality, however, depends upon the extent of inter-group trading as autonomous divisions of the company can be separately accredited. Hence, the company may have a number of accredited group companies to ISO 9001 , 9002 and 9003.

Training Organization. Here the company is providing a service rather than a product and is working primarily from the basis of identifying training needs and tailoring individual or group training programmes as opposed presenting standard training packages. Here the most appropriate level would be ISO 9001.

Understanding the 20 Elements of ISO 9000

The Standard is an extremely concise document which has been very carefully worded and therefore needs to be read in detail to be understood.

A definition of the terms used in Standard can be found in ISO 8402. In particulars the standard uses the following terms to describe the three components of business chain:

(a) Purchaser describes the customers of the company to be assessed to the Standard;

(b) Supplier describes the company to be assessed and this reflects that ISO 9000 is primarily a supply standard;

(c) Subcontractor describes the supplier of goods and services to the company to be assessed.

The other important term used in ISO 9000 is product which is used to describe the product or service at all stages of the process. With this interpretation raw materials, components, sub-assemblies as well as finished products are covered by the term 'product' in manufacturing, and similarly a service at all stages of provision is referred to by the generic term 'product'.

Each part of the Standard is basically divided into four sections as follows:

(a) **Section 1** defines the scope of application for the relevant levels of activity.

(b) **Section 2** details the documents referenced in the Standard.

(c) **Section 3** defines the terms used in Standard by basically referencing ISO 8442.

(d) **Section 4** is a description of the quality system requirements and is divided into 20 elements in Part 1 into 19 elements in Part 2 and into 16 elements in Part 3.

A practical interpretation of the requirements of each element of the Standard is given below.

Management Responsibility. This element requires the company to have a documented quality policy and to ensure that this is understood by all employees. Often this means issuing each employee with a copy of the policy statement or alternatively prominently displaying the policy. Organizational responsibilities need to be defined and the Standard identifies five specific areas to do with the actioning and recording of quality problems and the appropriate controls and corrective, actions. Adequate resources for verification activities are required by section 4.1.2.2 and particular note should be taken of the need for trained personnel in the areas of management, performance of work and verification activities including audits. A management representative who has ultimate responsibility for the quality system needs to be identified. This is usually the quality director in the case of large companies, the quality manager in the case of medium sized companies and the general manager for small companies. The 1994 revision also requires executive responsibility to be defined together with customer expectations and needs. Managers are requided to review the quality system performance periodically and this usually involves inputs from internal audits. reject records and customer complaints. The reviews normally take place approximately every six months.

Purchaser Supplied Product. Where a customer 'free issues' equipment or materials to the supplier, the Standard requires that these materials should be properly protected and their identity maintained.

Quality System. This element basically requires that the quality system should be documented in terms of policies, procedures and instructions. Guidelines are given as to the format of the documentation and the need for quality planing. The 1994 revision explicitly requires the documentation of a quality manual.

Product Identification and Traceability. This element lays down the requirement for the product or service to be correctly identified throughout the production process and that if it is required explicitly by the customer (in otherwords this is not mandatory) then the traceability back to constituent raw materials of batches should be maintained.

Contract Review. This element states that the customer's requirements (the 'contract') should be formally reviewed to ensure that the supplier is capable in both technical and organizational terms and that a record should be maintained of such reviews.

Process Control. The supplier is required to have formally documented work processes for all operations affecting. quality. Process equipment and personnel should all be capable of meeting the requirements. 'Special processes' are those which cannot be examined by subsequent testing prior to use for example, the packing of a parachute! Such processes should have particular attention paid to their capability and control and to the standards of workmanship. required. For the first time, the 1994 revision also requires the provision of equipment maintenance.

Design Control. This element requires that the design process should be documented and correctly planned and both the design inputs (specifications) and the design outputs (drawings etc.), should be formally documented. The supplier shall review the design to ensure that the outputs meet the input requirements and that any changes to the designs are properly controlled. The 1994 revision requires .the design reviews to be formally documented.

Document Control. The documents which form part of the quality system (procedures, specifications, detailed instructions, atc.) should be issued in a controlled way which indicates who has approved the document, the date of approval and the current level of issue revision. This ensures that everyone in the organization is working to the most up-to-date information and such documentation should be readily available to those who need to use it. Any changes to documents should also be controlled and approved by the originator and a list should be maintained of such modfications.

Inspection and Testing. The supplier should ensure that incoming goods are verified (not specifically tested, so the Stahdard does not compel 100% inspection). before use and, if required urgently, then a concession is required so that goods are capable of being recalled. Furthermore, the product or service should be tested at all stages of the process laid down in the quality plan and final release should only be allowed when the finished product has met the specified test requirements'. Records shall be kept of the testing undertaken indicating the person(s) responsible for testing and the acceptance criteria applied.

Purchasing. This element basically requires that the supplier should use 'assessed' sub-contractors, and whist the Standard does not compel a supplier to use only ISO 9000 approved sources (as clearly initially no company could get approval) this is an obvious and convenient approach. All purchasing drcuments should specify in precise terms with is required and who has approved the purchase and, where specified as part of a contract, the supplier should allow the customer to verify incoming purchases without, however, absolving the suppliers' responsibilities for checking.

Inspection, Measuring and Test 'Equipment. Affectionately known as the 'calibration' section, this element of the Standard basically requires that the equipment used to test the conformance of the product is in good working order and in a known state of calibration. The Standard requires that measurement 'certainty be known, which is often difficult with eertain subjective tests, and that the calibration should be traceable to established national or international standards. The Standard does not specify which equipment should be calibrated nor how often. The periodicity of calibration is regulated, however, by the requirement to assess previous inspection data when equipment is found to be out of calibration. Equipment should be properly identified and protected and records of the calibration information should be maintained.

Control of Non-Conforming Product. Product which is out of specification shall be controlled and not used, and the supplier shall review the product with a view to either rejecting/reworking; providing a concession or regarding. The customer can require in the contract to be told of any concessions and any rework shall be undertaken in the line which documented procedures.

Inspection and Test Status. This element requires that the supplier shall identify whether a product has been tested or not and if it has been tested whether it has passed or failed. Many different approaches to identifying test status are allowed including labels, segregation, test records, etc.

Training. Employees whose work affects quality need to be properly trained. The phrase 'personnel affecting quality' is interpreted quite liberally and the Standard states that the training can either be in the form of educational background, training courses attended or experience gained. The supplier should be able to demonstrate through documented records the training of such staff and must show that the training requirements are reviewed regularly.

Corrective Action. This element of the Standard requires the supplier to continuously review and amend the quality system in the light of non-conformances. The supplier shall review what went wrong, why and what to do to prevent' recurrence and must also analyze the system regularly to detect and correct potential non-compliances.

Handling, Storage, Packaging and Delivery. Sometimes referred to as the 'housekeeping' section, this part of the Standard requires that the product shall, be handled and stored in such a way as to prevent damage or deterioration. The product shall be packaged in conformance which requirements and, depending upon the contractual arrangements, the supplier shall also be responsible for protection of the product during delivery.

Servicing. Where a contract requires the product to be maintained after it has been supplied then again the supplier should have a documented method descri ing such servicing. These procedures will apply even if the servicing is carried out by a third party, for example in the case of an automotive garage. The requirements for servicing were introduced in Part 2 of the Standard (IS0 9002) in the 1994 revision.

Quality Records. The records of the performance of the quality system (contract reviews, sub-contractor assessments, test records, calibration data, etc.) shall be maintained in a readily accessible format for a prescribed period of tittle. The Standard does not, however, specify how long records should be kept as clearly the retention period for the test results for say biscuits with a shelf life of a matter of weeks would be very different from the commissioning data from a nuclear power station with a working life in excess of 20 years.

Statistical Techniques. Where the supplier uses data analysis methods, for example in market analysis, process control, reliability analysis, product sampling, etc., then the methods used should have a valid statistical basis and again shall be carried out in accordance with documented procedures.

Internal Qualify Audits. The Standard requires the supplier to 'police' their own quality system to ensure the laid-down policies, procedures and instructions are being followed. These audits should be undertaken by suitably qualified employees who are independent from the area being audited. Audits shall be carried out at appropriate frequencies (typically three to six months) and the resuhs reported to the managers responsible for the area audited to take any corrective actions identified.

Stages in the Implementation of ISO 9000

Most of the companies which have been accredited to ISO 9000 have undergone some form of implementation process whereby new quality system elements have been introduced within their organizations. All organizations employ a quality system to some extent but in order to achieve accreditation to ISO 9000 the system generally needs to be structured and presented in line with the requirements of the Standard.

The basic stages in the implementation of ISO 9000 are:

1. to define the quality objectives of the company and establish the existing systems and procedures;
2. to develop the existing system and introduce new elements in line with both the business objectives and the requirements of ISO 9000.

The mistake many companies make in the implementation of ISO 9000 is to attempt to adopt some form of 'off-the-shelf documented quality system rather than to develop and improve their existing business processes.

In terms of the detailed activities involved in developing quality systems to ISO 9000 these may be summarized as follows:

(a) Analysis involves an identification of the quality objectives, a review of the existing' quality systems the securing of the commitment of senior management and the development of the ISO 9000 implementation plan.

(b) Product or service specification involves developing contract review procedures, design and development procedures, the procedure for controlling the issue, approval and change of the quality system documentation to be generated and the production of quality plans.

(c) Process Control requires procedures for identifying the product throughout the conversion process and for maintaining traceability. Procedures are also required to describe the control of all the main production or business processes and any associated detailed work instructions. Methods should also be developed to control any non-conforming material throughout the process and standards of workmanship need to be defined together with criteria for acceptability of the product or service at the appropriate process stage.

(d) Material Control requires procedures for the specification of bought in goods or services, methods for assessing sub-contractors and procedures for receiving raw materials, including sampling plans and control procedures for any materials supplied directly by the customer.

(e) Quality records require procedures for the maintenance and storage of quality system records and also procedures for the periodic auditing of the system. Procedures are also required for the recording of employee training.

(f) Inspection and testing includes the methods for in-process and for checking on the producter service contract including the definition of acceptance criteria. Details are required of how the inspection status of the product is maintained and procedures for the calibration of equipment and the associated records. This stage should also include details of any statistical techniques used.

(g) Quality manual should be a relatively brief document (20 or so pages) stating the business policy with resped to quality and should be structuced in line with the sections of ISO 9000. Detailed procedures should be cross-referenced in the quality manual which should be seen as a means of promoting the company's approach to quality.

The advantage of this approach whereby the implementation is broken down into elemental stages is that the tasks can then be delegated to the appropriate managers responsible which promotes both the accuracy of the procedures and the organizational ownership.

The timescales for implementing ISO 9000 vary considerably depending upon company size and system complexity and also the organizational resources and commitment provided.

Similarly cost of implementing ISO 9000 will vary from company to company. The major costs involved include management time in the preparation of documentation the provision of secure storage areas, calibration costs including test equipment and assessment costs. Some companies, although by no means all also require additional personnel to either manage or operate the quality system.

Quality System Design and Structure

The formalized design of the quality system is a process which most companies undertake only once (ignoring subsequent modifications and amendments) and for this reason the process often benefits from the advice of an external consultant.

There exists as many different quality systems as there are companies, each one reflecting both the business objectives of the individual company and the requirements of ISO 9000. A basic design framework to adopt is to structure the quality system at three levels as shown in Figure 2.

The first level of documentation; widely termed the quality manual, should state the company's policy with respect to quality and identify the corresponding responsibilities and records. This first level of documentation should be structured in line with the sections of ISO 9000.

The third level of documentation is normally company-specific giving details of how individual work processes (for example, welding,

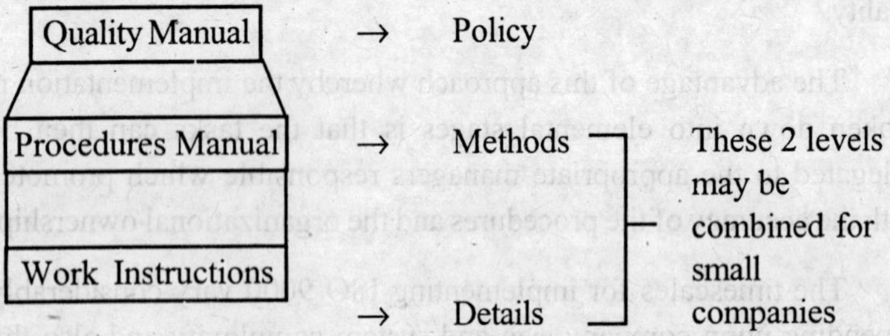

Figure 2 Basic quality system structure.

soldering, testing) are carried out within the company. These work instructions should in addition to specifying how the work should be done should also identify who should undertake the work and what records are maintained. Work instructions should be clear, concise and auditable.

At the second level of documentation, quality procedures, opinion is divided as to whether they should reflect the requirements of the Standard or the operation of the business. Most companies employ a hybrid approach whereby certain procedures relate specifically to the Standard (for example, 'Control of Non-Conforming Product') whereas others reflect the business processes (for example, 'Preparation of Quotations').

Certain elements of the ISO 9000 quality system framework lend themselves to generic design. For example:

(a) Vendor assessment requires some form of supplier identification categorization, a definition of the supply specification together with a record of the supplier assessment, as shown in Figure 3.

(b) The calibration system generally requires some form of gauge identification, a schedule for the calibration of equipment and finally individual calibration records showing details of the calibration method, accuracy, frequency etc.,

(c) The training element should contain details of the overall traning requirements of the quality system to identify which personnel have been trained and also the individual training records showing information on the training undertaken.

XYZ Engineering Ltd. Park Street Calcutta		Ref : SA/02 Issue : 01 Date : Jun 98
Supplier Assessment Record **Supplier category : A** **Supplier Name:** ABC Chemicals **Ref :** ABC 1 **Material :** Sulphuric acid (Spec. Ref. XYZ 07).		
Non-conformance	Date	Corrective action

Figure 3 Vendor asdsessment systems.

Preparation of Quality System Documentation

The procedures and work instructions written to describe the quality system should be clear, concise and auditable. In preparing the documentation, the first task is to establish the format for the documents to facilitate control purposes. This normally requires some form of document reference and issue status together with a document authorization mechanism. Some form of master list of procedures is normally maintained which records the procedures in use, the current revision status of each procedure and the circulation list. The basic structure of the procedures should be as follows:

(a) purpose which describes the activity covered in the procedure;

(b) scope which describes which aspects of the activity are covered in the procdure;

(c) related documents which are those documents referred to by the procedure;

(d) procedure which describes the details of the element;

(e) documentation which describes the documents produced in the execution of the procedure and the records required.

Consideration as to how the procedure is to be subsequently audited should be a key concern in developing the documentation and in particular attention should be given to:

(a) responsibilities as to who should carry out the procedure;

(b) description of any specifications, settings or acceptance criteria;

(c) details of the records which should be taken to illustrate conformance to specification;

(d) any special skills assumed or training required.

When planning the quality system documentation, attention should be given to the definition of which procedures are required (an overall system game plan) in order to eliminate potential overlap or, alternatively, a ballooning effect whereby proceduce after procedure is added to what appears to be an incomplete 'masterpiece'. The best approach is to encourage those (managers) responsible for the process to draft the procedure as this ensures:

(a) detailed understanding of the process described;

(b) ownership of the completed procedure.

In addition it is often good policy to circulate the procedure for comment to the employees for carrying out the procedure.

In developing a qulity system procedure it is normally good pracuce to create a flowchart of the process to be described. A common mistake is for authors to over-elaborate and to write procedures in what they perceive to be a required 'quality assurance speak'. This produces unworkable controls and unnecessary bureaucracy a criticism often levelled at ISO 9000 but in almost all cases self-generated.

Examples of ISO 9000 Quality System Implementations

Many different structures and formats of quality system have been accredited to ISO 9000 and therefore there is no single, successful approach. Individual procedures. however. should follow the format described earlier. An example of which is shown.

As below the procedures are usually either:

XYZ Engineering Ltd. Proc : QAP #

Issue: XX

Procedure: Receiving Inspection Date: YYYY

RECEIVING INSPECTION

1. Introduction.

 1.1 This document details the operation of (inwards goods inspection) in the inwards goods receiving area.

2. Scope

 2.1 This procedire appraes to all (inwards goods inspection) activities in the site.

3. Related Documents

   3.1 Company Documents

   (List of relevant company procedures/standards).

   3.2 Customer/National Documents

   (List of relevant documents)

4. Receiving Documentation

   4.1 On receipt a (Goods Received Note) will be raised - form (ABC 123) refers.

5. Inspection Routines

   5.1 On receipt of the GRN the Inspection area will examine the goods or materials against the purchase order and any relevant specifications.

   5.2 If the goods are acceptable they will be passed on to the next stage or process and the GRN marked accordingly.

   5.3 If the goods are defective the GRN will be marked accordingly and the goods physlcally identified and segregated. The procedure for hancling defective goods is contained in OAP #.

6. Records

   PREPARED BY: APPROVED BY:

Figure 4 Sample quality system procedure

quality-specific procedures for example Calibration or

business procedures for example Purchase Order Processing.

The document describing the quality policy usually termed the quality manual should be seen as an overview document which can be used to promote the company's quality system externally. The quality manual generally does not contain a great deal of proprietary detail describing how key processes are carried out but instead will refer to specific quality procedures or work instructions.

As described previously the quality manual should be structured in line with the elements of ISO 9000 as this assists the assessors in the comparison with the requirements of the Standard. A typical quality manual layout is shown in below:

The Stages And Depths of Quality System Audits

An audit is a systematic and independent examination to determine whether quality activities comply with planned arrangements. The reasons for auditing quality systems include:

COMPANY QUAUTY MANUAL ISO 9002-1994

0 Introduction

1. Scope and field of Application

2. References

3. Definitions-Quality Policy Statement

4. Quality System Requirements

 4.1 Management responsibility

 4.2 Quality System

 4.3 Contract review

 4.5 Document control

 4.6 Purchasing

 4.7 Purchaser supplier product

 4.8 Product identification and traceability

 4.9 Process control

 4.10 Inspection and testing

 4.11 Inspection, measuring and test equipment

4.12 Inspection and test status

4.13 Conlrol of non-conforming product

4.14 Corrective and preventative action

4.15 Handling, storage packaging & delivery

4.16 Quality records

4.17 Internal quality audits

4.18 Training

4.19 Servicing

4.20 Statistical techniques

APPENDIX —List of quality system procedures

Figure 5 Structure for a Quality Manual.

(a) internal audits are an explicit requirements of ISO 9000.

(b) audits are required to provide objective evidence that the quality system is functioning and assist in the 'policing' of the system to ensure the system does not deteriorate;

(c) internal audits provide important input to the management review of the performance of the quality system in achieving the quality objectives.

The main stages of an audit are as follow;

(a) planning 35%
(b) performing 40%
(c) reporting 10%,
(d) follow-up 15%

The percentages indicate the approximate amount of time to be devoted to each stage.

Audits can be carried out at different depths of detail upon the objectives of the audit. Basically the audit can be carried out at a 'systems' level which involves a broad evaluation of all elements of the quality system described in the quality manual or at a 'compliance' level which provides an in-depth evaluation of specific quality activities and procedures, as shown in Figure 6.

In terms of the organization carrying out the audit, the following distinctions can also be made,

(a) Internal audits are carried out by a company on its own quality system.

(b) External audits are carried out by a company to evaluate supplier's quality systems.

(c) Extrinsic or second/third party audits are carried out on the company by a customer or third-party organzation.

Based upon the above definitions the most common forms of audits therefore are:

Internal company audits-internal, compliance audits;

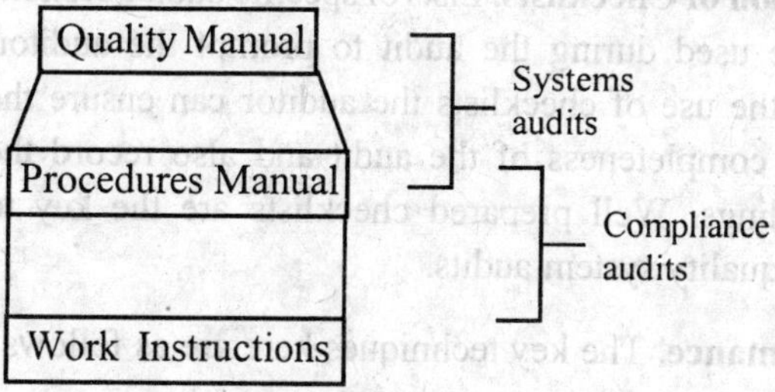

Figure 6. Depth of quality system audits.

(a) assessment of suppliers-external, systems audits;

(b) accreditation assessments-extrinsic, systems audits.

Audit Tools And Techniques

The two key viewpoints necessary when, carrying out an audit are:

(a) a clear understanding of the detail of the procedures audited;

(b) a clearing understanding of the requirements of ISO 9000.

In terms of each of the main stages of the audit the key tools and techniques are as follows:

Audit Planning

The key elements here are as follows:

(a) **Audit Schedule.** A matrix of the timing as to when each audit element is to be checked throughout the year.

(b) **Audit Persorinel.** The appointment of an auditor. or where the scope of the audit, is considerable, an audit team leader and team members.

(c) **Notification of the Auditee.** Request for all the quality system documentation relevant to the audit. Many people feel you should surprise an auditee—this is universally the wrong approach.

(d) **Preparation of Checklists.** Lists of specific audit questions which are used during the audit to prompt the auditor. Through the use of checklists the auditor can ensure the pace and completeness of the audit and also record the audit findings. Well prepared checklists are the key to effective quality system audits.

Audit Performance. The key techniques here are as follows:

(a) Entry meeting to initially brief the auditee and arrange escorts, and exit meetings to finally provide feedback on the audit findings.

(b) The audit itself is a very practical (and often unpredictable!) experience. Auditing is normally conducted on a sampling basis (illustrative records are examined) and objective evidence should be sought and recorded (both the affirmative and deficient findings). Checklists should be used as a guide and expanded if necessary.

(c) In terms of asking audit questions, Rudyard Kipling's rhyme should be borne in mind: I keep six ,honest serving men, they taught me all I knew their names were what and why and where and when and how and who. In other words open questions should be asked.

(d) Any deficiencies noted during the audit should be confirmed with the auditee, and not come as a surprise later.

Audit Reporting. This primarily involves the recording of any non-conformances and summarizes the audit findings for purposes of management review. The key elements are:

Audit follow-up. The key technique here is:

The audit close-out which ensures any CARs raised during the audit have been corrected and a record of this made.

If CARs are not closed out then the action should be escalated which normally involves referring to a higher level of management.

Audit Documentation

An explicit requirement of ISO 9000 is that a record should be kept of the internal audits. The they records which are normally expected are those associated with the audit planning (schedules and checklists), details of the corrective actions identified and records of the reporting of the audit to the quality system manager.

ISO 9000 Accreditation

Accreditation can be undertaken by anyone of the approved bodies. The basic stages to accreditation are as follows:

System Implementation. The company designs and implements its quality and carries out a complete set of internal audits. There is a normal expectation of at leas three months of evidence of the quality system' operation prior to the accreditation visit although this can present problems where process cycles (for example, a product design cycle) may take considerably more than three months and therefore all stages of a complete process may not be documented. This is sometimes overcome by sampling sequential stages irom different (say, design) projects.

Document Review. The quality system documentation is forwarded to the accreditation agency for review against the requirements of ISO 9000. It is normal at this stage to forward the quality manual, procedures manual and a sample of workinstructior's. The accreditation agency will then notify the company of any discrepancies (usually requirements ISO 9000 not covered by the company's documented systems) which will need to be aadressed prior to the accreditation visit.

Accreditation Audit. This is normally carried out by audit team of qualified lead assessors who ensure that:

(a) the requirements of ISO 9000 are being met in practice;

(b) the company's quality system is being implemented as documented.

The accreditation auditors adopt a very formal approach and set the scope of the audit at the entry meeting, basically following the agenda laid down by the relevant part of ISO 9000. Any non-compliances are identified at me time of the accreditation visit and normally classified as either major (absence or total breakdown of a system element) or minor (isolated incidence of non-conformance).

Accreditation report and surveillance. The company is normally informed at the completion of the accreditation audit whether they have been successful. Companies can fail due to:

(a) a major non-compliance;

(b) large numbers of minor non-compliances.

Most companies quality systems do have a small number of minor non-compliances identified at the accreditation visit and are given (normally) 30 days to inform the accreditation, agency of appropriate corrective action. Upon receiving accreditation, which is normally granted for three years, the company can advertise its quality system as being to ISO 9001 9002 or 9003 (but cannot advertise that its products conform to ISO 9000). The accreditation agency will then carry out surveillance audits approximately every six months to verify that the quality system is being maintained and issues non-compliance reports as appropriate. The cost in terms of the damage to a company's quality image means that very few organizations have allowed their quality systems to degenerate and thereby lose their accreditation to ISO 9000. Surveillance visits normally focus upon areas of weakness identified during the assessment or previous surveillance visits and provide the basis for continual improvement to the system.

THE REQUIREMENTS OF ISO 9000

Element 1. Management responsibility

1.1 To describe the organisation's 'quality polity' in writing and to indicate how it is communicated throughout the organisation.

1.2 To describe the organisation structure indicating individual and sectional responsibilities and authority.

1.3 To explain how the organisation proposes to implement and monitor procedures for ensuring workmanship and products meet customer requirements.

1.4 To specify the role of employees within the organisation, and in particular, their:

— experience;

— qualifications;

— responsibility for quality.

1.5 To nominate a management representative to.

— act as a focal point for enquiries;

— 10 be responsibte for the implementation of the quality system;

— ensure its continued effectiveness.

1.6 To explain how quality systems are reviewed and monitored at management team level.

1.7 To describe the recording methods pertaining to points 1.1 to 1.6.

Element 2. Quality System

2:1 To establish and maintain a documented quality system.

2.2 To identify the responsibilities of employees within the quality system.

2.3 To relate the organizations's operations to each of the individual elements of BS 5750: Part 1, 1987/ISO 9001/EN 29001.

2.4 To identify the responsibilities, commitment and participation of employees within the quality system.

Element 3. Contract review

3.1 To review all orders to ensure that customer requirements are clearly defined and understood.

3.2 To describe the organisation and documentation of contract review meetings.

3.3. To involve essential personnel and departments in decisions concerning the acceptance or rejection of customer orders.

3.4. To ensure that the process capability exists to meet contractual requirements.

3.5. To devise a system whereby changes to requirements can be properly co-ordinated, enacted and formally approved.

3.6 To explain how records are collected and maintained.

3.7 To identify responsibilities for the various aspects of contract review.

3.8 To specify criteria for ensuring the organisation is capable of processing a customer's order prior to its acceptance.

3.9 To explain the system for receipt and processing of orders.

Element 4. Design Control

4.1 To identify a plan for design indicating;

— the tasks involved;

— responsibility for each task;

— checking procedures:

— The-scales for completion.

4.2 To ensure all plans are controlled, updated and approved by authorised personnel.

4.3 To ensure that all employees participating in design and development activities are appropriately qualified.

4.4 To commit sufficient managerial, resources to design and development.

4.5 To establish the appropriate interfaces within design and development to ensure information is transmitted accurately.

4.6 To explain the procedure for receipt and initial processing of original design input documentation.

4.7 To ensure that all stages of the design and development process are properly documented and that adequate procedures exist for doing so.

4.8 To ensure that design and development requirements are clearly understood.

4.9 To ensure that authorised employees liaise with the customer in order to confirm that requirements are clear and sufficiently comprehensive and that modifications are discussed and documented.

4.10 To specify the organisation's design procedures; including design review meetings) drawings, purchasing specifications and alternative calculations.

4.11 To specify acceptance and rejection criteria.

4.12 To ensure documentation is readily available to employees at all stages of design and development.

4.13 To implement a documented system for controlling design changes, including employees responsible for authorising such changes.

Element 5. Document Control

5.1 To identify responsibilities for compilation, approval, issue, monitoring, recording and control of documentation and data pertaining to the quality system.

5.2 To devise a draft system for the compilation, approval and circulation of organisational procedures.

5.3 To establish a master file of current documentation and assign responsibility for its maintenance.

5.4 To establish procedures for the removal of obsolete documentation.

5.5 To ensure that documentation is readily available as required.

5.6 To ensure employees are trained to understand organisational documentation and data.

5.7 To explain how support documentation is controlled.

5.8 To create a control system for changes to documentation. Where possible, the originator to be involved.

5.9 To assign a unique numbering system to all documents.

5.10 To obtain customer approval of relevant documentation if contractually required.

Element 6. Purchasing

6.1 To explain the procedures whereby the organisation ensures that all supplies conform to requirements.

6.2 To ensure the organisation's purchasing requirements are clearly communicated to the supplier.

6.3 To create a system for the selection of approved suppliers- and subcontractors.

6.4 To plan and instigate supplier auditing.

6.5 To create and maintain a central filing system for all supplier and contractor records.

6.6 If appropriate, to implement a system whereby the organisation can check products and services at the supplier's premises.

6.7 To nominate responsibility for all tasks involved in purchasing.

Element 7. Customer-Supplied Product

7.1 To issue written instructions for the control of items supplied by customers.,

7.2. To provide segregation facilities to prevent any possibility of confusion with other customer products or store items.

7.3 To check the customer's supplied item against pertinent documentation and record receipt.

7.4 To provide adequate handling and storage facilities.

7.5 To record and report instances of non-conformance of supplied item to the customer before processing/utilisation.

7.6 To ensure that customer supplied items are periodically checked for suitability if stored for any length of time.

7.7 To identify responsibilities for control, recording and maintenance of all activities involving customer supplied product.

Element 8. Product Identification and Traceability

8.1 To be capable of identifying all products.

8.2 To ensure identification indicates whether or not a product has undergone a particular operation or process.

8.3 To set out internal traceability procedures pertaining to the isolation of suspect products.

8.4 To ensure customer traceability requirements are planned and documented.

8.5 To identify responsibilities for product identification and traceability and associated records.

Element 9. Process Control

9.1 To document work instructions, explaining how products or services shall be produced, including:

— any special requirements;

— working practices;

— samples of workmanship;

— criteria for acceptance and rejection.

9.2 To implement a system for ensuring products and services conform to requirements at all stages of production.

9.3 To implement a procedure for the commissioning of manufacturing processes and associated equipment.

9.4 To establish a comprehensive training programme for all personnel associated with process control.

9.5 To maintain records of all work instructions and to identify those relevant to quality planning requirements.

9.6 To identify any special processes, *i.e.*, those requiring supplementary information, training, work instructions or inspection.

Element 10. Inspection and Training

10.1 To implement inspection and testing procedures at appropriate stages of production and despatch.

10.2 To implement a recording system which clearly indicates that a product has satisfied acceptance criteria before it passes to the next stage of production.

10.3 To operate an inspection system at the following stages as appropriate:

— goods received;

— in process control;

— final inspection;

— audit inspection;

— 'first off';

— initial sample.

10.4 To implement a procedure for control of incoming products released on an urgent basis.

10.5 To provide quarantine facilities for products awaiting inspection.

10.6 To ensure no product can be despatched prior to inspection and recording of results.

10.7 To train employees in the proper use of measuring and test equipment.

10.8 To document the requisite tests, together with any special requirements such as equipments to be used, setting, calibration, etc. Documentation to be complied by qualified and authorised personnel.

10.9 To implement a procedure for the control and filing of certificates of conformity.

10.10 To identify responsibility for the acceptance of products against specifications.

Element 11. Inspection Measuring and Test Equipment

11.1 To document the calibration systems used by the organisation.

11.2 To provide suitable equipment.

11.3 To detail the method of calibration for various ectuipment.

11.4 To incorporate selection of measuring equipment as part of quality planning.

11.5 To determine intervals between Calibration for all equipments.

11.6 To ensure all itams of equipment possess a unique identification number and calibration record.

11.7 To ensure that employees involved in calibration are trained and clearly authorised.

11.8 To ensure that equipment deemed unsuitable is formally removed and destroyed.

11.9 To detail the methods for repair of equipment.

11.10 To detail the procedure for the introduction of new equipment.

11.11 To ensure calibration equipment conforms to national standards.

11.12 To ensure external calibration organisations are suitably accredited.

11.13 To ensure that all users of equipment are properly trained in its usage, storage and calibration system.

11.14 To record and retain all calibration certificates and other information.

11.15 To guard equipment from interference.

11.16 To ensure environmental conditions are suitable for calibration.

11.17 To instigate reviews of calibration systems and procedures.

Elements 12. Inspection and test status

12.1 To establish a procedure whereby the status of a product, *i.e.,* conforming or non-conforming is clearly evident at all times.

12.2 To ensure that the status of products is clear throughout the manufacturing process for instance, whether or not inspected, whether awaiting inspection or segregated as non-conforming.

12.3 Authorised employees to maintain verification records enabling products to be released to the next stage.

12.4 To ensure the status of all products passing from one stage to another is ascertained as soon as practicable.

12.5 To ensure that regular status checks are carried out by authorised employees.

Element 13. Control of non-conforming products

To ensure that any non-conforming products or workmanship are clearly identified as such with appropriate documentation, and segregated.

❐

11

Management of Quality Control Process

The control of quality can be explained very simply. Let's consider, for example, any manufacturing process whose output is required to fit within certain prescribed physical or functional limitations. To control the quality of this output, actual results must be measured both within the process and at the end of the total activity comprising it. The measurements will either confirm or deny adherence to the prescribed limitations. If they confirm that all the required results have been achieved, they secure acceptance of the product. If they cannot confirm that the required results have been obtained, they provide original data for corrective action.

The specific objective of corrective action is to return the manufacturing process to a condition of acceptance. The overall objective of quality control is to provide a series of planned measurements designed to verify continuously that acceptable products arc being produced. Thus, in its broadest sense, the control of product quality is a process of acceptance based on original measurements, or on measurements and corrective action.

Statistical quality control is a special case wherein any given measurement may initiate both acceptance and corrective action. This can occur when the measurements are used to determine trends within the manufacturing-process limitations or to determine that a condition of acceptance continues to exist. The technique is most applicable when a process has an inherent degrading characteristic, such as tool wear or the gradual dilution of a plating solution. Thus measurements can also determine when a manufacturing process needs to be readjusted for continued acceptance.

The full meaning of quality control becomes apparent when each element is considered in its broadest sense. Measurements of product quality can be made visually or by using suitable equipment. The most infallible measurement is one that is automatic; that is a measurement designed to be part of a process through the automatic use of equipment. When this approach can be utilized for all the necessary measurements of an entire manufacturing process, that process will be controlled in the most effective and desirable way. If documentation of results and out-of-control warnings could be automatically incorporated in the same way, there would be little room left for further quality control improvement.

Where measurements cannot be made automatically, specially trained personnel are needed. From this need has evolved the inspection function, which is the core of most quality control activities. Inspectors can be trained to provide measurements visually or through the use of many types of equipment. The complete spectrum of potentially necessary measurements can be fully appreciated by envisioning the variety of industrial processes to be controlled as ranging from the manufacture of a machine screw to the launching of a space vehicle.

This concept of quality control is enlarged still further when the potential needs for corrective action are examined. For each acceptance measurement to be made there always exists the possibility of error, both in the results being measured and in the measurement. itself. The range of possible avenues for investigation and, therefore, corrective action covers almost every area of company activity. It includes such stalwart fixtures as product design, tool design and design of the manufacturing process itself. It also includes procedures, work instructions, material specifications and supporting processes such as calibration and maintenance. Quite often it includes individual managers and workers, both of whom are susceptible to human error.

The picture of quality control's basic objectives now expands to incorporate the next logical goal documentation of results. If a company could perform perfectly, valid acceptance would always be achieved and no corrective action would be needed. The fact that companies do not perform perfectly provides the basis and the justification for corrective action. By the same token, corrective action provides the strongest basis and justification for the documentation of results. When something goes wrong for no obvious reason and an investigation begins, all areas that could have contributed to the problem are immediately suspect. Each area for which documented results exist can, however, be quickly eliminated from consideration, thus saving time and effort.

Justification for objective evidence is supplied by the customer. No matter how good a company's overall operation and quality control system are, there will be times when delivered products are regarded with suspicion. This happens when the customer has a problem and is conducting a corrective action investigation of his own. Just as in any similar investigation, all potentially involved products and processes will be suspect until the true cause is determined. A company is always in a position to help its customer and to enhance its own image when it can produce objective evidence of its own performance.

Up to this point, the control of quality has been presented as a programme of measurement whose aim is acceptance but also as one to which corrective action and documentation of results are necessary adjuncts. Normally, corrective action activity is best handled by an independent agency of the company, but this is not an absolute necessity. As long as the function is effectively managed, it can be placed almost anywhere in the company. Quality control usually is organized as an independent function and, in the process, has grown as a profession principally because quality cannot be thrown into the same hopper with cost and schedule. Effective management of many company groups, each with the freedom to measure and report on its own quality performance and corrective action progress, would be extremely difficult. It would be like having each group report on its own cost and schedule performance. The only logical exception might be a company dealing in services rather than products. In this case, the personnel providing the services should be trained to perform and document inspections of their own work, and these records could then be measured against customer complaints.

Establishing the function of quality control as a separate organizational segment of the company immediately generates such fundamental requirements as organizing, planning, and staffing. First, however, another important objective should be established. This involves organization of the quality control function to provide maximum prevention of defective work. In other words, the function should be designed to determine and to eliminate potential problems before they have an opportunity to occur. This can be accomplished only when quality control planning is an integral part of overall planning for activities which can affect end-product quality.

Taking advantage of the opportunity to prevent problems simply makes good business sense. It depends primarily on knowledge of past problems and of new requirements, both being basic to the repertory for a quality control function. Old problems with new applications seem to have a way of creeping into new programmes unless someone is specifically on guard to keep them out. New, or different, product quality requirements often are not fully understood until they have become problems; they too must receive sufficient preventive attention. Changing product requirements can create serious difficulties unless thoroughly reviewed for effect upon receipt. When problems cannot be planned out of a system, the next best option is to design an inspection program that will discover them at the earliest possible point in the total company activity. In this way, losses will at least be held to a minimum.

It should be evident, in summary, that the process of controlling quality begins with a need for inspection and corrective action. It then logically expands into documentation of results and prevention planning to enhance its original value. The implementation of these four specific responsibilities in all areas of company activity requiring quality control represents the basic and predominant task of the quality control function. Any additional effort on the part of quality control should be considered primarily on the basis of its ability to sustain or to improve the four prime requisites.

Every area where people work and can make mistakes requires inspection. Each has its own peculiarities, depending on the nature of the work and its specific need for control. The amount of inspection provided should depend on the importance or criticality of the function being inspected, the probability of error, and the history of past performance. When inspection and corrective action work hand in hand in the interests of overall company performance, the amount of inspection will be that required to maintain most economically a realistic level of outgoing product quality.

Normally, one expects to find inspection in production areas to find it working effectively in engineering circles may pose questions in the minds of some people. If one examines the work of engineering personnel beyond the role of pure design, however, it becomes apparent that they are subject to the same human failings found in other areas. In fact, they may well appear overly biased as engineering models are nursed through manufacture and test. They are particularly prone to taking short cuts in model manufacturing that will not show up in the production units and to rationalizing their test failures as not being a condition of production.

Inspectors are commonly used in all areas of manufacturing. In this major activity, they perform in-process and final inspections as well as process-compliance inspections. They also check material and its usage. Manufacturing tools require of them not only initial inspection but periodic reinspection to make sure that they will not turn out bad parts. Finally, inspection in manufacturing areas includes surveillance of all machinery, tools, and measurement equipment to be certain that they are receiving adequate calibration or maintenance.

The next major area for inspection is procurement. Here a potential vendor's quality capability is normally examined by the inspector as a member of an overall evaluation team. Resident inspectors are usually established at those vendors' plants where critical or high-cost items are being bought. All other items of procurement are inspected at a receiving station to assure that only usable material is flowing into the stockrooms. The amount of inspection in this area will be a trade-off between vendor quality performance and the risk of having defective material in stock.

Periodic inspection of all stockrooms is necessary to make sure that material is properly segregated, identined, and rotated and that all requirements with respect to time and temperature sensitive materials are being observed. In shipping, inspection is concerned with packing methods and the handling of accepted products. It can be just as embarrassing to a company to have damaged products delivered to a customer as it is to deliver defectively produced material.

Depending on its size and the nature of its business, a company may require highly technical inspections, such as X-ray and chemical or physical analysis of materials. When such a requirement exists, it is not unusual to find a quality laboratory performing the inspections. This function—when it exists not only fills a real business need but also provides an important additional capability for failure analysis. Many problems have been prevented or solved by the effective utilization of a quality laboratory.

The inspection of all measurement equipment for accuracy, or calibration, is important to the overall control of quality. Whenever such equipment is used for acceptance, responsibility for it logically belongs to the quality control function. Regardless of where responsibility rests, however, periodic rechecking of all measurement equipment is essential. Without it, a company is in the position of continually subjecting itself to the real possibility of producing defective material.

Also essential to the effective control of quality, where applicable, is performance testing of products. The usual dilemma in this area is whether to have the quality control function perform the tests or inspect the results. The conflict arises from the adverse effect of tying quality control into schedule performance as against the additional cost of inspecting the results of another organization's testing. Nevertheless, no affected company management needs to be reminded of the overall importance of product performance testing.

Organizationally, the requirements for specific inspection in each area are usually laid down by a quality planning function. (See Chart 1.) This group forms that part of quality engineering concerned with the technology and cost-effectiveness of quality control. As such, it is responsible for the operating procedures, or quality control manual, by which the entire quality control programme is conducted. Quality planning also is the agency of quality control responsible for reviewing and analyzing new quality rwquirements. Applicable requirements are then integrated into engineering, procurement, manufacturing, and inspection plans.

As stated previously, the ability of a quality control function to prevent problems depends to a large degree on quality planning's association with other planning functions. If quality planning can exercise before-the-fact influence and become integrated with planning personnel throughout the company, it will achieve maximum effectiveness. If it must work after the fact, it will be less effective and its output generally will be more costly and late-sufficient cause for the entire quality control activity to get off to a bad start.

The quality engineering portion of quality control is usually home base for all corrective activities. Corrective action begins with the writing of the first rejection tag for non-conforming material. Many problems then proceed through a material review function up to and including a formal material review board consisting of representatives from engineering, procurement, manufacturing, and the customer as well as from quality control. The purpose of the material review board or scrap committee, as it is called in some companies is to dispose of all non-conforming material and to obtain corrective action that will prevent its recurrence. When a company allows the material review function to become primarily disposition-oriented, with little more than lip service being paid to corrective action, it will, in fact, continually miss opportunities to reduce future costs.

Depending on the complexity of its products or their ultimate use in complex systems, a company may require a failure analysis laboratory. Where this need exists, the close association of failure analysis with corrective action-plus the additional need for a complete lack of bias-logically make it the responsibility of quality control. Smaller companies, particularly, miss a significant opportunity to understand their products and their manufacturing system thoroughly by not having a failure analysis function. It's bad enough when a customer has to tell a company that its product is defective, but when he also has to help determine what specifically is wrong, the rapport between company and customer may begin to deteriorate.

Customer relations represents still another important function of quality control. For products other than those sold directly to the public, quality control is often involved in obtaining formal acceptance from the customer. This is always the case when there is a resident customer representative. Each time a customer quality problem exists, the quality control function is automatically involved. Throughout all phases of its association with the customer, quality control can serve a company well by establishing an atmosphere of integrity and responsiveness. Although there is always the possibility of going overboard to please a customer, a stronger possibility usually exists that quality control may be prevented from achieving the desired results.

Whenever configuration control is an important factor in a company's business, quality control plays a major role in its accomplishment. This occurs in either of two ways: Quality documentation must be established in such a way that acceptance is always tied to a specific configuration, or the status of configuration must be confirmed at each point of acceptance. Costly and unnecessary problems will surely develop unless there is a closely coordinated association between configuration management and inspection.

If quality documentation is to serve as objective evidence of work performed, it must be collected from all areas and must be organized in such a way that it can be easily retrieved when needed. This requirement justifies the need for a quality data center where all such documentation can be sent. Once the need for it has been established, the organization of the data center will depend on its total responsibility. As a minimum, it will organize and file all quality documentation according to programme, product line, or whatever seems most appropriate to the expected use.

Depending on the needs or desires of the specific company, the quality data center is often used as a point from which useful management reports can be developed. In this role, it affords a convenient opportunity to review much of a company's total performance. With the expenditure of little additional effort, reports of quality performance and trends can be prepared. Moreover, combining quality data with other available information on costs, for example can result in more meaningful reports. Even though quality data may not be completely utilized, they provide many quality control personnel with the opportunity to become knowledgeable about the company's actual performance record. This alone should make them useful in management circles.

Because improved quality performance is always welcome, the quality control organization frequently engages in motivation programmes aimed at this objective. "Zero defects" programs, which fall into this category, have become well known throughout industry. Motivation programs may take different approaches, however, and there is no way to be sure which will be the most effective in a given area. Usually, a company benefits to the extent of its input: If management really expects to gain from a motivation programme, it must plunge squarely into it.

So, although the quality control process begins with the need for product inspection and corrective action, we can understand how depending on the complexity of the business it can logically and usefully grow into other areas of activity. (See Chart 1.) In fact, quality control has spread its tentacles into so many important areas of company operation that, in its own right, it deserves to be an important and influential member of the company team. If a particular quality control function does not qualify in this respect, yet is accounting for a significant share of total company costs, the management should be asking itself why.

Chart 1
Evolution of a Typical Modern Quality Control System

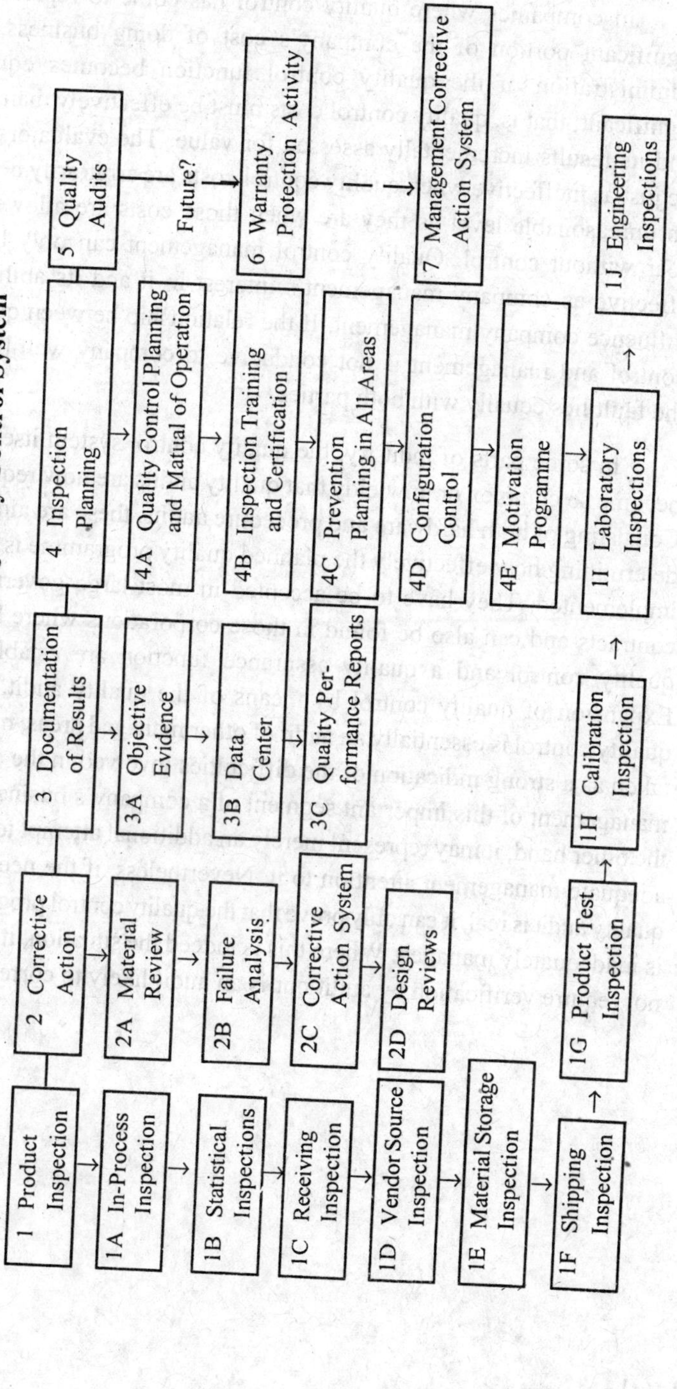

In companies where quality control has come to represent a significant portion of the company's cost of doing business, the administration of the quality control function becomes equally significant; that is, quality control costs must be effectively managed and its results incrementally assessed for value. The evaluators can be just as ineffective when quality control costs are arbitrarily held to an unreasonable level as they are when those costs are allowed to soar without control. Quality control management can only be as effective as company management's interest in it and its ability to influence company management. If the relationship between quality control and management is not conducive to company well-being, the fault lies equally with both parties.

In some parts of industry, the quality control system itself has become so complex or unwieldy that quality audits are now required. Consisting of both hardware and procedure audits, these are aimed at determining how effectively the planned quality programme is being implemented. They have to be accepted in most large government contracts and can also be found in those corporations where both a quality control and a quality assurance function are established. Expansion of quality control by means of the quality audit, when quality control is essentially an audit of other managed areas, must be taken as a strong indication of the difficulties involved in the overall management of this important segment of a company's business. On the other hand, it may represent merely an additional attempt to direct adequate management attention to it. Nevertheless, if the need for a quality audit is real, it can only prove that the quality control programme is inadequately managed. Where this is indeed the situation, it should not require verification by audit nor is an audit likely to correct it.

❐

12
Zero Defects Programmes

The highly publicized zero defects (ZD) programmes have attracted much credit and considerable controversy to the quality control profession in recent years. No one can deny that these programmes have focused more attention on certain fundamental problems of industry than has any other recent innovation. They also have provided many opportunities for management to be creative in overcoming these basic problems. After initial gains from effective promotional activities, however, the real value of zero defects seems unfortunately to have deteriorated into the maintenance of a facade primarily for prestige purposes.

Zero defects is a motivation programme having as its basis a concept of living and working which is beneficial to groups but particularly to the individual. Originating in the aerospace industry during 1961-1962, it grew out of the many perplexing problems facing the aerospace industry in those days. Chief among them was the realization that as complexity grew, success became more difficult. But the obstacles to success were being posed less by the glamorous new technologies than by a myriad of small, familiar, human-error problems. It became painfully obvious that advances in technology and complexity would have to be accompanied by parallel improvements in management and motivation. The zero defects programme was devised to meet this challenge.

ZD holds that people are conditioned throughout their lives to accept the fact that they are not perfect and will therefore make mistakes. By the time they begin working in industry this belief has become firmly rooted and finds its normal expression in the statement:

"People are human and humans make mistakes. Nothing can ever be perfect so long as people take part in it."

And it's true: People make mistakes, and so-called human errors are detrimental to progress and success. But it needn't happen. Zero defects can challenge each individual to establish a personal goal of superior performance and to strive conscientiously for personal excellence in everything he does. The crux of the challenge is to achieve perfect results by preventing and eliminating defects.

Attainntent of the zero defects goal is not easy; nothing worthwhile ever is. Errors are measures of the importance a man places on things; he takes better care of certain things than he does of others. In short, man has developed a dual attitude. In some things he is willing to accept errors; in others he is not. Mistakes have two causes: lack of knowledge and lack of attention. Knowledge can be measured, and shortcomings corrected, through established methods. Lack of attention is an attitude problem; it must be corrected by the man himself-who must make a conscious effort to do things right the first time. Anyone who commits himself to watching each detail and carefully avoiding errors takes a giant step toward setting a goal of zero defects in all things.

Each man must make this goal-setting decision for himself. The results can both enhance his personal reputation and add to the reputation of his company. But by far the greatest benefit is the tremendous personal satisfaction of having participated in a challenging new endeavour and of having achieved a heretofore unattainable goal.

The most significant feature of zero defects, and one that offers the greatest potential, is the opportunity it affords every employee from factory floor and office up to top management to participate in the programme and to develop self-improvement. This is the method by whieh it proposes progressively to achieve overall company improvement. It may be that any success realized to date has been concentrated for the most part at the working level of the factory and the office. There is little indication of sincere effort on the part of engineering and management to identify and eliminate problems for which they are responsible.

To the majority of managements exposed to ZD, it may have appeared to offer a low-cost, do-good programme, possessing certain features with which the company could ill afford not to be associated. Management doubtless recognizes that any real value deriving from zero defects will always be on the plus side of the ledger. The programme may even lessen management's burden in some areas and so prove acceptable. After giving its blessing, however, management usually proceeds merely to tolerate ZD and give it only lip service. Management fails to recognize zero defects as another attempt on the part of key employees to break the management barrier and to establish effective communication. The message that comes through loudly and clearly in any attempt to implement a zero defects programme is that management alone has the power to motivate personnel and to effect improvements. Lack of sincerity on the part of management not only is painfully obvious to everyone but makes the burden of implementation immeasurably more difficult and reduces the results to mediocre proportions at best.

To the majority of quality organizations that have been involved with it, zero defects probably has constituted both a boon and a headache. The benefits have flowed from renewed opportunities to discuss with management the configuration of the human error problem and the need for creative new methods of prevention. They include the spotlighting and publicizing of the meaningful activities of ZD, with the ensuing recognition of active participants. The headache is associated wholly with implementation. Although quality control is not always designated to handle the programme, it has been the principal candidate because of the zero defects leadership provided by the quality control profession. The first challenge of implementation lies in determining what specific activities should comprise a company's zero defects programme in the light of varied management support and participation. The next lies in mustering the necessary support from each company group to set up activities properly.

The choice of activities to be considered for any given programme has grown considerably since the inauguration of zero defects, thanks principally to the thriving ZD seminars and workshop found throughout industry today as well as to the numerous artcles and books written on the subject. There is an apparent contradiction between the ease with which attention on an international scale can be attracted to a new scheme to make workers more effective and the fact that improved effectiveness is seldom depicted as part of the basic responsibility of management or even, simply, as management effectiveness. At best, zero defects seeks and achieves management help and support rather than management leadership.

Zero defects has had major success in at least one area: It has captured the promotional talents of many people, as indicated by the outstanding kickoff ceremonies that have been publicized. Mass rallies attended by thousands of people and led by prominent speakers have been the order of the day, the result of successful teaser campaigns arousing maximum interest. These events have not only captured the imagination of the participants but have been effective in creating an initial atmosphere conducive to zero defects thinking and actions. The more difficult task has proved to be the support and further development of the early gains.

Among the methods used for sustaining the ZD programme are posters, slogans, letters to employees, give-away gimmicks, and the like. While all of these have some beneficial value, they are not in themselves sufficient. People need to feel personal satisfaction and receive personal recognition in order to be continually motivated. Consequently, activities involving performance measurement and personal or group awards have been most effective in promoting superior effort.

The well-publicized recognition of individuals has been the most successfully used reward in zero defects programmes. It has also provided an opportunity for a type of management which is most meaningful to both the individuals involved and the entire programme. The reason for this is obvious: Such awards combine an employee's need for pride in himself and for recognition with a strong desire for an indication of management's sincere interest in him as an individual. If management recognition of employee performance were the only benefit to be gained from a zero defects programme, the programme still would have been worthwhile.

Another common indication of a ZD programme in existence is a variety of performance goal charts. There are ZD goals for everything from percentage of discrepancies to employees' lost time. It is obvious that in some programmes goals are established merely for the sake of having goals. To maintain a facade of this type is merely to prove what constitutes the real motivating power of management. Where performance can be measured in terms of defects, charts based on motivating goals can be most effective. Where performance cannot be measured in this way, however, the value of charts is questionable.

In areas where performance parameters appear to be intangible, zero defects should ask: How does one measure performance? What constitutes improvement in this area? The answers to these questions will determine the parameters that should be charted to measure performance and to establish improvement goals. Any sincere attempt at goal setting will result in serious thinking about the real value or efficiency of a function, and it may even lead to the application of individual operations research to achieving a better understanding of how the group functions. Even if the questions cannot be answered finitely, any knowledge gained will benefit the management of the area in question, which is truly responsible for measuring performance.

One of the most significant activities that has been developed as part of zero defects is an error cause removal (ECR) programme. More than any other ZD activity, this fulfills the two basic objectives of zero defects: It guarantees improvement through the identification and removal of the causes of errors, and it allows every employee in the company to participate in the programme freely and effectively. Its implementation is simple. Initially, it requires an error cause identification form on which all employees are encouraged to write, without limitations, their thoughts on specific, potential causes of errors. Next, it requires a group of qualified personnel to evaluate all thoughts and suggestions, investigate them as necessary, and take positive management action on all those ideas that are valid.

An effective ECR programme identifies many mistakes and oversights on the part of one company group that find their way into the work of others. It also identifies many trivial annoyances that affect employee morale adversely but are easily corrected. Its greatest value in the prevention of problems, however, lies in its identification of possible applications of Murphy's law—"If something can be done wrong, somebody will do it.' Any company that suffers from so-called little problems can profit from ECR.

ECR is not unlike other potentially profitable activities. It requires management support to be effective, but actually the only support that is necessary is a willingness to act on valid suggestions. Many items, of course, are not valid; they require only a tactful "Thank you for trying." But those that are valid require timely response and action if the programme is not to suffer. Employees will not speak out when they know no one will listen to them. They devote to a programme the same attention, or lip service, that they see coming from management. And progressive management can ill afford to lose the value of individual inputs.

Most industry wide questionnaires on zero defects indicate that interest lies chiefly in cost of programme versus evidence of success and, naturally, in those specific activities to which success is attributed. But this information can be misleading in two ways: First, it is impossible to measure a state of mind or attitude; second, it is extremely difficult to differentiate between improvements caused by zero defects and those arising from other management action. For example, if a supervisor decides to increase significantly the training and certification of his people, his rejection rate may decrease drastically as a direct result. On the other hand, if the supervisor's action is a result of zero defects thinking the ZD programme may be responsible. Who is to know the truth of the matter?

The effective implementation of a zero defects programme or of any other so-called do-good programme invariably increases the burden carried by first-line supervision, and herein lies a real pitfall. These individuals already have one of the most important and time-consuming assignments in the company; thus it is unreasonable to expect them to review, analyze, and approve all the ideas solicited from their employees by management about every company activity. If a separate group of company representatives is set up to receive suggestions directly from individual employees, the supervisor can devote his full effort to the primary tasks. On the other hand, the supervisor's role is strengthened where he becomes the agent of recognition and awards due his employees through their participation in ZD and other programmes.

Zero defects should be sold strictly on the basis that any good that comes from it will add to the well-being of the company. Its potential is greatly enhanced where management provides leadership and sets an example of self-application. The programme should be designed to allow all employees to participate in it actively and be recognized; goals should be established where performance can be measured; and competition should be encouraged. Personal awards and recognition should be highlighted to the greatest possible extent, and supplementary promotional activities should be used to sustain interest in the programme. Finally, participation by contractors, suppliers, and customers should be sought.

Management can best support the zero defects programme by indicating a willingness to give ZD as much consideration as it gives to the problems that bother its customers. Employees will respond by pointing out the little things that are hurting overall business. In fact, when assured of a fair share of management's genuine interest, employees may even begin to feel important enough to act as though they owned the place, so to speak. The basic objectives of quality control will be furthered by this concern about problems and the greatest reaper of benefits will be management itself.

The same way of thinking can be applied to zero defects as was applied to the man-rating of such programmes as Gemini. When the moment arrived to push the button for a manned launching, it was too late to worry about whether the work had been done correctly. A similar moment of truth exists in the use of every product, and zero defects should attempt to instill this thought into each phase of the productive effort that can affect that moment. People can take pride in identifying with a quality. product and they will do so when they see that management shares their pride. The same motivation, moreover, underlies their understanding and acceptance of strict disciplines. When enforcement becomes a reality, the entire company from top management to lowest-level employee learns the difference between stating, "There are no obvious problems," and proclaiming, "Everything is completely right!"

❐

13

Motivation for Quality Development

The quality development of any organisation involves systems, techniques and its people. Experience shows that the most critical and yet most difficult of these three dimensions to develop are the people. The development of individuals and teams is quitessential to the quality development of any organisation. Development of quality systems and techniques are relatively simple and straightforward management challenges when compared to managing the cultural change associated with motivating people for quality. Proven methods and guidelines are available for development of systems and techniques but progress in third parameter, people is much less mechanistic or prescriptive and in general is much slower. Many organisations have not been able to achieve the expected results because insufficient effort or priority allocated to improving the approach and attitude of people involved. In terms of the stages of quality development described in Chapter 1, the extent of cultural (people) change increase as organisation move from a systems orientation through an improvement orientation to a preventive orientation. If two of the key elemens of cultural changes, teamwork and management style are considered in this context, it can be seen that:

(a) **Team Work** evolves from having a very small role within the systems orientation stage to bring an important but separate activity during the improvement orientation to being an integral part of the organization in the preventive orientation stage;

(b) **Management Style** evolves from awareness to involvement to commitment.

An integral part of the total quality approach is the harnessing of the skills of the people within the organization. When considering the assets of any organization (equipment, buildings, products, knowledge, capital, etc.) the only asset which is creative, which can take the company forward, is its people. In many immature organizations this latent talent of the people within is ignored as they are seen, in the words of Henry-Ford, as 'hands not minds'. Very often individuals who are seen as employees capable of only mundane tasks within the workplace are involved in creative, organizational activities outside the work environment such as managers of local sports teams. People have to be an integral part of the quality development of an organization. In fact the organizations develop at the rate at which their people develop.

Central to the organizational development associated with quality improvement is 'culture' change. Organizational culture, is an important concept when seeking to promote quality development although culture is difficult to precisely define or to measure. A simple definition of the, culture of an organization is:

The shared values and norms of behaviour of the individuals within the organization.

If for example, the managers within a company promote an attitude of 'let's try to cheat our customers by getting away with as much sub-standard product as possible then it should come as no surprise if the employees adopt this same attitude with the company. If the organization blames and criticizes individuals for mistakes or errors then the people will respond by being deceitful and evasive. If, however, people are trusted and respected then this will be reflected in their behaviour and values.

For people to produce quality work they must be motivated and care about the work they do. To be motivated individuals must have a motive and this sense of purpose must be clearly communicated to people. Motivating individuals and creating a culture change represents perhaps the most significant management challenge on the road to quality development.

People and Motivation

A great deal of the writing on management science during the twentieth century has been devoted to the relationship between people and work. Understanding the answer to the question of 'what motivates people?' is fundamental to managing the cultural change required for quality development. Along the more significant developments in understanding the relationship between people and work have been the contributions from:

— F.W. Taylor;

— A.H. Maslow;

— F. Herzberg;

— D. McGregor.

F.W. Taylor. The contribution of F.W. Taylor to management thinking in industry during the first half of the twerttieth century was significant. Taylor advocated a 'scientific' approach to management where the emphasis should be placed upon control and methods. This management approach was used extensively in the USA during this period and was attributed with the creation of a strong American industrial base after the Second World War. In many ways the style of management promoted by Taylor was appropriate to a situation where organizations were employing large, mainly immigrant workforces. Work measurement, method study and bonus schemes were very much part of this scientific approach to management, but increasingly from the 1970s onward these techniques were seen to be working against the development of a quality culture. Control and payment-based incentives were not delivering the quality products and service that were increasingly coming out of Japan. where managers had largely rejected the Taylor approach.

A.H. Maslow. A.H. Maslow in his work on people and motivation identified a hierarchy of human needs. Maslow suggested that as individuals developed and achieved the needs associated with one level then they would seek the needs at the subsequent (higher) levels. This model of human motivation, although proposed in the

1940s, is still relevant to quality management issues of the 1990s. As organizations develop and mature then the mechanisms for motivating people become more complex and abstract. Maslow's hierarchy of needs is illustrated in Figure 1 and also offers an important insight into the problems of international competition for developed nations where competitors in less developed (often low-wage economies) can achieve levels of motivation through the provision of rather more basic human needs.

F. Hezberg. F. Herzberg further developed the ideas relating motivation in the workplace to needs by classifying factors as either satisfiers or dissatisfiers. The factors affecting dissatisfaction were termed the 'hyginene' factors and included:

(a) salary;

(b) working conditions;

(c) policy and administration;

(d) supervision and arrangements;

(e) relationships.

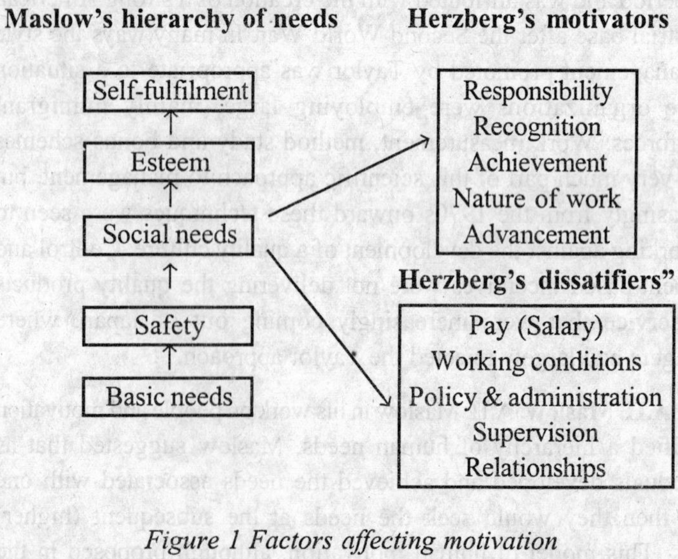

Figure 1 Factors affecting motivation

These factors were seen by Herzberg as potential causes of dissatisfaction but in themselves could not provide long-term satisfaction. In otherwords, individuals could only become demotivated by these factors (dissatisfiers) and never become sustainably motivated.

The factors affecting job satisfaction identified by Herzberg included:

(a) responsibility;

(b) recognition;

(c) achievement;

(d) nature of the work;

(e) advancement.

These factors were seen to produce satisfaction and were termed the 'motivators' because they could produce a positive attitude to work and often for a longer duration. This important distinction between concentrating on factors which have, at best, a neutral effect upon motivation and focusing upon more positive motivational factors such as responsibility is an essential management understanding. The cultural change in management state associated with quality development is very much concerned with the focus upon the positive 'motivators'. The experiences of organizations which are successful at delivering quality improvement has emphasized the need to manage both the hygiene factors and the motivators factors. Quality development that focuses only upon motivators will be naive. Similarly focusing groups on the hygiene factors will not produce long-term benefit. Both groups of factors need improvement in order to provide sustainable quality development.

D. McGregor. D. McGregor proposed two opposing behavioural models in terms of the way in which people approach work. The first McGregor described as Theory X, which states that humans:

(a) inherently dislike work and will avoid it if possible;

(b) need to be controlled and coerced to provide adequate work effort;

(c) wish to avoid responsibility and have little ambition above satisfying basic needs.

The alternative model was described by McGregor as Theory Y in which humans:

(a) see work as a natural activity as important as rest or play;

(b) exercise self-control and are committed to accepted objectives;

(c) seek responsibility and possess creativity which is largely untapped.

These opposing behavioural viewpoints are fundamental to the management perspective in dealing with motivation. Are people Theory X or Theory Y? The significance of McGregors's work is the link made between the way in which people are managed and the way in which they behave. If people are treated as Theory X then they will behave as Theory X. If, on the other hand, the management culture promotes a Theory Y viewpoint, then people are move likely to behave accordingly.

This maturing view as to how people should be managed and motivate reflected in the developments in quality management over the past 30 years. Increasingly the focus in recent years has been upon the involvements empowerment and motivation of the workforce. The systems and techniques of quality management will only be implemented effectively if the people believe in the process and support the objectives.

In service industries, quality starts and ends with the people. In the manufacturing companies, despite the advances in technology and automation, customer satisfaction is still largely delivered by the people.

Management Style

As with 'culture' the phrase 'management style' is an often used descriptor of the relationship between people and motivation and is generally a complex concept that is difficult to quantify. In simple terms management style can be defined as, "The collective methods and approaches used to motivate people within the organization."

The complexity of this concept lies in attempting to identify the subtle combination of explicit and implicit activities employed by managers within an organisation to achieve the objectives. Very often the management style and values are not implicity communicated and are therefore passed down through the management structure explicitly. For example, a young manager who joins an organisation will observe the way in which more senior colleagues behave and will also develop a set of criteria in terms of management approach that coincides with progression and promotion within the organization. If the senior managers in a company exhibit a control-orientated management approach based upon Theory X then this will promote this style of management among middle and junior managers and will inhibit cultural change (why should senior managers change a personal style of management that has brought them individual success in terms of promotion?)

To develop a quality-orientated approach firstly senior managers need to recognize the existing style of management identify a management approach which supports quality development and finally communicate the required culture in a credible manner to the organization. This means adopting an appropriate management style rather than simply expounding one. People listen to what managers say, but they also watch what they do!

Developing a quality culture is a senior management responsibility and involves:

(a) identifying a style of management to support quality development;

(b) effective communication.

There is of course no single style of management upon which to base quality development. There are, however, certain features of the approach to the management of people which support total quality and these include:

(a) adopting and 'enabling' rather than 'controlling'. style of management (the manager's viewpoints should be 'how can I help my people do their work better' rather than 'how can they help me to do my work');

(b) management values based upon respect for individuals for honesty and for integrity.

From this style of management derives the role of the manager in the organization who should be involved in the support and facilitation (rather than control) of subordinates. This role is illustrated in an alternative view-point of the 'organogram' shown in Figure 2 whereby the managers support rather than attempt to control the efforts of others.

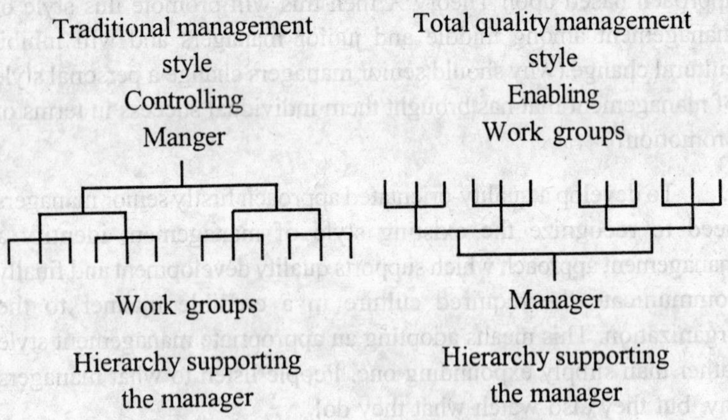

Figure 2. The manager's role in the organization

Hierarchy supporting the manager Hierachy supporting the work group

The second key element of management style concerns communication. In organizations arranged in functional 'chimneys' (where work is arranged on a functional rather than process basis) the communications are traditionally poor. Poor organizational communication inevitably leads to errors and hence to quality problems. Typical inhibitors to good communication within organizations include:

(a) lack of opportunity;

(b) fear of reprisal;

(c) people too busy;

(d) departmental boundaries.

Good communications are critical to good quality and good customer service and certainly as companies mature and develop an improvement orientation, a greater priority and emphasis is given to internal and external communication and to communication being a two-way process. Techniques such as briefing sessions or 'talk-back' sessions in which mangers scheduled time specifically for communicating are commonplace in organizations at the second stage of quality development (as described in Chapter 1). As companies mature yet further then reorganization often takes place to eliminate departmental boundaries through the use of teams arranged according to business processes.

Team Work and Quality Development

Research into the approaches used to implement quality development has identified many different methodologies for example:

(a) techniques led;

(b) 'guru' philosophy led;

(c) customer led;

(d) process led.

The common factor, however, is that all organizations on the road to quality development use teams. Team work is universally adopted as the vehicle for change and the organizational mechanism for involvihg people in quality improvement. The benefits of a team based approach include:

(a) improved solutions to quality problems;

(b) improved ownership of solutions;

(c) improved communications;

(d) improved integration.

Many of the quality improvement tools and techniques explicitly require team-based application and benefit from the range of skills and insights provided by teamwork. Perhaps the most'significant organizational change associated with quality development is the increased emphasis upon teamworking. The quality improvement stage of development described in Chapter 1 is very much devoted to the operation of improvement teams. Prevention-orientated companies integrate these team-based activities into the organizational framework. Rather than teamworking being a separate activity associated only with quality improvement projects it becomes part of normal operations within the workplace.

During this adoption of a more team-based culture: it is important for organizations to correctly understand the role of teamwork. It is incorrect, for example, to assume all activities or improvements need to be generated or derived from teams. Individuals are obviously still an important component of the quality developed organization it is simply the balance between individual and team-based activity that is changed. By harnessing the benefits of termwork, companies combine powerful techniques with improved motivation.

Building Effective Teams

The words 'teams' and 'teamwork' are used wide throughout organizations to describe groups of people and group activity. This widespread use of the descriptor 'team' has led to the concept of teamworking being taken rather for granted. Individuals may well be organized into identifiable groups but they may not be working as a team. Given that teamworking underpins much of the cultural change and the application of the techriiques of quality development, then it is important to ensure that teambuilding is carried out effectively. For example, if a quality improvement team is to be assembled, who should be included in the team? Basic guidelines for building effective teams suggest that team members should include:

(a) Those individuals affected by the problem;

(b) those individuals likely to be involved;

(c) those individuals with appropriate skills.

This responsibility or skills dimension to teambuilding is clearly important as all teams have a basic knowledge requirement and should involve those people who understand the objectives and will own the solutions. This functional viewpoint is, however, incomplete when attempting to build effective teams. The dynamics and balance of the team are equally, if not more, important to the eventual effective operation of any group of individuals. The work of Belbin at the Henley Management Centre clearly indicates:

(a) balanced teams usually succeed;

(b) unbalanced teams usually fail.

The balance of a team is achieved through and appropriate collection of individuals having different yet complementary team roles. As described below all individuals exhibit certain identifiable team roles and effective teams are built through balancing the combination of these team roles. The assumption that any group of individuals with the required skills can be brought together is naive and unlikely to succeed.

The climate in which the team operates is also important and this requires:

(a) a supportive atmosphere where individuals are not fearful of contributing;

(b) a welcoming atmosphere where individual contributions are encouraged;

(c) mutual respect;

(d) no one view or individual dominating;

(e) opposing views to be encouraged and handled positively.

Recognizing the significance of team roles and team balance and the importance of providing the correct climate are important prerequisites for enabling quality development through teamwork.

Team Leadership

As with areas of management, the leadership of the team is critical to the effectiveness of the team. The main roles of the team leader within the improvement team are illustrated in Fig. 3.

The team leader's role is therefore primarily concerned with the operation of the process. The team leader should not dominate the group but should provide impetus to the project through the efforts of the team members.

The question arises, however, as to who should be the team leader? Possible alternatives to the selection of the team leader include:

Figure 3. The role of the team leader

(a) the most 'senior' person in the team;

(b) the person most directly involved in the problem;

(c) the person with the most appropriate team role;

(d) election by the other team members.

Selection of the most senior manager as the team leader is not necessarily the most appropriate choice. Very often a senior manager within a team will simply reinforce existing organizational structures and may inhibit team contribution. Certainly a strong sense of ownership of the problem coupled with an appropriate team profile (for example 'chairman' or 'shaper') generally is a more successful recipe for effective team leadership. The problem with allowing the team members to select the leader is that this does not enable the team leader to select the members. With cross-functional improvement. teams it is normal to designate the leader who would then be involved in the selection of the team members. In functionally based teams it is more common to seek consensus for the appointment of the team leader.

❐

14

Quality Improvement Teams and Planning

Teams improve productivity as a result of greater motivation and reduced overlap and lack of communication in a functionally based classical structure characterized by territorial battles and parochial outlooks. There is always the danger that functional specialists, if left to their own devices, may pursue their own interests with little regard for the overall company mission. Team membership, particularly a cross-functional team, reduces many of these barriers and encourages an integrative systems approach to achievement of common objectives, those that are common to both the company and the team. There are many success stories. To cite a few:

(a) Globe Metallurgical, Inc., the first small company to win the Baldrige A ward, had a 380 percent increase in productivity which was attributed primarily to self-managed work teams.

(b) The partnering concept requires a new corporate culture of participative management and teamwork throughout the entire organization. Ford increased productivity 28 percent by using the team concept with the same workers and equipment.

(c) Harleysville Insurance Company's Discovery programme provides synergism resulting from the team approach. The programme produced a cost saving of $3.5 million, along with enthusiasm and involvement among employees.

(d) At Decision Data Computer Corporation middle management is trained to support Pride Team.

(e) Martin Marietta Electronics and Missiles Group has achieved success with performance measurement teams (PMTs).

(f) Publishers Press has achieved significant productivity improvements and attitude change from the company's process improvement teams (PITs).

(g) Florida Power & Light Company, the utility that was the first recipient of the Deming Prize, has long had quality improvement teams as a fundamental component of their quality improvement programme.

Teams for TQM

The several sub-systems or components of a TQM approach were examined in previous chapters. The most critical of these components is employee involvement, and it is the one around which the management system of TQM should he based, It is the most important of the components of TQM and also the most complex. Consider the analogy of an iceberg. Approximately 10 percent of an iceberg is visible, while 90 percent is hidden from view, Imagine that the organizational chart is an iceberg. The visible 10 percent is top management and functional management. The 90 percent, where the true potential for quality exists, is comprised of frontline supervision and non-management employees. Does it not make good sense to tap into the 90 percent which represents a reservoir of ideas for quality and productivity improvements? The vehicle for doing this is some form of team. A 1989 General Accounting Office study found that over 80 percent of all companies had implemented some form of employee involvement. However, the statistic is misleading because responding companies considered a suggestion system as an employee involvement programme, which is hardly a systems approach or a linking vehicle.

Quality Circles

The most widespread form of an employee involvement team is the quality circle, defined as a small group of employees doing similar or related work who meet regularly to identify, analyze, and solve product-quality and production problems and to improve general operations." Although the concept has had some success in white-collar operations, the major impact has been among "direct labour" employees in manufacturing, where concerns are primarily with quality, cost, specifications, productivity, and schedules. By their very nature, quality circles were limited to concerns of the small group of members and few cross-functional problems were considered. The major growth of the circles occurred in the late 1970s and early 1980s, as thousands of companies adopted the concept. Like so many previous movements, however, the concept never met expectations and widespread abandonment resulted. As many as 50 percent of Fortune 500 companies disbanded their circles in the 1980s?' The major reason for failure was a general lack of commitment to the "concept of participation and the lack of interest and participation by management." From a TQM perspective, quality circles lack the prerequisites of integration with strategy, company goals, and management systems.

Task teams are a modification of the quality circle. The major differences are that task teams can exist at any level and the goal cf topic for discussion is given, whereas in quality circles members are generally free to choose the problems they will solve. Task teams with the best chance for success are those that represent an extension of a preexisting, successful quality circle programme. Self-managing work teams are an extension of quality circles but differ in one major respect: members are empowered to exercise control over their jobs and optimize the efficiency and effectiveness of the total process rather than the individual steps within it. Team members perform all the necessary tasks to complete an entire job, setting up work schedules and making assignments to individual team members. Peer evaluation is another characteristic.

A number of common elements are characteristic of self-managed teams:

(a) **Job Design and Structure.** The team redesigns the work before implementation and controls the entire job.

(b) **Supervision.** Traditional supervisors could be absent altogether. Leadership may be assigned according to talent and preference.

(c) **Quality.** Tn addition to quality the teams may become involved in the entire job, including planning, cost, scheduling and even sales and distribution.

(d) **Decisions.** Decisions are not confined to quality but may involve all areas that affect the teams. Some may become involved in appraisal, pay, and selection.

(e) **Customers.** Internal customers are perceived as partners for the purpose of meeting needs of external customers. The primary focus is the external customer.

(f) **Authority.** If given complete responsibility for the actions of their areas, the teams may have authority and responsibility for growth and profitability.

Cross Functional Teams

Computer manufacturer DEC has integrated a range of proven TQM techniques into its programme, including cross-functional process improvement teams. One element is strictly home-grown. DELTA (DEC Employees Leveraged Team Activities) is a sophisticated. closed-loop suggestion system designed to discover and address problems. Under DELTA, only an employee who makes a suggestion can dispose of it. He or she also has the responsibility of working with other employees to implement or reshape the suggestion in order to determine whether it is feasible. Thus, DELTA empowers employees and promotes team building, two essential elements of quality management.

. The centuries-sold hierarchical form of organization with a vertical chain of command was the norm until recently, when organizational complexity demanded horizontal as well as vertical coordination in order to plan and control processes that flowed laterally. If no lateral coordination is achieved, the organization becomes a collection of islands of specialization without integration, a requirement of the systems approach. Linking business process improvement to the key business objectives of the organization is necessary if quality is to become real and relevant.

The quality manager (or chief inspector) reports directly to the plant manager and is responsible to determine by sufficient inspection that the company products conform to all pertinent company/customer specifications and drawings. Products deviating from specifications will be withheld from shipment and will be reviewed jointly by the plant manager and the quality manager for disposal and corrective action. Such a statement clearly identifies that quality is an independent function and that the task is limited to one of inspection and the accumulation of defect data for review. Inasmuch as no mention is made of the accumulation of historical data, it must be assumed that none is required. At the other end of the spectrum the statement of responsibility, accountability, and authority for the quality manager of a very large corporation can be extensive and detailed for example:

Under the policy guidance of the vice president and general manager, responsibility, accountability and authority is vested in the director/manager of quality as follows:

Responsibility

1. Plan, control, direct, develop, and evaluate the operations of the functional departments assigned to his or her area:

    a. Quality assurance, which includes:

        Product assurance

        Quality audit

        Laboratories

    b. Quality control, which includes:

        Internal quality control

        Supplier quality control

    c. Quality programme management

2. Ensure that products delivered to customers meet all standards of quality contained in contracts and specifications.

3. Ensure that operations or processes affecting quality standards and performance are tested, audited, and evaluated.

4. Examine quality policies, instructions, and procedures to ensure that they are effective, appropriate, and congruent with the accomplishment of division objectives.

5. Ensure that programme areas are supported and assisted in terms of systems, techniques, and trained personnel necessary to enable such programs to meet quality standards and requirements.

6. Establish a work environment that ensures the development and effective utilization of personnel and the proper combining of resources necessary to carry out quality programmes and meet objectives.

7. Communicate division goals; develop and disseminate concise statements of the quality groups tasks and standards of performance, and evaluate results against these standards.

8. Maintain a continuing liaison with customer personnel and agencies which generates a positive understanding of quality systems and commitment.

Accountability

1. Products delivered to customers meeting all specified standards of quality contained in contracts and specifications.

2. Achievement of required quality at cost within limits of allocated funds.

3. Prepare data that identify for management trends in hardware quality, costs related to scrap and production errors, and overall cost of the quality function.

4. The performance, morale, and motivation of assigned personnel.

5. The integration of his assigned functional departments with the remainder of the division.

Authority

1. The supervision, administration, and execution of programmes, policies and functions assigned, so as to ensure the division's capability of attaining its profit and long-range commitments.

2. Develop and maintain systems, controls, and techniques which provide for the timely detection, solution, and elimination of quality problems and their causes.

3. Approve programme personnel certification board requirements.

Whatever the dimensions of the task is it is clearly defined both the quality organization and the rest of the production operation understand what the quality department is required to do. An equally important element in organizing for quality is the recognition that the production of a quality product is the responsibility of every division of the company involved in the production process: engineering, manufacturing, material handling, and purchasing, as well as quality. This responsibility begins at the point of initial design and continues throughout the life of the product.

Basic Quality Task

An understanding of the basic task to be accomplished is fundamental to developing an organization. Although there are many variations of emphasis, the fundamental tasks of the quality organization can be identified as follows:

1. **Prevention of Defects Through Analysis of Requirements.** It is axiomatic that elimination of potential problems before production begins will result in lower cost and a better-quality product. Unaccountably, this is an area

all too frequently ignored. The inclusion of manufacturing and quality personnel in the early review of preliminary designs can reap handsome rewards by way of a more realistic tolerancing, dimensioning for easier machining, elimination of difficult assembly processes, better understanding of test requirements, and so on. Quality reviews at this stage can establish the proper sequencing of inspection requirements, eliminating unnecessary inspections which make no real contribution to product quality. The review will also pinpoint similarities in design to past products which have suffered from failures or defects. Early identification of such problems can lead to corrections or changes that will eliminate the probability of recurrence.

2. **Control of the Manufacturing and Test Operations.** To achieve product quality it is necessary to be certain that every manufacturing action is performed according to pre-determined standards and instructions. There is no substitute for the discipline that ensures this control. In theory it makes no difference who exercises such control. The factory workers who are properly motivated can be just as effective in controlling their output as the inspector who normally checks their work.

   In real life, however, the practicalities of meeting cost schedule commitment generally mitigate against production personnel being an effective force for sustained and improved quality. It falls to the quality organization to exercise this control or restraining activity. It is incumbent that they be equipped both mentally and technically to accept the responsibility. Failure to do an effective job has sometimes been due to the reluctance of quality management to accept the fact that the company really meant for them to control the production operation to the degree necessary to produce satisfacrory hardware.

3. **Detection of Defectives in the Hardware.** Detection of hardware and test errors is the traditional role of the inspection force within the quality organization. The effectiveness of this function has a marked effect on overall control of the product.

4. **Planning for a more Effective Operation.** One of the more noticeable shortcomings in many quality organizations is the absence of effort directed toward the future needs of the division. All too frequently the planning effort is concentrated on today's problems, with little thought given to future developments.

5. **Corrective Action to Prevent Repetition of Mistakes.** Repetitive mistakes are costly, interfere with schedules, and are unnecessary. Every company, however small must have a system to recognize repetitive problems and eliminate their cause. It is important to recognize that the elimination of some problems may be so costly as to prohibit any constructive action. A conscious decision to take no action must be carefully weighed against the possible results of such a decision.

Organizational Concepts

At the outset it should be recognized that there are no absolutes with respect to the manner in which the quality function is organized. The basic tasks of quality must be satisfied in some manner, but the organization required is dependent on a variety of factors. It should be developed to fit the job at hand: what is required for complex mechanical hardware is patently different from that required for a supplier of simple parts, a chemical processing concern, or a supplier of services. The opening paragraph of this chapter identified the need for a commitment by management; a definition of the quality charter-what, precisely, does the management expect from the quality group? The size of the task has a marked influence on the nature of the ultimate organization. The most effective group is one that accomplishes its task with a minimum of organizational requirements.

There is also no common agreement with respect to what the organization for quality is called. Quality Control, Quality Division, Quality Assurance, Product Assurance, and Quality and Reliability Assurance are all titles that appear on company organization charts, and it matters little what the organization is called as long as its charter is properly defined.

Quality assurance, for example, has been used to designate a total, complex quality organization; a small audit group in such an organization; a group responsible for all non-inspection quality tasks; and a separate organization independently auditing and reviewing all aspects of quality within a company. The specific task requirements may also influence the basic approach to organization. A limited responsibility may be best served by a quality assurance group acting in a staff capacity as mentioned above. Some large organizations consider it desirable to monitor the quality function by having a group of operating executives act as a quality committee, or quality council, establishing basic policy and ensuring that such policy is communicated to the operating divisions. The important factor is to recognize the scope of the work and organize for it.

In every company there are built-in contraints that can have an effect on how a task it organised, and these constraints must be recognized and taken into consideration. Identified below are a number of such constraints with a short paragraph outlining their effect. These are by no means all that could be developed, nor are they examined in detail. Rather, they are indicators of real-life situations that must be faced in the development of a good quality organization. Organizational theorists sometimes choose to ignore these constraints, but they are real and must be a consideration in any organizing effort.

1. **Company Operational and Organizational Guidelines.** Every company has developed over its history certain guidelines relating to how it organizes and operates. Usually, but not always, these are written down in the form of policy or standard practice manuals. Although these are not necessarily inviolate, the wise manager will find it prudent to stay within these guidelines unless they prevent the proper accomplishment of the quality objective.

2. **Management Style.** Over the years, most companies develop a management "style." This style or attitude, is reflected in the way the management team operates, both within the organization and in the marketplace, for example; some companies are highly disciplined, outlining in written procedures all possible situations and following the procedures to the letter. At the other end of the spectrum is the laissez-faire approach; nothing very formal, each executive doing his or her own thing and keeping in touch with peers in the organization. In some organizations nothing gets done unless the top executive personally decides. This is not the place to comment on the merits of the various styles but only to point out that the company style must be considered in organizing for quality.

3. **Customer Influences.** More frequently than not the quality organization is dictated/affected by requirements of the customer. This may come from specifications, process controls, or even certain administrative actions required in order to do business. This is particularly true for companies having contracts with government agencies, each of which has its own special set of requirements or regulations. One of the quality manager's more difficult tasks is to develop an understanding in all levels of management that these customer requirements are real and must be satisfied. Unfortunately, requirements of different customers are sometimes divergent to the point where multiple systems may be required. The challenge is to meet the intent of the requirements with the minimum disruption of the normal quality system. Quality costs can become exaggerated if the organization is expanded to over every eventuality.

4. **Diversity and Complexity of Product Line.** The diversity and complexity of the company product line have a strong influences on the development of the quality organizational structure. An organization that is suitable for the manufacture of a few, large, highly sophisticated, and individually costly

articles may not resemble at all that required to produce volume deliveries of small, diverse, highly precise parts from automatic machinery. It is erroneous to conclude that any given quality system or technique, however successful in the past, is necessarily useful when the manufacturing product-line changes radically or becomes completely different.

It is true that the same type of controls are often a requirement for entirely different products. It does not follow however, that the technique of application must be the same. Indeed, the technique may be so radically different as to require a different organizational pattern. For example, precision castings for a space vehicle may have the same tolerance requirements as those for an engine block on an automotive assembly line. Automatic gaging would be prohibilitively costly in the case of the space vehicle where the few castings involved would probably be checked individually by a highly skilled inspector, either by actual layout on a surface plate, or through the use of an inspection measuring machine. The automotive assembly line would probably have automatic gaging equipment built into the assembly line, which would be monitored by less-skilled checkers or by the production personnel. Both methods achieve the same end but through different techniques and a different organizational alignment.

5. **Company Size.** It would seem to go without saying that the size of the company itself has a marked effect on the Quality organization. Although the basic quality task must be accomplished, the function has to fit into the framework of the overall organisation. Large organisations have the facilities and finances to maintain systems and records, which, although desirable, may be well beyond the means of a smaller company.

6. **Stability of the Product Line.** Product stability can also have an influence on organizational structure. A product

line that is relatively the same from year to year can generate economies, both in the use of personnel and selection of the most useful and economic equipment. Less supervision, more use of production checking data instead of direct inspection, and elimination of formal corrective action teams are ready candidates for system improvement is a stable manufacturing environment.

Improvements such as the above cannot be achieved when the product line changes frequently. a different structure is required to identify problems as they occur and to take the required action to correct them. The manager of the quality function must be alert to recognize when a change in product requires a change in the quality system.

7. **Financial Stability.** Quality is a part of the business aspect of every company and its operation is dependent on the overall profitability of the concern. Quality managers cannot ignore, as some would have us, believe, the cost of doing business and the financial stability of the entire organization. Quality managers should get their fair share of the money but must recognize that the programme has to be developed to fit the funds available.

8. **Availability of Personnel.** The organization must always be formulated around the requirements of the task at hand. It would be unrealistic, however, not to recognize that the availability of certain by personnel may affect the formation of the ideal organization. Lack of certain skills in quantity may make it necessary for supervisory personnel to head more than one element where normally a separate grouping would be preferable. This can be true in lower-level technical assignments, where either cost or inability to hire creates a necessity for doubting up of responsibility.

The spectrum of functions that have been assigned to the quality organization is very broad. Some of these functions are universally accepted as a part of the quality role, whereas others are considered by many managements as being outside their conception of the quality charter. The following paragraphs identify the tasks that can be considered as part of the quality charter in the broadest sense. It should not be assumed that every organization must involve itself with each of these activities. The basic premise still holds that the organization should fit the job at hand, and cover only those tasks necessary to produce a quality product. Every production environment has need for different controls, and the quality charter should be structured around those needs, not to a list of possible functions. The general management of the company should be made aware of all of the personnel quality tasks in order to support and, indeed, demand the controls required. Further, the paragraphs below are intended only as a brief outline of the principal elements of the function.

1. Product Design Reviews. Inclusion of quality engineers in the design review process at the earliest possible time is the medium for accomplishing this object. Where formal design reviews do not exist, or where products are manufactured from another company's design, the quality engineers should still begin to critique the design as early as possible. This review should emphasize ease of manufacture and inspection, required process controls, similarity to past products which developed defects, and consideration of tolerancing problems in manufacture and assembly. It is not the responsibility of quality personnel to be the design checking function of the engineering department. Although glaring design deficiencies should not be allowed to develop without comment, the quality critique should be limited to matters that affect the manufacture and quality of the product. The danger in design reviews results from quality engineers frequently wishing to instruct the engineering department on how to design the product in its entirety.

2. Quality Planning. Every quality organization should have a planning function, however small. In very small operations it may be part of the department head's duties, but it must exist for quality to survive.

3. Purchase Order Review. The review by the quality group of all purchase orders for production materials is similar to the requirement for design review. History shows that purchased material is usually subject to more problems and uncompensated cost losses that that produced in-house. A considerable portion of these problems are the result of incomplete communication between the supplier and the company. Inasmuch as the department usually involved in stopping the flow of incoming material is the quality organization, it is imperative that they be represented as the order is placed. A review of purchase orders prior to release tends to minimize rejections by ensuring *(a)* that the proper specifications have been included, *(b)* that the necessary documentation has been requested, *(c)* that any additional inspection requirements are clearly stated, and *(d)* that the supplier selected is a satisfactory source and has been approved by the quality department.

This requirement for review must be organized as a function of volume. The quality group must make certain that the flow of the documentation through the division does not impede the placement of orders. The quality function can be handled by a single individual or a group, depending on the volume to be processed. In large organizations where the purchase order system is computerized, the quality input can be made a part of the system and input fed into the purchase order through a terminal located in the quality area.

4. Supplier Control. A large part of the dollar cost of many manufactured products is spent in the plants of suppliers: in some companies it is actually a majority of the total cost. Many of these companies, however, spend virtually no money in the control of this supplier effort. The role of evaluating and checking the performance of these suppliers falls largely to the quality organization. A separate quality function dedicated to ensuring that the suppliers are attempting to meet all the requirements of the contract can result in significant savings. This is reflected principally in the elimination of defectives found in receiving inspection or even after in the production cycle where delay can be more costly than the actual part. This identifiable quality function is one of the most undervalued, and often unused, tools in the quality system.

5. Stores Inspection and Control. Parts and materials need to be well controlled once they are manufactured or received from suppliers. It is the responsibility of quality to determine that the system devised by the company for this control is being followed and that different materials and parts are not mixed together or issued incorrectly. Depending on company size, this task can either be a separate function or an added responsibility of another segment of quality.

6. Tool and Fixture Inspection. The majority of manufacturing operations employ the use of specially manufactured tools and assembly fixtures. To minimize future rejection of hardware, the quality organization should be required to inspect such tools for adherence to the tool drawings and to inspect the first production lot for adherence to the engineering specifications prior to release of the tools for production.

7. Receiving Inspection. This group is charged with determining that the parts and materials received from suppliers do, in fact, meet the requirements of the purchase order, including the receipt of proper documentation. The tasks vary from simple inspections to highly sophisticated tests using the most modern computerized techniques. The receiving inspection group also develops historical records of supplier performance for use in the placement of future orders. Some companies include purchase order review as part of the receiving inspection function.

8. Product Inspection. Product inspection is the day-to-day chore of sorting the good from the bad. The Inspection force is divided generally into three groups.

(a) ***Fabricated Parts.*** All the piece-part hardware and the processes that produce them are controlled and inspected. This may be accomplished by sampling during a production run by lot inspection prior to moving to the next production station, or at the end of the production of the finished article. Depending on the repeatability of the production equipment and the experience of the work force, this

inspection can be very intense or simply an occasional check on a proven process.

(b) ***Final Assembly.*** The last critical inspection takes place during and after the final completion of the hardware. The degree to which this is emphasized has a relationship to the inspections and tests accomplished prior to this point; where sub-assembly inspections has been minimal, final inspection must be rigorous and all-inclusive. A system built on a heavy inspection and test cycle prior to final assembly may require only a rigorous final test. The variations in philosophy are limitless with respect to the degree of inspection at various stations.

(c) ***Sub-assembly Inspection.*** As individual parts are assembled into larger components or subassemblies, a further check is required to ensure conformance as well as completeness. Frequently, a part of sub-assembly inspection involves test routines where operating components have been installed.

9. Test Control. The role of the quality group with respect to the test function varies widely from industry to industry and from company to company. Each method has its strong adherents and it is sufficient to say that with the right management environment any of them can be successful. Some of the most widely recognized methods for quality monitoring and control are outlined briefly below.

(a) ***Quality Operation of the Test Department.*** In this system the quality division is directly responsible to write test procedures, design the test equipment, and run the actual tests as an independent agency.

(b) ***Direct Control of Test by Monitoring all Phases.*** The quality group is responsible to review and approve test procedures written by others,verify that the test setups are in conformance with the approved procedures, monitor the testing as it is being performed, and certify the test results as being acceptable. Their responsibility involves stopping the testing at any point where the results are not in accordance with procedures or specifications.

(c) **Minimum Role.** The minimum role that quality personnel can perform in the test area is to verify that written procedures exist, that they are being followed, and that a spotcheck of the test results indicates compliance to the requirements.

(d) ***Monitoring of Tests Written and Performed by Other Departments.*** In this system the quality role is limited to observing the tests as performed by a test organization and certifying that the results match the written procedures.

The gamut of quality participation actually involves combinations of systems outlined above. Again, the objective is to be certain that for the product involved sufficient independent quality control is exercised to ensure satisfactory hardware.

10. Final Acceptance. Final acceptance of the product prior to delivery is basic quality task. Organizationally, this can take different forms: a part of a test; the last inspection station; or in the case of large complicated items, a final review of product and paperwork in a separate department.

11. Process Control. The control of the basic processes used in the production of hardware and other products is fundamental to achieving acceptable end result. Heat treatment, chemical processing, batch mixing, surface preparation, and protection are examples of the types of processing that must be rigorously controlled if rejection costs are to be kept within bounds. In the non-hardware industries, such as petroleum, medicines, and foodstuffs, process control is the only real control prior to sampling the final product. The staffing of the process control function is dependent on the number and type of processes involved.

12. Customer Interface. The customer interface that pertains particularly to the quality organization is the one that has to do with those who make acceptance for the customer. The quality department, having the records and history of the product, as well as the customer's specifications, is charged with the task of interfacing with the customer to assure acceptance of the hardware. One of the pitfalls that some companies make for themselves is the mistake of having salespeople attempt to sell the customer the finished product, and then try to explain any questionable items.

13. Laboratory Operations. All quality organizations do not end the services of a full-time laboratory, but most need some laboratory work performed on a routine basis. Chemical and physical analysis of materials, process control checks, requirements for x-ray, and so on, are all laboratory operations essential to good quality control. These services may be obtained in a more cost-effective manner by the use of outside laboratory facilities.

14. Certification of Operators. In the somewhat distant past the journey-man machinist, welder, and so on, was exceedingly well trained, having served a long apprenticeship. Today when many critical production operations are, or can be, in the hands of newly trained semiskilled employees, a minimum level of proficiency must be obtained before new employees are allowed to proceed on their own. The practice of ensuring this skill level by a mandatory training and certification programme is becoming increasingly common among companies anxious to protect their reputation and their profits. After classroom training, on-the-job experience, and testing the employee is "certified" capable of doing the work assigned. Achieving this certification may take only a few hours or several weeks, depending on the assignment.

15. Calibration of Equipment. Calibration of equipment presumes the existence of non-production use standards to which the day-to-day working equipment can be compared and adjusted. These working standards must, in turn, be regularly checked against master standards, usually traceable to the U.S. Bureau of Standards. The services of special laboratories for this service are often employed in preference to developing an in-house capability. The use of these special laboratories is a perfectly satisfactory method of maintaining calibration as long as the system employed is under the control of some element of the quality organization. As mentioned previously, where a quality laboratory exists, calibration, or at last the maintenance of standards is often an element of the laboratory organization. Organising for the collaboration function must encompass all equipmelits used througout the operation-developmental equipmental as well as production. A common mistake is to assume that engineering equipment used for product development does not need the rigorous calibration requirements that production equipment requires.

16. Statistical Analysis and Data Reporting. Adequate record are paramount in any quality system. The "build history" of a products is often required to prove exactly what actions took place during manufacture or processing. Such records are usually the output of the planning operation. Equally important is the gathering and analysis of statistical data relating to the production output from the viewpoint of the quality management. The availability of computer storage and printout has increased enormously the ability of quality personnel to produce data. These data can include every aspect of the quality function. Receiving inspection reports, process and manufacturing trend data, repetitive non-conformances, test yields, and so on, must be produced in a form that when reviewed by other than quality personnel is understandable and complete. Data are useful only when their meaning is clear and leads to some constructive action. It is a common fault of programmers to load data into the system that will never be retrieved for use. Only that information required for regular management use should become a part of the permanent data base.

17. Audits. Audit of the quality function-indeed, of the entire manufacturing process is a historical element of the quality system. The degree of responsibility given to the quality audit function varies with respect to the size of the company, the historical performance of the product in the marketplace, and the desire of the company management to have independent reviews of the performance of the manufacturing operation. Some companies extend the audit function in areas other than those closely related to manufacturing on the premise that such audits identify problems that might otherwise go unnoticed, and can be wasteful of both time and money.

18. Corrective Action. Corrective action is the quality function designed to review discrepancies, determine their cause, and ensure that a solution to the problem is implemented. Corrective action is more than finding a solution corrective action is not complete until the solution has been implemented into the system. The solution may affect various divisions of a company: engineering, manufacturing, quality, purchasing, and so on. Repetition of mistakes represents an unnecessary loss of production dollars that fast, accurate, and complete corrective action can minimize. Organizing for corrective action can be as simple as assigning the responsibility to an area quality supervisor. In the smaller company this supervisor is the one relatively unbiased person who has access to all the information pertaining to the problem.

19. Administration. The administrative element of the quality organization is charged with the responsibility for writing and issuing quality procedures; developing hiring and training plans; preparation and control of the quality budget; and frequently has the added responsibility of some elements identified previously, such as data accumulation and certification or operators. In organisations where such elements represent few actual personnel, the administration department offers the leadership capability that can be used to minimize supervisory overhead. Most often the administrative department manager reports directly to the top quality executive.

20. Advanced Quality Technology. In today's rapidly changing engineering and manufacturing environment it is incumbent on the quality department to keep abreast of these techniques and to determine what new quality methods are required. In recent years many larger organizations have funded separate quality research programmes to advance the state of the art in measurement techniques, process control, computer applications, and defect detection.

21. Facilities Acquisition. The acquisition of the necessary facilities for the quality operation is an increasingly important element of developing quality system. The equipment available has become more diverse and in some cases very sophisticated. Selection of such equipment requires more detailed analysis, both from the standpoint of application as well as cost effectiveness. Where and how this analysis should be performed is not as important as the concept that the quality organization is a part of the approval cycle. In smaller companies the details of selection and ordering are often done by a separate facilities group with the head of quality approving the package and suggesting rivisions. Larger organizations, where considerable quantities of equipment/tools are to be ordered, require a group of quality engineers who review requirements, search for acceptable equipment, evaluate the alternatives for cost-effectiveness, and make the ultimate selection for presentation to the management facility control group.

22. Additional Responsibilitie. Some management have seen fit to strengthen the quality role by assigning tasks not traditionally accepted as a basic quality function, although they do have a bearing on the customer formulation of a total quality system the following elements should be reviewed to make a determination as to the best organizational assignment.

(a) ***Reliability.*** Reliability studies, projections, and analysis have, for the most part, been a traditional element of the engineering department. Recent history indicates that this role, at least in part, is being assigned as a quality function, particularly with respect to reliability assurance, the degree to which the product meets the predicted reliability.

(b) ***Product Liability.*** Although safety and product liability go hand in hand, it is not mandatory that they be assigned to the same personnel. We must remember that we are considering product liability and safety in terms of design, manufacture and use, not in terms of the legal aspects that prevail once a product liability suit is instigated. Safety, for example, might respond to a problem regarding assembly practices with the plant which would have no affect whatever on the ultimate use by the customer. Product

liability, on the other hand, may be concerned with an ultimate fatique failure, one which never could occur during manufacture and test.

(c) *Safety.* Safety, particularly as relating to the design and manufacture of the product, is also being assigned to the quality organization. The independent and impartial assessment tbat can be made by quality is the principal reason for this approach by top management. Safety has become such an important part of the manufacturing scene that an impartial review is mandatory.

(d) ***Field Service Reporting.*** Reporting of field service usage, including warranty claims, is a certain indicator of the reliability and usability of the product. Failure to analyze these reports and compare them to in-house failure rates can lead to ctastrophic warranty and reshipment costs. The quality department is the keeper of the in-house failure history. Some organizations have simplified their handling and correction of field failures by making them a responsibility of the quality organization.

(e) ***Configuration Management.*** In more complex products where changes to the design are to be expected the configuration management system must be accurate and timely to preclude delivery of incorrect material and to ensure updating of hardware with a minimum cost impact. Before the general use of computers to maintain and update configuration data, it was usually the responsibility of the quality department to manage configuration control by means of a manual system.

Types of Organization

We have defined the basic quality task, discussed some organizational concepts with regard to quality, and outlined the functions that must be considered when developing a quality system. The form of the organization can now be considered. It must be emphasized that all the elements previously identified are not a requirement for every organization. Only the larger and more diversified company would need them all. In developing the organization all functions must be considered, however, and a conscious decision made with respect to each one. To overlook or disregard an obvious need can only lead to catastrophy. There are certain fundamental organizational patterns that should be considered when putting the quality group together.

Staff Versus Line Function

An important philosophical concept concerning organizing quality group is the determination of its role as either an operating department in the line organization or as a quality assurance group operating in a staff position reporting to the chief operating executive. A staff group has the ability to move freely outside the normal operating environment, monitoring the results of the system and reporting its findings to management. In such a setting the inspection work is usually performed by personnel reporting to an inspection chief. Other functions relating to the quality system may be assigned to departments within the manufacturing or engineering organizations. A major disadvantage of this type of staff assignment is that the group is often not empowered to do other than report the situation.

The group must achieve corrective action by discussion and persuasion, with the chief operating executive as the final arbiter. In the absence of any operational authority there arises a normal reluctance to force many problems to their ultimate solution, the result being that proper corrective action is never pushed to a conclusion. There is the tendency to become more interested in finding fault that in eliminating troublesome company problems. This attitude can develop when the quality assurance group is made to feel like "outsiders" and not part of the team. There are, of course, companies that empower the quality staff to enforce corrective action by literally stopping the work effort if necessary.

When the quality function is established as a part of the operational line organization the quality department manager should report to the same management level as those in charge of manufacturing, engineering, and material. As an operating executive the quality manager has the responsibility not only to assure that acceptable hardware is delivered to the customer but also to minimize operational costs through rapid and responsive creative action and preventive quality control. The form of the organization may vary, but the focus should be on implementing the controls necessary to carry out the established quality role.

The problem of the smaller company is to achieve the proper result with resources that are limited by comparison to larger organizations. Personnel must be selected who are capable of doing more than one function. Specialists are a luxury that can seldom be justified. Once the quality charter has been identified and agreement reached relative to the scope of activities to be pursued, the work must be organized in as simple a manner as possible. Smaller companies tend to adopt the horizontal from of organization, with all the principal supervisors reporting directly to the department head. This simplifies communication and allows for rapid top level decision making. As a case in point, consider a shop whose output is relatively straightforward sheet metal and machine shop detail parts. The quality task has been described as:

1. Inspection, including raw materials
2. Collection of data regarding shop defects and losses.
3. Process control of certain chemical operations, such cleaning, painting, and chemical finishing
4. Monitoring customer complaints.

A more effective alignment would be to have a strong supervisor over all of the inspection effort, with all the other functions continuing to report to the quality manager. Such an arrangement would still give the manager Instant access to problem areas from both plant and customer, and at the same time minimize the number of upper-level supervisors required. As the organization increases in both size and complexity of function, the need develops to reduce the span of control of the upper-level supervision. The organization tends to change from a horizontal orientation to a more vertical alignment. This allows the department manager to devote time to those matters which he or she considered important to the well-being of the department and the company. It presumes more highly qualified leaders reporting directly to the manager: supervisors who are expert in their particular discipline and capable of making decisions regarding their part of the operation. No set rules govern the choice of organization but in a quality group it is particularly important that sufficient leadership be available to respond quickly to problems that affect the production process. There is an everpresent danger in very extended horizontal arrangement that problems may get set aside because of the press of other business demanding the attention of the top decision maker. As has been stated previously, the best organization is one that gets the job done effectively at minimum cost, recognizing that cost sometimes gives way to certain preferences in organizational concepts. What cannot be allowed to suffer is effectiveness. The large organization has the need for specialists in many of the quality disciplines. The generalist who has broad knowledge and responsibility appears higher and higher in the organization and his or her skills are managerial as contrasted to technical.

In a every large corporation that is involved with the majority of the functions outlined. as the quality task, the organizational possibilities are endless. Certain reallife situations tend to establish patterns; for example, grouping of similar activities, such as receiving inspection, source inspection, and control of stores. These are not only related but are often physically located in proximity to one another. The ability to share equipment and space may also dictate an organizational alignment. If the quality laboratories and receiving inspection are close together, a sharing of equipment offer substantial savings. Some companies require that very expensive equipment be shared between divisions, such as quality and engineering. These considerations should be uppermost in the mind of the quality executive when planning an organization. The second plan reduces the number of people reporting to the quality executive from eight to five; 'it raises the quality audit to a more important level, reporting to the director; all the projects are consolidated under one project manager; and the inspection and test group now has responsibility for all inspection, including source and receiving. The large comapany with more personnel available has a better opportunity to match skills with job requirements and to organize around the elements of the job, whereas the smaller company may have to organize more around the available talent.

Multi-divisional or International Corporations

Many multidivisional or internationally oriented corporations have a headquarters staff group for quality. A vice-president or director of quality reporting to the chief operating executive is responsible for corporate wide activities in the quality field. These responsibilities generally include:

1. Development of general policies, objectives, and standards
2. Preparation of basic training criteria
3. Consulting and audit service to the divisions
4. Preparation of reports to top management
5. Review of capital equipment requirements
6. Representing the corporation in interchanges with government and industry groups

It must be noted that the responsibility of such a quality executive is frequently not supported by the authority necessary to achieve the objective. Different product mixes, the degree of autonomy of the individual division managers, and even cultural differences in the case of multinational corporations mitigate against much real achievement by a headquarter's staff unless the chief executive is constantly and pointedly supportive. Even with such support the quality headquarter's staff personnel must be persuasive and tactful if they are to obtain the necessary cooperation from the divisions.

Final Organization

There is no "best" way to organize the quality function. The definition of the quality role identified the scope of the job and the elements needed to satisfy that role. The organizational framework to support that role must be tailored for every company, keeping in mind the various influences that have been described. It is particularly important that the organization be oriented toward those elements that have the greatest impact on the ultimate worthiness of the product and the cost to produce it. Several alternative organizations have been suggested, but they should not constitute a boundary, only a basis for further development.

Quality Planning

Quality planning can be defined as the sum of those actions taken in preparation for the accomplishment of the assigned quality task. In the early stages of the development of inspection systems it was usually limited to planning where inspection points were to be identified within the production cycle. Planning now involves a myriad of tasks, depending on the size and complexity of the production operation. The development of the organizational structure determines to a considerable degree how much planning is required and who must do it. Wherever there is a requirement a quality task there must be a plan to accomplish it. Someone in the quality department must develop and identify the steps and actions to be taken. The scope of the quality planning effort is therefore similar to the basic role identified in the quality charter. The number and type of plans required become a function of the complexity of the work effort and the experience of the work force. The requirement for detailed planning usually increases in proportion to complexity of product or system, lack of experience in the work force, and the amount of customer regulation imposed. Conversely, "plans can simplified when the products or system are less complex" where the personnel are highly qualified and the amount of customer regulations are minimal. In the real world, where these factors may vary from department to department, it is necessary to be certain that the plan prepared recognizes the conditions that exist.

Administrative Planning

Administrative planning begins with the preparation of the overall quality programme plan for the company. It is a reflection of the basic quality charter agreed to between chief operating executive and the quality manager. In many cases it is one and the same. Other administrative plans are:

(1) **Policy and Procedures Manual.** A quality policy and procedures manual is the resources document for all additional planning, as it contains the guidelines for the entire quality activity. The procedures themselves are often the actual step-by-step plan of operation for certain tasks, particularly ones that are repetitious and unlikely to change suddenly. The manual is the framework on which the rest of the quality plans can be overlaid.

(2) **Special Program Plans.** The customer/company programme leadership may require that special quality plans be developed. Such plans usually describe special paperwork and reporting systems, but they may also dictate the manner in which certain inspections or tests are to be accomplished. These controls may be more stringent than normal or they may call for a relaxation of some existing controls. Such plans are usually developed by the quality personnel assigned to the programme. They must be carefully controlled in order that the personnel working on the shop floor will not be confused by the exceptions to the normal procedures.

(3) **Personnel Planning.** Every organization must have well-identified requirements for the number and type of personnel required for the year ahead, with acquisition requirements by the month. The employment department must be given adequate time to hire the proper personnel. When ample numbers of qualified people are not available in the area, a training plan and schedule will also be required. Even in the smaller company where personnel acquisition is handled personally by the quality manager, a plan must be made to indicate when additional personnel are needed.

(4) **Planning for Audits.** The audit group, regardless of size, must develop audit plans and schedules in order to have a

consistency of approach and reporting within the company. Audit plans must be sufficiently detailed and clear that changes in the audit personnel will not affect the efficiency of the audit programme.

(5) **Equipment Acquisition.** Equipment acquisition is similar to personnel acquisition in that it requires a plan that indicates month by month the new equipment required, the justification for its use, estimated lead time, and cost. Irrespective of the approval cycle for such equipment, the quality department is responsible for planning to meet its needs and for justifying the expenditure of the capital dollars.

(6) **Other Administrative Plans.** Depending on the size of the organization and the charter given the quality department, many other plans of an administrative nature may be required, such as:

(a) Long-range forecasts of personnel, equipment, and space

(b) Accumulation of cost data by work center/department

(c) Plan for the accumulation, storage, and retrieval of non-conformance and yield data

Product-oriented Planning

All of processing or manufacturing work effort is controlled by some type of written plan or instruction. Such plans may be written by a singular group within the manufacturing organization, or they may be distributed to a number of different elements, such as tool engineering, manufacturing engineering, manufacturing test, or in the case of test design and planning, may come from the engineering organization. In every case the quality group must be a part of the team developing the plans to ensure that the product will meet the requirements of the contract. Insertion of specific inspection points in the processing and test cycle must be a part of every manufacturing plan.

In addition to those plans generated for use by production personnel the quality department develops other plans relating to the product:

1. **Supplier Plans.** An overall methodology for the approval and control of suppliers to the company is usually contained in the quality procedures manual. In addition, specific instructions/inspections are frequently required. These should be transmitted to the supplier as a part of the purchase order.

2. **Laboratory and Calibration.** The amount of laboratory testing and the general rules for the maintenance of standards and calibration of equipment are usually contained in the quality procedures manual. Individual calibration and laboratory testing procedures must be separately planned and maintained in a current file in the work area. In an organization with much diverse equipment, this can be a very heavy planning load. although some calibrations can be done by the use of the equipment manufacturers' manuals, the planners must be certain they meet the requirements of in-plant usage.

3. **Receiving Inspection.** The quality department must develop the inspection/test plans for the multitude of parts and equipment that are received by the company from outside sources. These plans must recognize what has taken place at the plant of the supplier and what subsequent inspections will be dope during the in-house processing cycle.

4. **Process Control.** Plans for the control of special processes used during the production process are an extremely important part of the quality control operation. Heat treatment, metal finishing, batch control, and chemical formulation are examples of processes that must have well-written for each step of the process and an indication of what physical action the quality group must take to unsure a successful result.

5. **Planning for Inspection.** The actual inspection of parts, components, and assemblies is the original and traditional function of a quality organization. The plans associated with this effort range form the very simple (such as a dimensional checkoff card) to an extensive step-by-step document outlining in detain the plan for acceptance of the product. There is no substitute for the planning required to assure a satisfactory product. As in all aspects of quality control, it is possible to over-emphasize the planning of inspection points and produce more paper than product. The mark of the proficient quality planner is to cover every important element without inserting unnecessary checkpoints that are unproductive in terms product use.

6. **Planning for Test.** Testing of many products has become the major element in the proof of acceptability and usability. Testing covers an extreme breadth of activity, from simple tension tests of material samples to hours-long runs of equipment undergoing changing environmental conditions. Organizationally, the quality group may not be the leaders in the formulation of test plans and the development of test equipment. The quality organization in all cases must have competent personnel reviewing and approving both plans and equipment, In some cases the level of testing required at receiving inspection may be so sophisticated that a special quality engineering group may be required to write the test plans, set up the equipment, and monitor, if not run, the tests.

Organization of the Planning Function

The manner in which planning for the quality operation is organized is similar to that of the overall quality organization in that it depends on the scope and size of the assigned quality task. The most effective planning operation is one that gives the quality department all the necessary tools (*i.e.*, direction, documentation, and equipment) at a reasonable administrative cost. In some small companies the planning can be accomplished by consultation between the inspectors and the supervisors, with the ultimate plans being produced on simple inspection forms.

Central Versus Decentralized Planning

Centralized planning implies that all planning is performed by one group. Such an approach is not practical because of differences in both discipline and physical location. It is, however, possible to group large segments of the various planning operations into one or two central operations, usually with substantial savings in efficiency and cost. For example, all inspection and test type planning could be located in one area adjacent to the corresponding manufacturing planning organization. This could include piece-parts inspection, process control, subassembly and assembly inspection, and all associated test operations.

In addition to probable cost savings in the number of personnel required, such a central planning group would ensure uniformity of inspection between different products and programmes. The preparation of receiving inspection plans could also be a function of such a group. Similarly, all administration planning could be grouped together, either as a part of the quality engineering function, or as the responsibility of a responsibility of a quality administrator reporting directly to the department head. As the responsibilities and size of the quality function increase, it is doubly important that the control of the business aspects of the department be grouped together and monitored closely.

Some quality planning, such as laboratory and calibration work, are most effectively handled in the functional areas involved, where the personnel are particularly those with several large, important, and non-similar programmes, prefer to decentralize a large part of the inspection, test, and administrative planning and have it done within the confines of the quality programme staff. The peculiar requirements of each programme may differ to such a degree that special instructions are required.

Programme funding restrictions usually prohibit the use of specialists in every discipline, so the programme planner has to be more versatile and qualified to plan a variety of inspection requirements. Certainly this approach is proper for cases where the requirements differed extensively from the rest of the plant operation, but the quality department head must be ever watchful to be certain that the need for decentralization is real. The tendency for overall programme management to want everything under its control does not necessarily lead to the most efficient quality effort.

Skill Requirements for Planners

All skilled quality personnel do not make good planners, even through their technical capability may be very high. It requires a special talent and disposition to do a good planning job, day after day. Some employees are temperamental unsuited or the task because of its confining nature, and planners must be selected by temperament as well as technical ability. A checklist of planner prerequisites would include:

1. An understanding of the technical process
2. The ability to recognize what elements are truly important
3. The ability to use simple language and terminology in order to help the inspector to understand the requirements
4. The ability to foresee "what if" situations in order to have a recovery plan available
5. An understanding of the inter-relationships that exist on the production line so as not to create unnecessary delays
6. A personality that can accept and work under the pressure of constant changes in plans and requirements.

Organization and planning are the keys to success in quality control. They both begin with the establishment of the quality role by management. The development of the organization to fit the task also establishes the basic parameters of the planning required. Organizational development or improvement should not be used as an excuse for growth. Organization implies an orderly approach to a defined goal, which is achieved by the use of intelligent planning.

Quality Control. Quality control is concerned with observing a process, identifying the variable characteristics of its content, and then tracking these variables through scientifically devised statistical methods. The measurement of the variables while they are being accomplished, permits holding the process its specified performance limits. This prevents defects from occurring or at least finds them at the earliest possible moment.

Quality Management. Quality management treats the company as a process and the various management systems within that process as the variables that require measurement and control. However, each of these variables is devised and conducted by a group of individuals, whereas in quality control the variables are accomplished by a chemical or physical process. That is why quality management requires an understanding of the way the whole company operates. It also requires a comprehension of the company goals, which are not spelled out and a process plan or blueprint; a familiarity with other functional management systems, such as marketing, engineering, finance, and purchasing; and a willingness to spend time helping other function measure and control their own operating characteristics.

Quality control is thing and process oriented; quality management is people and system oriented. The purpose of quality management is to make the company run more smoothly and more profitably by preventing problems. It also serves as the key element in solving those difficulties that do escape the prevention system. In many ways quality management serves as a catalyst-bringing together activities with a common purpose and different methods. Quality management must report organizationally in such a way that it is free of control by those whom it is measuring and assisting.

Quality Engineering. Quality engineering is major element contained within the quality management function. It is responsible for activities within other departments and particularly engineering assists the appraisal function in establishing acceptance methods and procedures, conducts failure analysis, and reports results and needs for corrective action.

Purchasing. Quality engineering assists purchasing in vendor selection. Prepares the buyer rating results, and trains supplier personnel in quality concepts and techniques. It determines the need for sources control or inspection and sets up the appraisal plan for products or services in conjunction with purchasing.

Engineering. A major role of quality engineering is to help arrange design reviews, products qualification, life testing, and other objective performance measurements oriented to preventior. It provides engineering with data concerning manufacturing and customer experience with products.

Marketing and Sale. Marketing depends on quality engineering to provide product performance data to assist in the selling of the product, conduct quality seminars for the customer, and handle consumer affairs activities. Quality engineers share results with marketing concerning specific causes of complaints and ways or preventing them. They also experience data to assist in developing new specification.

Comptroller. Quality engineering assist the comptroller in identifying the characteristics of the cost of quality within both product and service areas. Another responsibility would be to devise quality control programmes to evaluate clerical accuracy.

Manufacturing. In the manufacturing area, quality engineering determines appraisal activities for each product and process, assists in selecting test equipment and devising sample techniques, and conducts quality orientation or manufacturing personnel.

Administration. Quality engineering arrange new employees orientation programmes in cooperation with personnel and conducts company-wide quality awareness activities.

Top Management. Top management is furnished quality status information showing areas where problems are occurring and listing specific causes, responsibilities, and actions under way. Quality engineering also provides continuing status chart visible in work areas (both white and blue collar) and gives smaller, desk-size copies to key management.

Quality Department Activities

Appraisal Analysis. The inspection a test functions-ranging from suppliers' plants, through receiving, in-process, assembly clerical, engineering, field, and wherever applicable for the company should be designed specifically by quality engineering. No appraisal activities should conducted by chance; all must be part of the overall concept of treating the company as one large process that continually needs to be measured.

Appraisal. All appraisal function having to do with the acceptances of the company's products or services must be accomplished by the quality department. In turn, quality engineering assume responsibility for training and leadership of the personnel involved. The data generated by appraisal are the quality department's most significant product.

Failure Analysis. This is one of the most important jobs in the quality engineering task list. Analysis must be conducted primarily to determine the integrity of the overall quality management system, as well as getting the specific problem surfaced and resolved.

Consumer Affairs. Customer with complaints need someone to talk with who one their side. This function must be carefully oriented to think in customer's terms. All complaints must be handled within two working days and departments that caused the problems must take corrective action immediately.

Product Quality. The handling of product safety problems must be assigned to special teams consisting of quality engineers, lawyers, and appropriate specialists. Quality must chair this team.

Quality Education. Administering the professional and other employee training necessary to maintain the competence of the quality function itself and the awareness's of other departments is a key function. Actual training will be accomplished by quality management's functional personnel, but quality education must provide the spark and coordination.

Environmental Quality. This function is the liaison between the regulatory agencies and the company to make certain that all regulations are known and met. It must conduct continual self-audit within the company manage, the environmental quality functions policies.

Strategy of Quality Management. Installing a quality management system in a company is a never-ending, long-range effort. There are six phased of evolution. They are listed in sequence, yet all of them occur in parallel since a company is a growing entity with new members coming and old member leaving on a regular basis.

Comprehension. There must be a solid understanding of what quality is all about, how the company feels about it, and a recognition that the goal is to do things right the first time. In the case of management this is the stage when it decides there has to be a better way reaching its goals than continuing with the waste that faces it.

Correction. When people contribute ideas and participate, management must be ready to do something. Most of the problems that occur in a company can be corrected only by management. When employees see that management is really taking action, thy will believe that management is serious about the whole business of defect prevention. Corrective action should be organized through natural interfaces and a methodical listing or problems taken to the proper activities for correction. Follow-through should be in a disciplined manner. Employees who list term must be notified immediately that their input has been received and be told of the disposition of the items.

Commitment. Everyone must in some way signify that they understand the quality concepts, agree with the goals, and will do their best participate. The method of accomplishing this depends on the personality of the individual company. Some companies from a "quality club," some just request show of hands, some sign pledges, some take group photos. No one way is best. However the strategist should recognize that the step cannot be ignored. If the commitment is not registered as a conscious act, it will not be remembered.

Communication. Quality awareness activities expose the desire on the part of employees (of all levels) to have their problems heard. It is best to reach out early and ask to hear the problemmes rather than wait to be approached. Error-cause identification programs, group meetings, and discussions are very helpful and practical, particularly when set up on continual basis. Professionally designed and marketed programmes such as Buck-A-Day provide employees with an interesting programme that will improve moral and communications.

Competence. Committed people who understand what has to be done will want to put their own houses in order. This is where the functional department can begin its won internal quality control programmes with the assistance of the quality management function. Also, it is very important that quality function assurance that all its activities are accomplished with the maximum effectiveness. There is a significant responsibility and burden in leading quality improvement programme you must always work harder than anyone else in getting things right the first time. Zero effects has to be the performance standard of the quality department at all times.

Continuance. As noted, the phases must be conducted on a continuing basis. However, this will not happen unless they are scheduled exactly and someone is responsible for continuing and conducting them. Planned acts range from a visit to a new executive in the manner of "welcome wagon," to the orientation of new employees as they join the company, and to the recommitment of the entire population to quality improvement on an annual basis.

Policies. A company management must state clearly its method of operating if it wants its employees to understand and implement it. The six C's apply to running a company, as well as to installing a defect prevention quality programme. Managers of all functions and professions traditionally blame their senior management for not supporting them or for not providing the proper leadership. In reality, individual managers must make certain that the polices necessary to their functions exist and that everyone understands them.

In quality management there are three key policies that have to exist to smooth the way for installing the company-wide programme.

1. The company management must state its standards concerning the subject of quality. The policy should be couched in words typically used within the company, but the policy should state these things.

   It is intent of the X Company and its management that all products and service supplied by this company will conform exactly to the specifications and advertisement our customers have used to purchase from us. The quality department is responsible for assuring that all products or services received by the company met this requirement and for reporting any difference immediately so that corrective action can take place.

   Quality means conformance to the requirements. Our standards is zero defects, which means "do it right the first time." Our performance measurement is the cost of quality, which is the expense of doing things wrong. The comptroller reports the cost of quality.

   Each department will conduct its own internal, continual quality improvement programme (with support from the quality department) to guarantee is ability to meet these standards, and each employee is expected to do everything he or she can to help all of us accomplish this necessary goal. Communication programmes will be conducted continually to assure that each of us can hear the other on this subject.

2. The management must cleariy state the organizational responsibility and reporting relationship of the quality department. The department itself must issue an operating policy concerning all the activities that take place within it.

   The company quality department must always be organizationally independent of those operations it is charged with measuring. For that reason the quality director will report to the chief executive officer. The quality department will assist other departments in division and conducting the appropriate internal quality control programmes, and will conduct company-wide quality awareness functions. In addition, the department will perform all appraisal activities, report the results, and conduct corrective action systems. Quality engineering, consumer affairs, environmental quality, product safety, reliability, and other appropriate functions shall be included in the department's responsibility.

3. The management policy must stake what it means by requiring other departments to.

   Conduct appropriate internal quality control programmes in their operation. This means spelling put of how those departments can identify the necessary actions to develop comprehension (rewriting the quality logic so that it fits the terms of their professions); Commitment (deciding to do some reviews and inspection inside); Competence (conducting internal audits with the support of quality engineering); Communication (conducting quality awareness and error-cause removal or make certain activities); Correction (setting up an action team); and Continuance (having their own quality improvement team to review status continually). The astute quality department will supply guideline to other functionswhich they will be delighted to receive-concerning some actions to be taken and methods of measuring non-hardware activities. All of these policies, and the procedures necessary to implement them, should be included in the company quality manual. Quality management and the defect prevention system it creates must be treated as a living system requiring continual nourishment and attention the quality department does not need to be large in terms of numbers of people or budget.

Dimensions of Quality

We have beliefs about quality as about other things. Some of these beliefs are hidden. Some are complementary. Some are true and we act in accordance with them. Some are not true and we act in accordance with them as well.

The fact that quality has at least two independent dimensions was made very clear to me about eight years ago. Figure illustrates the two dimensions of quality. In one direction is the conformance of the product to the requirements. It focuses on a uniform, consistent product meeting specifications. It is concerned about doing things right the first time. The place where the quality of conformance becomes an issue is typically in the factory. The second dimension of quality occurs in the marketplace. In this dimension the issue is the perceived grade of the product. It is concerned with the competitive position of the product relative to other products that are being sold. It is concerned with doing the right things.

Some beliefs about quality have been identified, studied, and in some cases quantified. Three beliefs about quality are the following:

1. The quality of conformance decreases the cost.
2. Most errors occur because the criteria for self control are not met.
3. Perceived quality increases the selling price.

Belief 1: The Quality of Conformance Decreases the Cost

The first dimension of quality is the quality of conformance. Improving the quality generally reduces the cost. Products that do not have to be reworked or scrapped can be made more efficiently. The American Society for Quality Control has standardized the quality cost structure. The categories are listed here:

1. **Prevention.** The cost associated with personnel engaged in designing, implementing, and maintaining the quality system. Maintaining the quality system includes auditing the system.
2. **Appraisal.** The costs associated with the measuring, evaluating, or auditing of products, components, and

purchased materials to assure conformance with quality standards and performance requirements.

3. **External Failures.** The costs which are generated because of defective products being shipped to customers.

4. **Internal Failures.** The costs associated with defective products, components, and materials that fail to meet quality requirements and result in manufacturing losses.

The committee recommends that systems be esta~lished to record costs according to the following detailed categories:

Prevention

1. Quality planning and process control planning:

   (a) Quality planning—quality control engine-ering type work

   (b) Process quality control—that portion of compensation and costs associated with implementing the quality plans and procedures

2. Design and development of quality measurement and control equipment

3. Quality planning by functions other than quality control

4. Quality training

5. Other prevention expense

Appraisal

1. Receiving or incoming test and inspection

2. Laboratory acceptance testing

3. Inspection and test

4. Inspection and test material

5. Quality audits

7. Checking labour
8. Setup for inspection and test
8. Outside endorsements or approvals
9. Field testing
10. Internal testing and release
11. Maintenance and calibration of test and inspection equipment
12. Review of test and inspection data
13. Evaluation of field stock and spare parts

Internal Failures

1. Scrap
2. Rework and repair
3. Troubleshooting
4. Scrap and rework-fault of vendor
5. Reinspect, retest
6. Downgrading
7. Material review activity

External Failures

1. Complaints
2. Product of customer service
3. Returned material processing
4. Engineering error
5. Factory or installation error
6. Returned material repair
7. Warranty replacement

Studies Relating Failure Costs and Profits

Although quality-related cost is a good tool for thinking about the distribution of quality-related cost, there may be better indicators that correlate better profit..A study, by Francis X. Brown and Roger W. Kane at Westinghouse, indicates that failure costs may be better correlated with profit than other measures. This study, which was based on 64 business units, showed that every dollar decrease in failure costs, profits increased an average of $5.45. One possible explanation for this multiplier effect is that many of the costs of quality failures are not easily identified as failure costs, but that they affect profit anyway. Failure that cause shortages at subsequent operations increase production downtime. Some rework is absorbed in productivity and reported as labour variance. Chronic rework or excessive shrinkage may necessitate scheduling of overtime or purchase of additional production facilities.

A completed product that fails in final test may result in increased work-in-process inventory and reduced billings for the month. Product failures in the field can, at least in the long run, contribute to reduced market share or poor price realization. They may also contribute to past-due or uncollectible receivables. The second dimension of quality is the grade of quality. Products may conform to the specifications, but there are differences in specifications. For example, there is a perceived difference in quality between a Chevrolet and a Cadillac although each may conform to its respective specifications.

The higher selling price for a perceived higher quality can be summarized in a statement by Stanley Marcus, past chairman of Nieman-Marcus: "As long as oranges are two different sized, people will pay more for the largest and juiciest." This can be verified by taking a five-minute survey of food prices in your local grocery store. Compare the prices of the generic foods with those of the brand name products. This has also been researched and documented on a scientific basis. One of the first studies to try to identify and analyze the factors that impact profit was the Profit Impact of Marketing Strategies (PIMS) research. The PIMS team studied the effect of hundreds of variables with long-term financial performance. The analysis gave strong support to the proposition that market share is a major influence on profitability. It also identified other factors that had significant impact. One was perceived product quality. The score for the perceived product quality was appraised in the following terms: What was the percentage of sales of products or services from each business in each year that were superior to those of the competitor? What was the percentage of equivalent products? Inferior products? These factors included various quality and service delivery traits.

The best of all possible worlds is to have both hight market share and superior quality. Businesses in this category averaged 28.3% return on investment. Even with a weak market position, however, superior quality producers earned 17.4%. There have been other studies conducted since the initial PIMS research that are wholly consistent with the analyses of the PIMS team. In Search of Excellence, for example, researched 75 of the most financially successful companies. Of these 75, 5 were in the resource-extraction business. For those companies, efficiency may be an apropriate first principle.

❐

15

Marketing Aspects of T.Q. Services

Educational institutions have an obligation to make learners aware of the variety of learning methods available to them. They need to give learners opportunities to sample learning in a variety of different styles. Institutions need to understand that many learners also like to switch and mix-'n'-match styles and must try to be sufficiently flexible to provide choice in learning. Miller, Dower, and Inniss make the same point in Improving Quality in Further Education. Their argument, which applies to any other type of institution, is that the FE college should ensure that learners experience a range of teaching and learning styles so that their chance of success is maximised.

Much work has still to be done on how to use TQM principles in the classroom. Some of the elements might involve the following pattern. A start could be made with the learners and their teachers establishing their 'mission', which could take the form of 'All Shall Succeed'. From this, negotiation might take place about how the two parties will seek to achieve the mission—the styles of learning and teaching and the resources they require. Individual learners may negotiate their own action plans to give them motivation and direction. The process of negotiation may require the establishment of a quality steering committee or forum to provide feedback and to give the learners an opportunity to manage their own learning. Parents or employers might will be represented on it. Detailed monitoring through progress charting will need to be undertaken by both teachers and students to ensure that all are on track. This is important to ensure that timely and appropriate corrective action can be applied if there is a danger of failure.

The establishing of a strong feedback loop is an important element of any quality assurance process. Evaluation should be a continuous process and not just left until the end of the programme of study. The results of evaluation processes should be discussed with the students, perhaps by means of completing a record of achievement. The very act of being involved in evaluation will assist in building up the students' analytical skills. It is important that the institution uses the results of the formal monitoring to establish the validity of its programmes. It must be prepared to take the necessary corrective action if the customers' experiences do not meet their expectations. None of this is easy as teachers who have pioneered such processes know. It can be an emotional experience and one that can take unexpected turns. What it does is to provide students with motivation and the practical experience of the use of TQM tools which are transferable to other situations.

Barriers to be Overcome when Introducing TQM

TQM is hard work. It takes time to develop a quality culture. By themselves hard work and time are two of the most formidable blocking mechanisms to quality improvement. TQM needs a champion in the face of the myriad of new challenges and changes facing education. Quality improvement is a fragile process. All major changes are, cultures are essentially conservative and homeostasis is the norm. Most staff are most comfortable with what they know and understand. However, to stand still while competitors are improving is a recipe for failure.

If TQM is to work it must have the long-term devotion of the senior staff of the institution. They must back it and drive it. Senior management may themselves be the problem. They may want the results which TQM can bring, but be unwilling to give it their wholehearted support. Many quality initiatives falter because senior managers quickly return to traditional ways of managing. Fear by senior managers of adopting new methods and approaches is a major barrier. This is potentially the most serious of blockages. If senior management do not give TQM their backing there is little that anyone else in the organization can do. The sheer volume of external pressures also stands in the way of many organizations attempting TQM. Although quality programmes are introduced with considerable publicity, too often they can be overtaken and submerged by other initiatives. There is a need to ensure that despite other pressures quality always has an important place on the agenda. This is where strategic planning plays such an important role.If TQM is firmly a part of the strategic role of the institution, and if there are good monitoring mechanisms in place, then there is a good chance that quality will keep a high profile. This makes it harder to ignore, and increases the chances of its being taken seriously.

The strategic plan can help staff understand the institution's mission. It helps to bridge gaps in communication. There is a need for staff to know where their institution is going and how it will be different in the future. Senior management must trust their staff sufficiently to share their vision for the institution's future. Visions are often not shared because of a fear of a loss of status and disempowerment by managers. When coupled with a fear of delegation by managers this can make quality development nearly impossible.

A potential problem area in many institutions is the role played in it by middle management. They have a pivotal role because they both maintain the day-to-day operation of the institution and act as one of its most important communications channels. They can often block changes if they have a mind to or they can act as the leaders of teams spearheading the impetus for quality improvement. Middle managers may not define their role as one of innovation unless senior managements communicate to them their vision of a new future. Senior managers must be consistent in their behaviour when advocating and communicating the message of quality improvement. They cannot say on thing and do another and then expect to engender enthusiasm among their staff or loyalty and commitment in their middle managers. They have to persuade others that new working methods will pay dividends.

Quality has a variety of contradictory meanings. As Naomi Pfeffer and Anna Coote have observed in their discussion of quality in the welfare services 'Quality' is a slippery concept'. It implies different things to different people. Everyone is in favour of providing quality education. The arguments start because there is a lack of agreement as to what it means. It is, therefore, necessary to have a clear understanding of the various meanings of quality otherwise there is a danger that it becomes a mere catchphrase, a word with high moral tone but little practical value. understanding of the diverse meanings of quality is a necessary starting point for our discussion of TQM.

A possible reason for the enigmatic nature of quality is that it is a dynamic idea.The emotional and moral force which quality possesses makes it a difficult idea to tie down. There is the danger that much of its vitality can be lost if it is subjected to too much academic analysis. Westley and Mintzberg make the point that this happens to many important concepts which are freely used in practical settings. A strange process seems to occur as concepts such as culture and charisma move from practice to academic research. Loosely used in practice, these concepts, as they enter academia become subjected to a concerted effort to force them to lie down and behave to render them properly scientific.

Some of the confusion over the meaning of quality arises because it can be used both as an absolute and a relative concept. Quality in everyday conversation is mainly used as an absolute. People use it to describe expensive restaurants and luxury cars. As an absolute, quality is similar in nature to goodness, beauty, and truth; an ideal with which there can be no compromise. In the absolute definition this which exhibit quality are of the highest possible standard which cannot be surpassed. Quality products are things of perfection made with no expense spared. They are valuable and convey prestige to their owners. 'Quality cars', for example, are hand-built and expensive and have interiors of walnut and leather. Rarity and expense are two the features of quality in this definition. Quality in this sense is used to convey status and positional advantage, and the ownership of things of 'quality' sets their owners apart from those who cannot afford them. It is synonymous with 'high quality or top quality'. To use the words of Pfeffer and Coote again, 'Most of us admire it, many of us want it, few of us can have it'. Used in the educational context this concept of quality is essentially elitist. By definition only a few institutions are able to offer such a 'high quality' educational experience to their learners. Most learners cannot afford it, and most institutions cannot aspire to provide it.The absolute notions of 'high quality' have little to do with TQM.

Quality can also be employed as a relative concept. This is the sense in which it is used in TQM. The relative definition views quality not as an attribute of a product or service, but as something which is ascribed to it. Quality can be judged to exist when a good or service meets the specification that has been laid down for it. Quality is not the end in itself, but a means by which the end product is judged to be up to standard. Quality products or services, in this relative or ascribed definition need not be expensive and exclusive. They may be beautiful, but not necessarily so. They donot have to be special. They can be ordinary, commonplace, and familiar. Overhead projectors, ballpoint pens, and the school catering service may all exhibit quality if they meet simple but crucially important standards. They must do what they claim to do, and do what their customers expect of them.

The relative definition of quality has two aspects to it. The first is measuring up to specification. The second is meeting customer requirements. The first usagemeasuring up-is often summed up as 'fitness for purpose or use'. This is sometimes called the producer definition of quality. Quality for the producer is achieved by its products or services meeting a pre-defined specification in a consistent fashion. Quality is demonstrated by a producer having a system, known as a quality assurance system, which enables the consistent production of the good or service to a particular standard or specification. A product exhibits quality so long as it consistently meets its maker's claims for it.

Organizations who follow the TQM path regard quality as being defined by their customers. The reason for this is simple.

Customers are the final arbitrators of quality and without them the institution does not exist. The TQM institution has to use all means at its disposal to explore its customers' requirements. Total quality means knowing them in ways and depths never fully explored before and using this knowledge to translate needs into innovative new products and business approaches'. Quality can be defined as that which best satisfies and exceeds customers needs' and wants. This is sometimes called 'quality in perception'. Quality can be said to lie in the eyes of the beholder. This is a very important and powerful definition, and one that any institution ignores at its peril.

Tom Peters, discussing the pivotal role of the consumer in quality in *Thriving On Chaos*, argues that the perceived quality of a business's product or service is the most important single factor affecting its performance. Peters argues that quality as defined by the customer is more important than price in determining the demand for a majority of good and services.His unequivocal findings are that customers will always pay more for the best quality regardless of the type of product. He has also found that employees become energized when they have the opportunity to provide a quality service or produce a quality product.

Quality Control, Quality Assurance, and Total Quality

As well as providing a definition of quality it is necessary to understand the difference between three other important quality ideas. These are the distinctions which are made between quality control, quality assurance and total quality.

Quality Control is historically the oldest concept. It involves the detection and elimination of components or final products which are not up to standard. It is an after-the-event process concerned with detecting and rejecting defective items. As a method of ensuring quality it may involve a considerable amount of waste, scrap and reworking. Quality control is usually carried out by quality professionals known as quality controllers or inspectors. Inspection and testing are the most common methods of quality control; and are widely used in education to determine whether standards are being met.

Quality assurance is different from quality control. It is before and during the event process. Its concern is to prevent faults occurring in the first place. Quality is designed into the process to attempt to ensure that the product is produced to a predetermined specification. Simply, quality assurance is a means of producing defectand fault-free products. The aim, in the words of Philip B Crosby, is 'zero defects'. Quality assurance is about consistently meeting product specification or getting things 'right first time, every time'. Quality assurance is made the responsibility of the workforce, usually working in cells or teams, rather than the inspector, although inspection can have a role to play in quality assurance. The quality of the good or service is assured by there being a system, which lays down exactly how production should take place and to what standards.Quality standards are maintained by following the procedures laid down in the QA system.

Total quality management incorporates quality assurance, and extend and develops it. TQM is about creating a quality culture where the aim of every member of staff is to delight their customers, and where the structure of their organization allows them to do so. In the total quality definition of quality the customer is sovereign. It is the approach popularized by Peters and Waterman in *In Search of Excellence,* and which has been a constant theme of Tom Peters' writings since. Many companies, such as Marks and Spencer, British Airways, and Sainsburys have been pursuing this approach for a number of years. It is about providing the customer with what they want, when they want it and how they want it. It involves moving with changing customer expectations and fashions to design products and services which meet and exceed their expectations. Only by delighting customers will they return and tell their friends about it.

The 'Product' of Education

It is always necessary to ask two fundamental questions when trying to understand quality in any station. The first is, what is the product? and the second is, who are the customers? These questions are equally applicable to the discussion of quality in education. What is the product of education? There are a number of different candidates for this title. The pupil or the student is often spoken about as if they are the product. In education we often talk as though learners are the output, especially with reference to the institution's perceived performance over discipline and behaviour. Terms like 'the supply of graduates' make education sound like a production line with students emerging from the end of it.

For a product to be the subject of quality assurance process the producer needs firstly to specify and control the source of supply. Secondly, the 'raw material' must pass through a standard process or set of processes, and the output must meet defined specifications. Such a mode! does not easily fit education, although there are those that might wish that it would. Such a model would clearly require an initial selection of learners to be made. Some sectors of education do this, but many, following the comprehensive principle of open access, do not. However, it is from there on that the analogy begins to fall apart. While processes such as the national curriculum and the specification of standards and competencies in NVQs have improved the standardization of the process, nevertheless the process of education is anything but uniform.

It is impossible to produce pupils and students to any particular guaranteed standard. As Lynton Gray has put it in his very useful discussion of the issue: Human beings are notoriously non-standards, and they bring into educational situations a range of experiences, emotions and opinions which cannot be kept in the background of the operation. Judging quality is very different from inspecting the output of a factory, or judging the service provided by a retail outlet. The idea of the learner as the product misses the complexities of the learning process and the uniqueness of each individual learner.

Service Quality

Service quality characteristics are more difficult to define than those for physical products. This is because they include many important subjective elements.The causes of poor quality and quality failure are different for services and products. Products often fail because of faults in raw materials and components. Their design may be faulty or they may not be manufactured to specification. Poor quality services, on the other hand, are usually directly attributable to employee behaviors or attitude. They often result from lack of care or courtesy. Indifference, lack of training or concern are often principal reasons for a breakdown of service. The different nature of service quality characteristics needs to be borne in mind when discussing educational quality.

Service differ from production in a number of important ways. They are major differences between delivering a service and manufacturing goods.The first difference between the tow is that services usually involve direct contact between the provider and the end-users. Services are delivered directly by people to people. There is a close relationship between the customer and the person who delivers the service. The service cannot be separated from the person delivering it or from the person receiving it. Every interaction is different, and the quality of the interaction is in part determined by the customer. The quality of the service is determined both by the person delivering the person receiving the service. Unlike production there can be no absolute consistency or homogeneity in service delivery. The consistency of the service can only be within boundaries. Time is the second important element of service quality. Services have to be delivered on time, and this is as important as their physical specification. Additionally, as a service is consumed at the moment of delivery the control of its quality by inspection is always too late. The close personal interactions found in services allow multiple opportunities for feedback and evaluation and these provide the main, but not the only, means of judging whether customers are satisfied with it.

The third differences is that unlike a product, a service cannot be serviced or mended. A poor meal is a poor meal. It cannot be repaired for this reason it is important that the standard of services should be right first time every time. Paradoxically, it is the high possibility of human error and failing that makes is difficult, if not impossible to achieve the right first time standard. Nevertheless, this should always be the aim.

Fourth, services face the problem of intangibility. It is often difficult to describe to potential customers exactly what is being offered. It is equally difficult on occasions for customers to describe what they want from the service. Services are largely about process rather than product. It is usually more important how an outcome is arrived at than what the outcome is.

The fact that services are usually rendered directly to customers by junior employees is the fifth distinguishing feature of a service. Senior staff are generally remote from customers. Most customers never have access to senior managers. The quality of the initial interactions colors the view customers have of the whole organization, and so the organization has to find ways of motivating front-line employees to always deliver of their best. This is why training and staff development are crucial importance. While senior managers may not serve at the front in service organizations they must lead from the front and convey to their staff their vision of the service and the standards they want set for it. Lastly, it is very difficult to measure successful output and productivity in services. The only meaningful performance indicators are those of customer satisfaction. Intangibles or 'soft' measures are often as important to success and to the customer as are hard and objective performance indicators. 'Soft' indicators—care, courtesy, concern, friendliness, and helpfulness are often uppermost in customers' minds. Intangibility makes it very difficult to turn round poor service, because it is sometimes impossible to convince dissatisfied customers that a service has changed for the better. Consumers judge quality by comparing their perceptions of what they receive with their expectations of it. Much of this is also true for education. Reputation is crucial to an institutions' success, but the origin of that reputation often defies analysis and measurement.

For the purposes of analysing quality it is more appropriate to view education as a service industry than as a production process.

Once this view is established the institution needs to define clearly the service it is providing and the standards to which they will be delivered. This needs to be carried out in conjunction with all its customer groups, including discussions with governors, parents, and with industry directly or via local Education Business Partnerships.

Education and its Customers

We have defined education as a provider of services. Those services include tuition, assessment, and guidance to pupils and students, their parents and sponsors. The customers—the stakeholders of the service—are a very diverse group and need identifying. If quality is about meeting and exceeding customer needs and wants it is important to be clear whose needs and wants we should be satisfying. It is at this point important to say something about the idea of a 'customer' in the context of education. To some educationalists 'customer' has a distinctly commercial tone which is not applicable to education. The prefer to use client instead. Client, with its connotations or professional service is seen as more appropriate. Stakeholder is another term often used in this context. Others reject all such language and would rather stay with pupil or student. Language is important if an idea is to be acceptable. In this book customer and learner are mainly employed, but there is no quarrel with those who might wish to substitute other terms.

There are others who should make a distinction between 'clients' who are the primary beneficiaries of the education service, and 'customers', who are those who pay for it but who may be at one remove, such as parents, governors, employers or government. In this book customers will be used for both sets of relationships and the distinction will be made between 'primary customers' who directly receive the service, 'secondary customers' such as parents, governors, sponsoring employers of FE students who have a direct stake in the education of a particular individual or in a particular institution, and 'teritiary customers' who have less direct but none the less crucial stakeholding in education such as future employers, government and society as a whole. To some extent this distinction is at odds with schools' legislation. The 1988 Education Reform Act makes the parents the primary customers of the process. This provides an additional, but not irreconcilable, difficulty for schools. The diversity of customers makes it all the more important for educational institutions to focus on customer wants and to develop mechanisms for responding to them. It is important to define clearly the nature of the service an institution provides to its customers.It is equally important to maintain an excellent and continuing dialogue with them.

The overall aim of the initiative is to link the demands for accountability with the desire for improvement; often they are seen to be mutually incompatible. Improving can be a statistical exercise, fulfilling requirements in terms of performance indicators but, when linked to the qualitative process of developing a narrative related to classroom practice, the two processes can be both developmental and powerful. A keynote of the Initiative is to gain the commitment of identified teams of staff in FE colleges to the idea of monitoring and evaluation as a positive and educative process in itself. Too often, quality is associated only with audit, review and inspection. If quality is genuinely inbuilt and integral to the whole institution, the integrity of the process may eliminate the fault-finding, problemsolving focus of many quality systems. The identified teams are asked to work through 20 tasks in the handbook over one year. This is supported by systematic staff development and accredited training in evaluation techniques for team leaders. The teamsidentify 'quality gaps' in the area of provision for which they are responsible. These 'gaps' are then converted to quality targets that are tackled by the team itself. Nationally each team will identify 3 targets to be met each. term. In order to address these targets, the team formulates an action plan identifying what is to be tackled, by whom, how and where. This provides the basis for a bid to a central college group which will then approve or modify the bid for funding. The funding may take the form of release time, equipment or materials. This forms the basis of reciprocal contracting—where the team contracts to deliver on its targets. The Senior management team would contract to deliver on its targets in the same way as all other teams. All targets and time scales are 'public knowledge' and conform to the College strategic framework for quality. This means that the College Development Plan can be enacted through the contracting process and the regular review of progress each term.

Implementing the Initiative

The first stage is to agree some key principles that provide the focus of improvement. Many teams include classroom practice, the quality of teaching and learning or the interaction between lecture and students. These concepts need to be dis-aggregated into a series of developmental tasks. At this stage, it is useful to being the process of identifying critical success factors or criteria for making judgements about the success of the improvement process. Although a necessarily lengthy process, it is essential to ensure a commitment through ownership—the team decides what the issues are, and what the criteria for success will be. The accredited training programme provides the necessary support for key individuals to lead the programme as 'professional evaluation'. It is important that the central group that receives bids from teams undertakes a monitoring and evaluation role for the whole college.

Methodology of the Initiative

The methodology of the initiative is based on the work of David Kolb and D A Schon. This model of experimental learning and the reflective practitioner, exemplified through the research and development function, is not usually part of the FE College system. If time for 'reflection' is built into the teaching and learning programme, it becomes possible to identify needs and meet planning requirements within "normal practice". The teams therefore use a variety of monitoring and evaluation techniques, each suited to its own purpose. The widespread use of questionnaires is generally found to be of limited use. Both students and staff can become "anaesthetised" to their use and the quality of some information is doubtful. By using a variety of methods, it is possible to triangulate on issues, and gain a much closer insight into the origins and nature of the issues. Many of the so-called problems identified by some quality systems are products of the system itself rather than being symptomatic of real underling course culture.

Evaluation techniques call be built into learning programmes, using tutorials, seminars and workshops. The common complaint is that "we don't have time...(for quality)." Teaching hours are being reduced and many staff are under considerable stress as a direct result of increased administration. A possible solution lies in revisiting teaching methodologies, timetabling and room allocations. It becomes necessary for the team to have increasing ownership of the means to deliver the curriculum that meet their identified needs and the needs of the students more effectively.

Traditionally colleges have been driven by SSRs and the requirements of resource allocations based on student numbers. Increasingly, the notion of performance related funding may produce a more efficient and effective way of delivering learning programmes that will incorporate "self-critical academic maturity". These are the issues that can be picked up very quickly by the 'empowered' course team. Their initial solutions to perceive problems may be crude, but they offer a genuine Rand D function that many commercial operations value highly the emphasis on discrete elements of college operations ego marketing, recruitment, quality, tends to fragment and dispel responses such as—"its someone else's responsibility".

You cannot delegate or subcontract quality and the fundamental approach of TQM lies in a set of values and attitudes that embody commitment to continuous improvement. In the same way, quality is not a project, nor is it a standard to be achieved. This serves only to limit achievement and leads to a "lip-service"model of the way that things should be done.

Quality Improvement

The "steps" to quality improvement begin with a view about "what do we mean by quality". Programme Area teams may have a different view to that of the management teams; providing interesting perspectives on the college's view of quality. Agreeing common principles is part of the first reflective stage. It is based primarily on experience, and may be a function of a series of critical incidents, concerns, problems, good ideas or hunches. These form the basis of the keynote principles to be outlines in the college Quality Development Action Plan, that outlines the "mission" and incorporates commitment to specific quality attributes.

Secondly, decisions about the composition of teams will provide a basis for identifying areas of "common effort". In itself an interesting exercise, this can identify the "black holes" of provision and the "team that never meets" or the "team that never was". Team forming provides a basis for more collaborative working and for improved communications and shared resources. Indeed, the benefits of this single exercise often promote a more integrative approach to all aspects of the college provision and lead to consideration of structured responses.

The third stage is for each team to identify their own response to "quality gaps", as perceived by the team. These gaps should become targets for improvement, recognising that in some cases there are resource implications for management attention. Initially, it is useful to identify smaller (incremental) issues for improvement, rather than medium or long term targets. If all teams engage in the process, by contracting to deliver, the whole college can move rapidly to a stage of critical mass. At this point the management strategy should incorporate a moderating influence, ensuring a degree of realism and consistency in both targeting and methodology. This is important to ensure that diversity of approach does not preclude a corporateness of purpose.

Perceptions and Expectations of Quality

The quality debate in higher education traditionally focuses on whether profit-orientated private sector concepts can be readily transferred to the public sector. This is a complex issue but even the limited view of the student, as a customer or client, goes against the grain of many in HE. They are very reluctant to empower a group who are traditionally treated as passive recipients of education. Both the broad consumer perspective, that service quality can be equated to the extent to which the perceived level of service delivered matches consumer expectations and the more specific view that service satisfaction equals consumer perception minus consumer expectation is not without problems in the HE context. However, the implication that satisfaction will result if perceptions are greater than expectations has a great deal of intuitive appeal.

This balance between consumers' perceptions and expectations as a measure of service quality has been fairly widely-discussed and appears to be useful. Nevertheless antagonists to the quality initiative often argue that in the HE context it is futile to attempt to define quality in this way because student expectations are poorly developed, variable and unpredictable. Validly measuring student perceptions and expectations is not a simple matter but can be approached in a systematic way to reveal useful information. To complicate matters further, antagonists to the quality initiative often point out that different stakeholders in HE will all have different sorts of expectations from a particular institution or service. Consequently they claim that different stakeholders will have disparate ideas about "quality" jeopardising any attempt at valid assessment. Clearly there is more than one client group to be considered in examining the perceived value of higher education, but this does not mean that these various perceptions cannot be systematically studied.

The work of the SSRU

Unit recently, students' views of their academic experience had been of interest only to a handful of educational evaluators but increasingly the value of this information has been recognised. The realisation that students' attitudes and perceptions are not only interesting that may play a central role in shaping the decisions of those who manage our higher education institutes has widespread implications. Since its inception in 1988, the Student Satisfaction Research Unit (SSRU) at Birningham Polytechnic has produced an abundance of information related to student perceptions of educational quality and their satisfaction with their educational experience. Our interest in quality and their satisfaction with their educational experience. Our interest in quality and our attempts to measure it through student satisfaction have three broad aims. First, we are attempting to identify and examine the components of satisfaction and the components of quality and to consider how these two domains are interrelated. Second, we are investigating whether there is a common core to students' perceptions of satisfaction and quality third, we are attempting to model student satisfaction and quality of education and to represent this model in ways which are designed to inform management decision and policy-making. Nowadays, collecting information about student satisfaction in educational establishments is a growth industry. Information of this kind has the potential benefit of guiding management decision-making with respect to the planning and provision of educational services. Those HE managers who can clearly identify and subsequently measure client-centered quality will be able to capitalise on student-based information to support their claims for resources.

Eliciting Areas of Student Concern

One approach to directly eliciting students' views of the Polytechnic which has proved to be particularly productive over the last few years is a form of Nominal Group Technique which we have dubbed the "Group Feedback Strategy" (GFS). Essentially this takes the form of a structured participative discussion with groups of students in order to provoke a span of student nominated indicators of satisfaction and dissatisfaction. Experience has shown that engendering an atmosphere of frank and open communication encourages students to talk freely and honestly about what their education means to them. These sessions, facilitated by experienced group leaders, generally result in eliciting a wide and diverse range of satisfiers and dissatisfiers which are used on an annual basis to update the design of the instruments used to student satisfaction in Polytechnic.

Areas of Student Satisfaction and Dissatisfaction

The outcomes of the GFS procedure were consensus, but wide-ranging, lists of satisfiers and dissatisfiers elicited from students in each of the 16 parficipating classes. In order to provide a framework for analysing these unstructured statements, each "good" or "bad" statement was allocated to one or more of 44 core activities which had been identified through synthesising categories used in our previous work these core activities are reasonably exhaustive of students' concerns and are clearly associated with student satisfaction and dissatisfaction.

The Personal and Interpersonal area which includes such activities as "broadening my experience and outlook". "socialising with other students" and "talking to staff freely and openly" is seen in a very positive light (77%) whereas Spending and Budgeting has little potential for satisfaction (5%). Teaching and Learning Activities can provide some satisfaction (37%) whereas Using Facilities generally trends to be a focus for discontent (18%). In other words students tend to stress negative aspects or grievances when considering their finances or using polytechnic facilities.

In addition to expressing their opinions about their likes and dislikes, students were also required to each of the 44 core activities with respect to 5 two aspects of importance. The first rating was of the importance of each activity to enhancing the effectiveness of study; the second rating was of the importance of each activity to enhancing students' personal sense of well-being. Part of our purpose was to investigate the relationship between these twin aspects of importance in order to provide information about students' priorities.

Both satisfaction and importance are essential ways of considering students' perceptions of their educational activities. Polcyn has suggested that importance and satisfaction can be represented as quadrants on a graph and each quadrant has different organisational implications.

The major concern in the management literature in the 1980s has been the development of management competences. Since the purpose of the study of management is to improve performance, it is not surprising that attention should be focused on an analysis of what abilities managers need in order to be effective and various categorizations have emerged. The beginnings of the research for generic management competences can be traced back to the 1970s when the American Management Associations (AMA) launched a project based on observation and analysis of 1,800 management jobs.

In the AMA managerial competency model which emerged competence is defined as 'a generic knowledge, motive, trait, self-image, social role, or skill of a person that is causally linked to superior' performance on the job.' The model identified, in addition to specific knowledge competence, four clusters of generic competences which they identify as intellectual, entrepreneurial, socio-emotional and interpersonal. In Britain academic study and research was given a marked stimulus by the Management Charter Initiative (MCI), a large-scale industry-led management development programme supported by central government which now involves over 200 UK leading private and public organizations. A price to be paid for government support, particularly in the British political scene, given the relatively short periods between elections, is that results have to be visible, immediate and measurable. Consequently there has been an inevitable tendency to produce checklists often containing an undifferentiated collection of personal characteristics, mechanistic skills, management processes and much more complex abilities.

In the field of education the growing recognition of the crucial importance of good management practices in school was dramatically strengthened by the impact of 'local management of schools' imposed by the 1988 Education Reform Act. Central government clearly regards management development as a key element in its declared strategy for ensuring improvement in the quality of education to meet the needs of industry and the economy. Fortunately the years that followed the Act have coincided with the period when serious doubts are being expressed about the basic idea of analysing a professional management task into itemized elements of competence. It is increasingly recognized that the overall ability to perform effectively is more than the sum of a set of subordinate abilities. Jacobs makes the point that while it is possible, by obtaining and carefully analysing performance data, to identify clusters of behaviour that can be reliably and logically classified as competences, what is obtained is only a partial and fragmented view of the complexity of management. Management performance involves other activity which is difficult to isolate and describe; it involves qualities and abilities which are not easy to observe or discover; it has outcomes which defy measurement.

The Management Task Force set up by the Secretary of State for Educations to identify and explore some of the issues involved in management development in schools has largely rejected the prescription of training in an arbitrarily determined set of skills as the way forward. This has contributed to a growing conviction that those who manage are in the best position to identify what their needs may be. This approach is reinforced by a current general political philosophy that 'the customer knows best'. Thus the identification of need is a major concern among providers of management development and it is generally held that it is essential for schools to feel ownership of the programmes through being fully and directly involved in planning their content, style and procedures.

The Research Methodology

In determining an appropriate method of enquiry the researchers were informed from three sources: The Peer Assisted Learning Project of the Far West Laboratory for Education Research and Development, San Francisco. Effective peer group interaction, an integral part of the action research approach, is the cornerstone of the Master of Science programme at the University of Ulster. Groups are encouraged to engage in reflective enquiry which seeks to analyse and understand their own and others' practice leading to courses of action for sustained improvement. Creative thinking is also encouraged as a complementary activity by which is meant the ability to form novel associations from looking at the elements of managerial reality in an open and unconstrained way. This approach offered the possibility of uncovering, if they existed, elusive generic capabilities from complex realities.

The focus group as a form of qualitative research has many characteristics in common with features of the above approach: 'The hallmark of the focus group is the explicit use of the group interaction to produce data and insights that would be less accessible without the interaction found in a group'. The style of approach is exploratory rather than hypothesis testing and based on interview and interaction. Surprisingly focus groups have not been widely used in research in the social sciences or education, but the method clearly offers a valuable vehicle for group members experienced in rigorous reflective analysis. For this research six head teachers were chosen from the primary, secondary and further education sectors and two female members were included to allow for possible differences in style and practise. All are alumni of the MSc programme and had the advantage of three years of cognitive development in the group dynamics described above. The researchers acted as moderators, adopting a detached style which allowed members to raise and explore issues they felt were significant but maintaining proximity to the focus of enquiry.

Balanced Judgement

The ability to exercise balanced judgement was also seen as critical. Group members saw it as related to problem-solving in that, once a situation has arisen or a problem has been recognized, analysis follows and key factors are identified and evaluated in the process of choosing a course of action. It was clear that as the group distilled their thinking over a number of sessions they did not see it as an exercise in mechanical logic: 'It is not merely clinical analysis but a combination of that with intuition.' There was considerable agreement that the kind of judgement necessary is significantly different from judgement in the legal sense: 'You have to be prepared to base decisions on much softer evidence than would be accepted in a court of law. You very rarely have time to collect all the evidence you would like and you have to exercise judgement on a partial picture. Values also can't be left out of the picture.' The issue of values arose in a number of contexts but particularly in relation to the context created by the new legislation: 'You must be aware of the values you are perceived to embody and perceived to protect.' 'Does school reflect the world out there as it is or should it project what the world out there might be?'

It is interesting that while many writers speak about making sound judgments the recurring theme in the discussion was about balanced judgement. The group saw the examining and weighting of the advantages and disadvantages of factors in often ambiguous and conflicting circumstances as important and the testing of decisions against the priorities' and values of the school. Balanced judgements was seen as particularly important in time of crisis and dilemma.

Intuition

Intuition was seen as serving judgement, following a long debate about the relationships between experience, creative thinking, judgement and intuition. The group did not agree with a conception of intuition as devoid of thought. 'Intuition is more than mere hunch or guesswork. It may start as a gut feeling but is tested against the bank of your own experience.'Two key elements recurred in the attempt to capture the essence of intuition: the part played by experience and the part played by a thinking process. The groups saw stored memory and ordered experience as important. It is interesting that they independently derived a conception close to that outlined by a number of recent writers, who suggest that the basis of intuition lies in the ability spontaneously to tap the mind's compressed store of experience, knowledge and understanding. A top executive in industry express a view, reported in Vaughan, which would clearly be accepted by members of the group: '1 don't think intuition is some magical thing. I think it is a subconscious drawing from innumerable experiences that are stored: You draw from this reserve without conscious thought.' Similarly, the group perceptions of the role of thinking in intuition are similar to aspects of the concept of creativity developed by a number of writers. Henry regards creativity as associated with imagination, insight, invention, motivation, ingenuity, inspiration and intuition'. The cerebral aspects of intuition were constantly stressed by the group.

Strategies for Management Development

At the outset it might be. helpful to define our understanding of 'management' and therefore refer the reader to two existing definitions of the word. Both are task-focused and point to the central role of the people, the human resources, in an institution to achieve the tasks. So 'management' is 'the process of securing decisions about what activities the organisation will undertake, and mobilising the human and material resources to undertake them'; or it is, 'achieving goals by, with and through people and managers and all those responsible for the world of other adults'. In this context 'management development' can be defined as, 'the process whereby the management function of an organisation is performed with increasing effectiveness'.

There is clearly an imperative to improve strategies for management development at all levels in the education service. For example, Her Majesty's Inspectors reporting on school and college inspections during the period 1982/86 wrote that, 'one of the most significant determinants of a good school was high-quality leadership and good management'. This was followed by a statement from the Senior Chief Inspector reporting on the state of England's education service and quoted in the *Times Educational Supplement* in 1990. He said,'...the management of schools leaves much to be desired. In only about a third of those inspected was senior management judged to be particularly effective'.[...] Therefore, the need for more coherent and effective strategies for school management development has never been more urgent.

The effective delivery of management development must begin with strategic planning at several levels in the education service. Schools There is now much good practice available in terms of the effective planning and delivery of staff development, and within this broader context for management development, at school level. Such good practice must now become normal practice in all schools. The planning should have three main strands. The first is the drawing up of an institutional development plan (IDP) which is informed by an evaluation of the school. The IDP, a relatively brief and readable document, will then be available as a basis for all other aspects of school planning such as curriculum development, staffing, budgeting and making decisions about the priorities for staff development. The second is the establishment of a staff development committee which is broadly representative of all groups on the staff and has appropriate delegated authority to plan and deliver a school's programme of staff in-service education and training within the agreed framework of priorities set out in the IDP.

The third is a scheme of staff appraisal which is adequately resource and provides information about individual development needs. Suitably anonymized, the outcomes of staff appraisal should be used as an additional source of background information by the staff development committee as they plan the use of the resources allocated to them.

Local Network. Local networks can help to prevent school-focused staff development from becoming too inward-looking by providing opportunities to work with colleagues fro, other schools in the area.

Regional and National. Effective planning for management development also requires a broader perspective at regional and national levels to help avoid too much 're-invention of wheels' and also to address strategic issues of more than local importance like the accreditation of programmes of management development and the preparation for headship.

Other Agencies. Several other agencies will continue to make a significant contribution to management development at all levels,

(1) **Industry.** One of the most encouraging features of school management development over the past few years has been the increased involvement of personnel from industry working on the basis of a partnership with education. A less regular feature of such co-operative arrangements in the movement of personnel from industry into schools or other aspects of the education service.

(2) **Professional Associations.** The teacher associations have also shown an increasing commitment to the professional development of their members and many now offer a wide range of courses and other forms of in-service education and training.

(3) **Higher Education and Independent Providers.** Higher education and, a growing number o independent providers will continue to contribute to school manpgement development at all levels. In the future their success or failure in this role will depend much more on the pressures of the marketplace, Schools, consortia and other networks of institutions or individuals will be shopping around for the best and most appropriate opportUnities for management development at prices which they can afford.

An overall strategy for management development should embrace the maintenance and development of institutional management structures as well as the personal development, of individual managers. From time to time key people will leave an institution for a variety of reasons and, although man individual resignations are unpredictable, local a regional patterns in vacancies are discernible. Succession planning begins with this type Df analysis and uses the results to consider the action required to increase the chances of filling vacancies with a minimum loss of overall management performance in an organization.

Large organizations are more able to implement in house systems of succession planning and can fill many vacancies through internal promotion. Schools on the other hand are preventative of small and medium-sized organizations which can do much less to predict succession problems and must usually resort to external appointments to fill their vacancies. This means that they are more vulnerable to market forces over which they have little control. There is a danger that the move towards the local management of schools will compound the problem of fragmentation in the education service and put further limits on the possibility of succession planning at local level. However, the education service as a whole has usually 'grown; its own managers. It is therefore quite possible to envisage on approach to succession planning which has a local perspective provided that overall data about teacher supply and conditions is available at national level. Such data could then be supplemented by regional and local knowledge of staffing structures in schools, age structures, wastage rates and recruitment patterns which are potentially available to local education authorities. Armed with this knowledge, LEA s and consortia of schools would then be in a position to adopt a more positive approach to succession planning. For example, they could take steps to increase the number of qualified application for particular types of vacancy in the locality by joint advertising, training and development programmes.

Individual career development is clearly an important concomitant of succession planning. In school staff development and the wider provision of inservice education and training must find the right balance between the requirements of the present job, personal professional growth and preparation for promotion. Certainly careers advice and appropriate support in the planning of a personal development programme should be available to all teachers as should opportunities to gain experience of management responsibilities at a higher level.

Without some assessment of need, the time and money spent on the management development of an individual can be wasted or, at least, be of only limited value. Staff appraisal and self-analysis questionnaires may help to inform development needs but both are relatively limited and blunt instruments. There would be greater coherence at all levels of management development if we could approach the assessment of need, and then the provision of development, using a micro-surgeon's knife rather than the traditional blunderbuss, firing off development opportunities in the hope that a few will strike individual targets. There is also much to be gained by raising the profile of personal and generic management competencies as a vital component of development programmes alongside the more traditional tasks-related and job-specific aspects of middle and senior management roles in schools.

The Educational Assessment Centre project, started in September 1990 and based in Oxford, worked with 28 clients from the maintained and independent school sectors in England, Wales and Scotland. It is an important and ambitious attempt to meet both the requirements outlined above by providing senior staff with a detailed diagnostic profile for further professional development based on 12 generic management competencies. The initial aim of the EAC project is to improved the management competencies of further headteachers so that they will be effective managers as well as successful educators. It should be emphasized that the project is applicable to management development in all aspects and phases of the education service.

Assessment centres have been used in both the public and private sectors of employment. for over 50 years to inform the process of developing and selecting senior managers. Their use has been restricted to senior levels primarily because assessment centres that productive valid and reliable data are relatively expensive to establish and operate. Establishing an assessment centre in particular occupational setting is a complex and technical process which draws on the expertise psychologists and professionals.

❐

16

Quality Audits

If quality control could be defined as an extension of management to assure the maintenance of discipline and consistency of performance, an audit of quality control performance might be considered a measure of management effectiveness. Yet nothing could be further from the truth. Too many managements are so busy getting things done that no one is overly concerned with how well they are being done. To even consider let alone tolerate-measuring management's effectiveness is unheard of. Nevertheless, quality audits have come into being for big business at least, and apparently they are here to stay.

What precisely is their purpose?

Quality audits either were started or first attained a degree of notoriety in some of the larger systems-management-type programmes; they are now required by most sizable government contracts. They came along as part of a continually growing extension of contractual quality control requirements, all aimed at improving the total quality control effort. This extension alone should have been an indication to management of the need for improvement, but it was necessary to add the audit procedure to emphasize the importance of each quality control requirement. The audits represent an attempt to force and to guarantee tangible compliance. That they have failed to accomplish their mission fully is evidenced by the position they now hold. Like certain other quality control requirements, quality audits have become mired in that nebulous area where quality control contrives to conform without seriously embarrassing management or forcing it into undesirable or expensive action.

All audits share one characteristic in common: unpopularity. Nobody likes to be audited. Audits find mistakes and deficiencies, and these, in turn, reflect on individuals. Usually, individuals fear the destructive force of facts more than they crave a truly constructive atmosphere, yet their performance makes audits necessary. Where would the banks, for example, be today without audits?

The fact that quality control itself is essentially an audit of other people's performance may be one of the principal reasons why it is so often unwelcome and why it generally faces an uphill struggle. This same fact, moreover, in the light of management's responsibility for overall performance, actually places quality control in the role of performing management audits and thus may very well be chiefly responsible for the barriers that too often exist between management and quality control. In one sense, there is no difference between management and an individual when it comes to an audit.

The specific intention, in quality auditing, has been to make a separate organizational segment of the quality control function responsible for reviewing the balance of the organization's performance. Although they are primarily procedural, audits at times include product or hardware. The principal target has been the quality procedures manual, which defines quality control's responsibility and provides implementing instructions. The manual also is likely to receive the lion's share of attention so far as the customer is concerned. With the customer requiring internal audits, audits of quality procedures, and surveillance of procedure implementation, it is abundantly clear that all the customer really wants is a set of effective quality control procedures, realistically implemented.

When the customer's willingness to pay is added to his explict desire for an effective quality control system, one wonders why the task of supplying effective procedures is so difficult and why reuirements must be periodically changed in a continued attempt at improvement. The answer is that no quality control procedure can be effective unless it requires disciplined action or management by another company function. If no need existed for discipline in that area, there would certainly be no need for quality control. Add to this the fact that quality procedures generally do not direct other people to do things, and the paradox of quality procedures and quality programmes should begin to come to light.

Unless the stated and accepted objective of a given quality control programme is to achieve quality and the objective of controlling quality is to become an integral part of overall company operations the net effect of quality procedures will be limited to quality control personnel only. Thus any hope of exerting significant pressure on the rest of the company is more dream than reality. Quality procedures under these circumstances have a strong tendency toward restrictive self-correction when they run into specific difficulties; that is, to correct deficiencies in other groups, they keep adding requirements for quality control personnel. Allowed to grow in this way, the complete set of procedures in time becomes so complex and unwieldy as to be almost totally ineffective and, very possibly, indicate the need for auditing.

An audit performed at this moment to determine the precise degree of unwieldiness characterizing any given quality procedures manual would very likely reflect certain sensitive key points. The first is somewhat academic! Compare the amount of instruction given to quality control personnel, as represented by the quality manual to the amount of instruction given to personnel who must perform the work that quality control reviews. If the workers are inadequately instructed, the point is made no further arguments are needed. Next, review the results of customer audits for two significant findings: *(1)* an excessive number of failures to comply with the written word as opposed to basic deficiencies and *(2)* a preponderance of quality procedure changes in the corrective action column. Finally, review the results of internal quality audit in the same way. If the findings indicate that here, too, quality control personnel and quality procedures are the chief targets, the question ought to be asked: Are we really seeking effectiveness or merely trying to keep one step ahead of the customer?

Whenever a quality control organization plays this "follow the customer" game even to a small degree, it finds itself caught in a giant web. There is almost no way out, and the web keeps getting bigger. The quality manual itself becomes more difficult to handle than the functions it was originally intended to provide a guide for. Quality control personnel become so entangled in its procedures that other, more important work suffers. There is so much wheel spinning within the quality control organization that someone company or customer—ends up paying for efforts of no real value, and opportunities to contribute to overall company performance and management effectiveness are lost. This, then, is the paradox that quality audits have been deemed necessary to discipline the very people who themselves should represent the epitome of discipline for all others.

When quality audits are limited to the instructions contained in a quality procedure—as often happens—they are not likely to improve on the intent or objective of the procedure. When strongly pursued and supported they can, on the other hand, force the procedure to become more important than the objective. When this occurs, quality control will have taken a great step backward. Unfortunately, it is not difficult to locate symptoms of this insidious condition, which can be avoided entirely if the specific purpose of the quality audit is stated as measuring the total effect of a given quality procedure against the overall objective of the quality control function.

In pursuing the value of a given procedure, other questions immediately come to mind. For example:

* What is this procedure's objective?
* Does it require others to do something? If so, what?
* Does it enforce discipline already required of others?
* Is it a crutch for discipline or action that is lacking elsewhere?
* What does it contribute to the overall business?

* Is it too wordy to be understood and utilized effectively by individuals?

* Is it really necessary?

The value of answering these and many similar questions is not limited to quality control. They are representative of the type of information general management should want about its quality control function. The use of quality audits for the pursuit of value will not only improve the usefulness of audits but lead to more meaningful and more forceful quality procedures. Since the real measure of quality control's effectiveness is how well it has succeeded in getting others to control their operations, failure to use quality audits in this manner falls into the category of missed opportunities.

An essential ingredient in any audit is the auditor himself. If one were to list the reasons why audits fail, the selection and training of the auditors would stand high. To be effective, a quality control auditor should have broad knowledge and experience. Like all auditors, he must be impartial and capable of dealing with people at all levels, but above all he should have the intelligence to assess the value of any given situation and turn it into an avenue of progress. Each actual problem he uncovers can provide an opportunity for quality control to make a contribution to the company's performance and, hence, profits.

Often the quality auditor is adversely affected by circumstances. If management is a destructive user of facts, facts are more difficult to obtain. If meaningful action is not generally forthcoming as a result of auditing, the spirit of cooperation dwindles. If too many problems are reflected in the summary report, quality control management may be embarrassed. When circumstances such as these are added to the natural resentment and normal roadblocks auditors are likely to encounter, it becomes evident that the auditor who aspires to be truly effective faces real challenges. Management courage is demanded to overcome the obstacles and make auditing profitable. After all, an audit summary that reflects no actual problems and accomplishments is not a good report; for those who crave honesty, it spells "lip service." The quality control programme that cannot be improved is obsolete.

Quality control management is of course not alone in being subject to auditing, although more should perhaps be expected of quality control because of its experience in auditing others. Many large corporations and certain U.S. Government agencies employ formal management audits at times to find out what is really happening in specific areas or programmes. Since these areas or programs are deliberately singled out for review, such audits usually carry with them the stigma of suspicion and this suspicion inevitably is directed toward management. Members of the auditing teams generally are selected on the basis of their established management capability, their all-round acceptability, and any special experience they may have which could be beneficial to the area or programme being audited. The conduct of such audits can follow any line; after a review of background material, they customarily start with interviews of key personnel; then they proceed into any specific avenues that may be highlighted by the interviews.

Like most other audits, management audits have built-in problems. For example, the individual who can make the most constructive use of the results is the same individual on whom the deficiencies that are discovered reflect most unfavourably. For this reason, there is a strong tendency toward conservatism on the part of both the auditors and the audited. In other words, the paramount question in everyone's mind is: Do they really want to know the truth? Reluctance to either probe for the truth or divulge it immediately sets in because of the very personal fear of its misuse. Under these conditions, most management audits turn out to be nothing more than mild surface-skimming ventures.

If only half of the statements made in this chapter thus far were true, it would still be obvious that the greatest deterrent to a useful audit is the lack of a truly constructive atmosphere. Since most people inherently wish to build up both themselves and the organizations with which they are affiliated, it is unlikely that they are actually contributing to this lack except as a defense mechanism. It is much more likely that thc few people who represent management are controlling the atmosphere. The authority of management places these individuals firmly in a position to do so; their actions, not their words, set the pace for all the actions that follow, and only they have the power to change such matters.

Provocative examples of the failure of management's actions to keep in step with its words exist almost everywhere in industry. The name of the game is "management directives," "management procedures," or "company operating manual." Why some of these are written at all will probably remain a mystery forever. Company operations manuals, in fact, can become so complex and unwieldy that they more closely resemble quality manuals. Many managers obviously use them merely to suit their personal needs or desires at a particular point in time. Some directives are issued in answer to legitimate complaints but with no idea that they will ever be enforced; others are followed only for the sake of political expediency; while still others, once promulgated, are eliminated quietly and informally. An extreme case is represented by the manager who insists on conformance only when lack of it will get him into trouble for example, with industrial relations and finance, where strong controls usually prevail. The net effect of this type of management action is to develop an organizational environment which can best be described by such a declaration as, "If they don't care, why should we?"

When management allows itself to break down in this fashion, it has in effect laid itself open to wholesale game playing. It might just as well say, "Anything is O.K. as long as you can get away with it." This helps to encourage the kind of people who will try to "get away with it" and who thus resemble management closely, but it creates nothing but obstacles for those who really have the best interest of the company at heart. Little better is the management that vacillates between insistence on conformance and complete tolerance of non-conformance. While there may be an explanation for this vacillation, too often it is known only to the individuals involved, and the phenomenon of subordinates having constantly to adjust to keep in step continues to be a fact of life in industry.

Complete management integrity demands the kind of courage that is sadly lacking today that, in fact, is not often sought. One may disagree with these statements, feeling that any decisive action constitutes a display of courage. But the kind of courage referred to here does not include acts of daring or even of panic in response to a setback arising from previous action. The management courage needed today is best represented by a steadfast approach to the continuous improvement of every aspect of the company's operations. It is intelligent, unbiased, and relentless, facing adversity calmly because it is aware that perils are omnipresent. And it is this kind of courage that demands a constructive atmosphere; in anything less, it would begin to suffocate.

It is unlikely that many existing managements fit a pat description exactly. Instead, they are neither extremely courageous nor extremely chaotic. Probably the atmosphere they create is neither constructive nor suffocating—it falls somewhere between these two extremes. On the other hand, hardly a management in existence today has never experienced some of the symptoms of such extremes. What organization, for example, has never felt the sting of impending chaos or had to do battle to take advantage of a new and exciting opportunity? While the results are not always related to management effectiveness or failure, often they are. In such cases, management will want to take credit where it is due.

Instead of waiting for the performance ledger to show a deficit, management should steal a page from the best quality control thinking and establish preventive measures. If future problems and risks are really going to be kept to an absolute minimum, it is not enough to gauge performance and progress merely by the fact that major milestones are being reached on schedule and within cost limits. Some indication of the quality of an achievement tells more about the future than does a mere notation of its having occurred. If either ineffectiveness or negligence on management's part is not caught in its early stages, it becomes so firmly rooted in the organization that it almost inevitably produces disaster.

At first glance, a company may appear to have an extremely challenging and difficult task when it sets out to measure in detail the relative effectiveness with which its component parts are being managed. Management, after all, comprises only a few individuals, and there is only so much time in a day, with so many things to be done. This is all very true but, if management really believes that measurement is important, it will find a way. It has overcome bigger challenges in the past. One solution to this difficulty is so logical that it is almost obvious: Briefly, management needs help to handle the measurement task, but only help of a very special kind—help that has no bias except in the direction of the company's total interest. Was not quality control created for the very purpose of measuring other groups' performance, of preventing problems in other company areas, and of protecting the company's interest in those areas?

Effective utilization of the quality control function by management is an ideal way for management to keep its fingers firmly on the pulse of almost every operation that can affect its well-being. Quality control is already functioning to some degree in most of the areas in question. All that is needed to change its environment from one that is at best somewhat suffocating to one of genuine management value is a decision on the part of management. Once this decision is made and its intention verified, management will be amazed at how much can be learned so easily and conveniently. Quality control has been around a long time; what is more, it has been stationed in the midst of all the potential trouble spots companies have been able to accumulate. Its knowledge of problems and their prevention far exceeds its ability to communicate that knowledge. Whatever the reason for this state of affairs, quality control represents an untapped reservoir of the most intimate information on the ways in which people work and the kind of difficulties in which they can involve a company.

In support of any movement to capitalize on the inherent potential of quality control for improving overall management effectiveness, two features of a U.S. Department of Defense specification for quality-programme requirements (MIL-Q-9858A, dated December 17, 1963) should be examined. This specification clearly recognizes that a quality control programme must encompress more than the functions of a quality control organization. It goes so far as to suggest that fulfillment of quality requirements need not rest solely on the shoulders of a single organization. This opens the door to the broadest possible type of management action. Recognizing the overall responsibility of management toward the total quality programme, it merely asks that management clearly determine which organization is responsible for the control of each work element that can affect the quality requirements stated in a contract and that it regularly review the status and adequacy of the programme.

This Department of Defense specification is the result of many years' experience and extensive analysis of quality control programmes. In spite of these impressive credentials, its fundamental plea is that management should recognize and fulfill its responsibility for product quality, and it allows management whatever leeway it needs or desires for fulfillment. Actually, this makes a good deal of business sense, because quality deficiencies have a way of insinuating their way into a company and destroying or at least damaging an otherwise healthy atmosphere. Since there are so many different company units capable of creating a quality deficiency, what better way is there to fulfill this management obligation than to make each one responsible for its share of the load, with quality control as an audit type of enforcing agency? And what surer way could there be for management to extend its ability to satisfy important customers' requirements completely?

A management decision to pursue maximum utilization of quality control whether in response to customers' demands or the results of objective analysis—carries with it the power to set up an extremely dynamic situation. Depending on the degree of non-conformance to procedures that has been tolerated the decision will send out shock waves of varying force. Everyone will be required to work to the established management plan or have it changed.

Corrective action will become a constructive way of life; nothing less than fully responsible statements will be permitted. This atmosphere will be too rich for the thin-blooded, some of whom will fall by the wayside.

In making what may well be termed an action-incorporating decision, management in all likelihood will not have to change its written policies very much. The impact of this decision is primarily one of attitude; hence written statements regarding quality control need only be expanded in the area of quality audits so as to include all management documents defining responsibility and procedures for work which can have an effect on product quality. Note that only the scope, not the magnitude, of the effort is affected. With its expanded scope, quality control can be required to apply the same kind of thinking to company procedures that was previously prescribed for quality procedures.

The sum total of the specific procedures under discussion constitutes the management plan or system for accomplishment. An audit of the implementation of these disciplines can, in fact, be a measure of management effectiveness. As a first step, however, an overall review of the basic purpose and content of the procedures will have the effect of weeding out those that are unnecessary and of establishing the rest on a firm basis. Procedures should be generated by management only when formal delineation and control of specific activities is essential to the effective, coordinated performance of the tasks involved. Any given procedure should assure uniformity of understanding concerning a particular task and the method of handling it, fix responsibility for it, assure continuity of action, and provide a sound basis for the evaluation and control of performance. Compliance must be mandatory, with deviations authorized only by the issuing authority.

If, however, implementation is to be mandatory, in any realistic sense, two fundamental problems frequently associated with established procedures must be avoided. One such problem concerns the complexity arising from too much detail: the other, the discouraging prevalence of red tape which normally accompanies change. This red tape sometimes causes flagrant disregard of procedures.

Procedures can be kept simple but fluid by adhering to fundamental objectives and eschewing mechanics. For example, procedures designed to integrate the efforts of three separate organizations to achieve a single goal should be limited to those fundamental facts necessary to all three groups for proper understanding and coordination. If the procedure incorporates every detailed instruction that will be needed by each group, it may confuse all three and thereby defeat its basic purpose. Instructions for individuals or for self-contained groups should be handled separately. When detailed mechanics are absolutely essential to an integrating procedure, the use of simple flow charts generally proves superior to a flood of words that will only bewilder the reader.

With any procedure, a fast-reaction change mechanism is needed to prevent disruption of the productive effort. But red tape is not limited to such a change mechanism. Often the real culprit is the individual or the organization responsible for approving and processing the change. In fact, the eontrihuting factors are legion: among them, unavailability of the necessary personnel when needed; inability of personnel to make decisions or commitments because of management restrictions or for other reasons; and remoteness of personnel, physical or mental, from the real world of industrial operations. Remedying any of these conditions may require a major policy change. And might not the intimate knowledge of operating problems, habits, and needs possessed by quality control personnel be a most valuable asset in any such analysis or decision? If the red-tape problem is purely mechanical, the solution can be as simple as introducing a procedure-change notice similar to engineering's drawing change notice (DCN) or that commonly used for a test-procedure change (PCN). Both are geared to the need for quick response. That this type of change notice is not commonly found in conjunction with management procedures may be just another indication of the slight overall regard in which management procedures are held.

Nor should the implementation of company operating procedures overlook the establishment of basic responsibilities. For example, every supervisor should be held responsible for a general knowledge of all applicable procedures. Next, individual employees should be held responsible for complete knowledge of each procedure which specifically relates to their individual tasks and responsibilities. After this, supervision should be encouraged to perform periodic self-audits in a continuous attempt to maintain discipline and to ascertain whether a particular procedure may no longer be effective or necessary.

Regardless of the initial requirements, company procedures can be made more meaningful and effective through the application of a well-designed and rigorously executed audit plan. However, the net effect on management effectiveness of any given audit whether it be conducted by quality control or by any other groupde pends almost entirely on the sincerity of management's original intentions and on the prevailing management attitude. The capability exists; still to be proved is whether it will be allowed to flourish. Moreover, no set of company operating procedures was put together in a day; each one requires constant renourishing.

Theoretically, an auditor examines samples of existing facts, then appraises the condition they represent. He is the first to realize that audits are no more than samples, that they are only indicative or symptomatic of the total condition. How widespread a particular undesirable condition may be, for example, will require a further investigation by management. The auditor will have merely seen and communicated the signs of the condition. And, one may hope, he will also have included and emphasized in his report those signs of really efficient and effective operation. The auditor should not be led astray by sensational distractions, such as technical problems. These should be left to the experts in that particular field.

If a certain prominent management auditor were to wander from company to company, reading the signs of management effectiveness, he doubtless would encounter indications of almost every possible management ill. Were this not true, the still growing volume of management literature and the training and development that have become essential parts of today's business world would be without substantive support. Nevertheless, the surest and the most fundamental sign of ineptness in any management is a lack of adherence to its own system of operation as defined by its own procedures. Where there is no discipline, any sort of mismanagement can follow.

Although business failures occur for many reasons, they are almost always related to some specific failure of management. On occasion; managers have miscalculated the cost of a programme or the size of a task, yet most failures are far more likely to be directly related to a serious miscalculation of an organization's or a product's ability to perform. The sad fact is that utilization of quality control as proposed here could have done much to prevent either source of trouble. This may sound like a simple remedy to an old and serious problem; but, if the signs of miscalculation are there, it would be a shame not to recognize them before it is too late.

❐

17

Quality's Function in Testing

Testing is an important and expensive part of the overall operation of many companies. Its importance lies in its significant effect on the performance of a company's produets. Its expense derives from the high level of skills and the costly test equipment usually involved. Thus testing cannot be treated lightly in the overall management seheme of things. Lack of sufficient attention to basic responsibilities and objectives ean easily make it more costly from both points of view.

Quality control's involvement with testing begins with its basic responsihility for acceptance of company products and becomes complicated hy the similarity of impection to test. The similarity can readily be seen in the growing development and use of precision measurement and test equipment for inspection purposes. This continued growth has tended to highlight certain fundamental questions regarding the definition and purpose of testing. For example: Is testing merely an inspection of the functional characteristics of a product? Is product acceptance its primary or its sole purpose? The varied answers to these and other pertinent questions have contributed in large measure to the controversy surrounding the role of quality control in testing.

The nub of the controversy is whether quality control should actually perform tests or merely witness them and verify the final results. The diversity of implementation throughout industry indicates that neither approach is obviously superior to the other. In those cases, where quality control does not perform testing, the responsibility most frequently is assigned to manufacturing. In certain cases, however, engineering is given the responsibility; in still others, it falls to an independent test organization. The basis for this varied organizational implementation of the testing responsibility may lie purely in business economics or in differing fundamental concepts about the purpose of the quality control function.

Inherent, fundamental faults are associated with both basic approaches from an economic as well as a quality control viewpoint. Assigning all of the testing to quality control on the premise that to do so constitutes the cheapest way of handling the job may well turn out to be false economy. In these cases, quality control frequently becomes entangled in the web of schedule pressures and bends or trades off basic control responsibilities to a point where the company's performance image may be jeopardized.

When manufacturing or some other agency performs the testing under quality control's monitoring, the issue of the additional expense of witnessing tests invariably arises. Unfortunately, this dual implementation will always present the appearance of being costly and unnecessary. It is, in fact, the most costly and the most difficult way to control testing. Yet there are times when it is the only way to protect the company's interests in this important area. Nevertheless, to have quality control automatically witness all tests may prove to be more uneconomical than to have quality control perform all tests.

What is needed in testing as in quality control itself is a policy that accurately fits the specific needs of a company. This policy should be the result of economic trade-offs among all significant factors, each being considered in its proper perspective with regard to its ultimate value for the company. The factors that should be considered include the ultimate effect of each specific testing requirement on the end product of the company's business, the cost of each different approach to a specific testing requirement the basic policies and capabilities of each potentially involved function and the level of performance disciplines that can be achieved.

In order to develop such a policy, the entire gamut of potential testing requirements should be examined in the light of all available management approaches and logic as they apply to each situation. To avoid confusion, testing will be considered to involve all measurements that are not visual and dimensional in nature that is, all activity designed to determine the physical, chemical, or functional properties or characteristics of a product or process. In this way, everything not clearly in the realm of inspection can be considered.

The first need for testing is usually generated by engineering on the basis that a company's business starts with design of product. Engineering then becomes involved with design tests, prototype tests, and possibly qualification tests. Such tests may call for anything from simple bench setups to extensive testing laboratories. They may involve parts, processes, components, assemblies, sub-systems, or entire systems. The requirements may range from tests on basic properties or functions to complete environmental or life testing of a product.

The next need for testing is generated by the procurement activity. The testing of procured products is an essential ingredient of many purchases. For the most part, this testing is performed by vendors and varies in magnitude according to each company's procurement needs. It may also range from the simplest type to the most complex. Involved in most procurement programmes are the tests to be performed on receipt of the vendor's products as part of the receiving in sped ion activity. Occasionally, outside testing services must be procured because of the lack of adequate in-house testing facilities.

The greatest need for testing ordinarily occurs in manufacturing or production, and it is here that the latest developments in testing devices come iuto play. A wide variety of test methods and equipment is available, depending on the product, the processes it goes through, and the accuracy of the measurements required. While non-destructive methods are continually sought and used, many situations demand that samples of product or processing material be destroyed to determine its characteristics. Most destructive testing is conducted in laboratory support areas, either because production-type test equipment has not yet been developed or because the duplication of necessary laboratory equipment would be too expensive.

When functional testing of the end product is a requirement of the business, production testing can take many forms and can reach almost limitless proportions. It may involve a piece of completely automatic test equipment or an accumulation of testing devices assembled into a manually operated test station. As the complexity of products increases, production testing may require an entire facility for the testing of a complete system or a combination of facilities for the checkout of such products as a complete aircraft or space vehicle. In certain sectors of industry, testing represents a major part of the total activity.

Regardless of the type or magnitude of testing, the total value of all test results depends on two supplementary activities: test documentation and calibration of test equipment. Calibration insures the validity of results and is a major test activity in itself documentation provides the means for utilizing results. Results are utilized in several important ways. Initially, they are used as the basis for all decisions to proceed or to stopor, in the less complicated applications, for all decisions to accept or to reject. Another application is in support of "trouble shooting" investigations of failures and anomalies. Still another application is in the prediction of future results, which generally involve reliability requirements or the analysis of trends. Finally, documented test results supply part of the protection a company needs against the discovery of latent defects or failures. In view of the wide variation in the magnitude and scope of testing throughout industry. it seems unlikely that a single management approach could satisfy all the needs. Testing in engineering at vendors' plants, in the factory, and at the customer's house all pose different management problems, objectives, and viewpoints. Traditionally and practically, engineering, manufacturing, and quality control regard testing from the vantage points of different sets of values. Each has its own opinion of what is important, how to make the best use of testing and what its specific worth is to the company.

Engineering, for example, may feel that the highly technical nature of testing demands that only engineering be permitted to conduct tests. At the other extreme, it may take the view that, as long as no one interferes with the conduct of engineering tests, it couldn't care less how other tests are managed. Engineering is not likely to be overly concerned with calibration, except as applied to original design considerations. With regard to documentation, it usually is concerned only with test data it requires for its own use. In general, the engineering viewpoint of testing closely parallels those aspects for which engineering is held responsible in the overall scheme of things.

Where manufacturing or an independent test organization is responsible for production testing, its viewpoint is always strongly influenced by production schedules and budgets. The natural instinct and practical experience of both groups tell them that today's pressures and problems affecting delivery come first. That is, they will if necessary risk tomorrow's management anger that could stem from customer problems in order to forestall today's wrath for missing schedules. Their attitude regarding documentation is that data constitute a deterrent to getting the job done. With regard to calibration, passiveness is the rule of thumb which generally applies. Before discussing quality control's viewpoint, it should be noted that other departments as well often have an active interest in the company's testing activity. As already stated, considerable testing is performed at vendors' plants; this is basically the management responsibility of the procurement group. It has become traditional that procurement delegate such responsibility, along with all acceptance responsibilities, to quality control except when an entire team is assigned to a major subcontract. In general, procurement's attitude is one of "Let George do it." If we recognize that procurement's needed skills are different, there is nothing basically wrong with this approach from a practical point of view. The approach is wrong, however, when procurement has no feeling of responsibility for seeing that George is on the job acting on this delegation of authority.

In many applications, the contracts and configuration control groups of a company must become involved in test activities. Their involvement encompasses specific contract test criteria and test data packages in association with specific configuration levels. Requirements such as these must be factored into the overall test plan, and compliance must be communicated back to the originator. Achievement of this task for large and complex programmes has proved to be extremely challenging for many companies, and there is a growing history of results that are less than completely successful.

Quality control's viewpoint on testing differs from that of other groups chiefly because it is so broad in scope. Unlike engineering or manufacturing, each of which has one principal objective and responsibility coupled with many secondary ones, quality control's principal function is to see that all company requirements and obligations are met in each affected area or activity in which it has a responsibility. Hence quality control is equally concerned with all aspects of testing. Important requisites such as documentation, calibration, and configuration status are not allowed to take a back seat to other considerations. All are equally necessary for acceptance and delivery. If quality control were suddenly given a prime responsibility for meeting production test schedules as would occur if it were entrusted with production testing it would no longer be able to provide proper emphasis on those tasks for which it was created.

Even if the foregoing were only partially true, it is still obvious that total responsibility for testing in today's industrial environment cannot be effectively assigned to anyone previously established department. Once this is fully recognized, prime testing responsibilities can be considered individually and can be assigned to fit the company's needs and capabilities, with supplementary responsibilities and controls assigned where necessary. In this respect, management would do well to follow the quality control viewpoint, since it is in essence a management viewpoint. Every customer requirement or company commitment involving testing must be met this is management's responsibility.

In adhering to the quality control viewpoint, management will recognize the total scope of requirements affecting testing as well as quality control's normal role in the acceptance of product. In this light, management should establish useful guidelines which will guarantee inclusion of control requirements and may also help to pinpoint the most effective and efficient way to proceed. Thinking in this vein will also bring out the need for and the value of, strict disciplines in test procedures, trouble-shooting techniques, retest requirements, and documentation.

Guidelines for quality control's participation in testing should be based on the total effect of each testing requirement on final acceptance of the end product. In this connection, only three conditions can exist and therefore need to be evaluated. The first condition is represented by tests that have no bearing whatsoever on the quality characteristics of delivered products; that is, tests that are not performed on products to be delivered or on samples of such products and whose results will not be used to establish test criteria for deliverable products. In this case, quality control participation generally is not required unless, for some other reason, it becomes involved in such research projects. For example, research into new or improved measurement techniques not only concerns quality control but may well have been initiated by it.

The next condition is represented by in-process tests designed primarily to preclude discrepant conditions in the final test operation for the end product. In all such cases, further opportunities to determine compliance to the acceptance criteria are provided. Since this type of activity is essentially a screening operation, it may be established on a purely economic basis, and qualitv eontrol's role should be determined on the same basis. In other words, quality control need not participate at all except as it can also contribute to the cost trade-off with the final acceptance operation. In some cases, it is logical for quality control to perform the screening—as, for example, in receiving inspection tests. Where this is not logical, the participation should be no more than surveillance to the extent necessary to protect the company's investment.

The third and most common testing condition is represented by those tests that have a direct and final bearing on the acceptability of product for delivery. Here the role of quality control must be absolute with respect to its fundamental charter, and here it is likely to receive its most serious challenge. The reason: A simple matter of economics is involved whenever two departments appear to be spending a considerable number of dollars to produce a single result. The awful truth is that this situation can occur only when the role of quality control has actually been overplayed or when the actions of quality control are properly conceived but their vital value lacks recognition.

The available management approaches to quality control's role in this final test area are threefold: full responsibility, sample testing, or monitoring. Full responsibility is undesirable except in those cases where completion schedules need not be overemphasized. But in those cases and where the capability exists within the quality control function there is no more economical way to proceed: For example, quality control often assumes full responsibility for materials testing. There is nothing fundamentally wrong with this. What can be wrong is to force quality control to forgo its basic heritage.

Where giving quality control full responsibility for test is impractical, the next most desirable approach is sampling. When the economics of production quantities or flow permit the establishment of sampling procedures, this is perhaps the most effective way for quality control to fulfill its purpose. It is the only way in industries where product is the result of a continuous process or of a series of contiguous processes. In fact, the epitome of quality control in its finest form might well be the periodic sampling of a controlled process to assure management of its continued acceptability.

The least desirable of all quality control roles for testing and yet the only one most frequently available is that of monitor. Test monitoring is expensive, it is difficult to manage effectively and it has probably done more to alienate other groups or departments involved in testing than any other single factor. It is expensive because it requires the same level of skill as is required for testing, and, by design, it is always redundant. The sole exception occurs when the testing is done by automatic testing machines; in that event, someone must monitor the machines.

The difficulties involved in the management of test monitoring center on two points: Most technically skilled personnel prefer to work directly with the hardware; and, when they are engaged in such work, they resent the implication that they can't be trusted to perform without a "traffic cop." The first point makes it difficult to attract skilled personnel initially and then make them realize the importance of the test monitoring job. The second point adds to the difficulty because the resentment exerts a negative effect on individual test monitors. In fact, this resentment occasionally takes the form of personal harassment or even, at times, of abuse.

It is a regrettable fact that people in testing do need to be watched. Examples of products which have failed to perform because of a test deficiency are so numerous that they must appear on almost every company's records of performance. Deficiencies occur in spite of test monitoring, and the reason, doubtless, is as fundamental as is the reason people speed on highways. It is unnatural for people to pursue two different objectives simultaneously. On the highway, if the road appears clear, we tend to pursue our own personal objective of speeding toward our destination and ignore the objective of observing the speed laws. In testing, if it appears that the product will not suffer, one may be similarly inclined to speed toward schedule objectives rather than to adhere strictly to procedures.

Successful test monitoring must begin with test planning. To have test monitors without having specifically defined and planned tasks is to ask for trouble. A man cannot be assigned as monitor to a group of testers and be held completely responsible for the group's total output. Such assignments will discourage the man and might even lead to an informal alliance between testers and test monitors, with the company the loser. This type of situation generally develops a pattern whereby both parties protect each other at someone else's expense. The only thing worse than this is to assign test monitors solely to demonstrate compliance with an unwanted requirement and then to limit them to keeping out of the way and not interfering with the progress of the task at hand.

In addition to avoiding the potential pitfalls that go with the lack of planning, the establishment of specific test monitoring responsibilities is a sure way to keep necessary monitoring costs to a realistic minimum. That it also provides meaning and purpose for such tasks is one more point in its favour. The test monitor with specific, planned, clearly defined responsibilities can become a valuable member of the company test team. He can be attracted to the company, sold on the merits of the test programme, and motivated to make a personal contribution to it. It takes this kind of vision to lift the clouds of confusion and concern which often shroud the quality control test area.

A test monitor is responsible for verifying results at key test check points and enforcing the continued maintenance of basic testing disciplines. Determining appropriate test check points can be more or less difficult, depending on many factors. Essentially, check points should be established each time a final measurement is being made of an end-use function which the product must perform for the customer. This automatically provides the company with verification of the most important test parameters against which its delivered products will be evaluated. Going back from this end point, further check points should be added as they are needed to insure the integrity of the final measurements or to fulfill specific contract requirements or company commitments.

The use of test monitors often attains peak value during times of trouble rather than when testing is running smoothly. Maintenance of sound documentation and of trouble shooting and failure analysis disciplines when technical problems develop has averted the loss of valuable failure data and conditions for many companies. This, in turn, has minimized the total cost of each failure, of its resolution, and of the ultimate corrective action. Maintenance of test procedure disciplines, calibration requirements, and configuration control when applicable is also invaluable. Problems that are allowed to erupt in these areas are always extremely costly as well as embarrassing, and pinning down the number of products involved is almost impossible without complete reinspection or testing. The enforcement of test disciplines proves the old adage true: An ounce of prevention is worth a pound of cure. The next step in building a better test programme with monitoring is the development of teamwork. Once test monitoring has been clearly defined and its value has been recognized, it can be properly integrated as an accepted element of the test operation. The bigger and more complex the operation, the easier it is to develop teamwork between testers and monitors. Consider, for example, the confidence a test conductor must have when he is about to launch men into space. When the final key test parameters have been remeasured for the last time, he listens for the final message he wants to hear from his testing team: The results have been "verified by quality." Now he can proceed, backed up by the maximum confidence his team can provide. That's the way it was with the Gemini programme, where the teamwork of all parties involved really paid off.

Although the importance of teamwork is more readily apparent in today's widely known and much publicized systems management programmes, it is equally important in any test programme where profits depend on results. Relatively speaking, poor results can be just as dramatic and costly to the owners of smaller test operations as they are to the owners of large operations; only the degree of notoriety that attends failure varies with the size. Test monitoring, wherever it is applicable, can provide maximum service only when it is promoted as a distinct but integral and necessary part of the total test operation. Where testing is of real importance, following this path to the development of a professional test team will greatly improve its chances of success.

Once the entire scope of testing has been examined and the possible approaches have been explored, the role of quality control in individual test situations should be easier to determine. At times the difference in value of available choices may not be significant, and, for some reason, what seems to be the best choice may not work. In the long run, nevertheless, the end results will be determined by the validity of the analysis, by the lack of bias in the decisions, and by the firmness of implementation.

Where engineering tests are concerned, it seems logical that engineering be assigned the performance responsibility and that the need for monitoring be limited. For design tests, there should be no need for monitoring; the design engineer should be given a free hand and full responsibility to work out his own design. When a design reaches the prototype stage, however, other interests such as production test criteria and engineering baseline for configuration control begin to develop. Some test monitoring, which could easily be coupled with initial inspection requirements, should be established at this point. This small effort could provide sufficient production and acceptance viewpoints to offset gross errors or oversights that would be costly later.

Qualification testing which is usually assigned to engineering has a profound effect on the acceptability of products. It is generally designed to test prototype or early production units to the limit of the environmental criterion within which they are required to operate and to serve as proof that production units can meet this criterion. Any physical difference between these units and production has the potential to nullify the basic objective. Unusual handling or nursing of the units through qualification testing can have the same effect. Close quality control surveillance is therefore needed in this area. A close scrutiny may even reveal that the evaluation of a design to determine whether it can meet its ultimate purpose would best serve the overall interests of a company if it were conducted by an independent and unbiased agency.

Testing laboratories are often required both for engineering or development tests and for production controls. Therefore, they have a direct bearing on acceptance. Examples include materials testing; hydraulic, pneumatic, and contamination control; and the like. If we assume that regardless of its departmental management a particular laboratory would also service the needs of other departments, the logical assignment of responsibility for the laboratory is to the department with the greatest need. Because laboratories are not ordinarily envisioned as strictly integrated with production flows or schedules, this evaluation should certainly include quality control as a potentially effective assignee.

In some cases, laboratory equipment must be shared; but this arrangement has drawbacks that would never exist if one department had complete control. Regardless of the arrangement, however, quality control's role in the laboratory must be one of direct involvement in those tests that have a direct bearing on the acceptance of product. In each case, its involvement can be as doer or monitor. Organizational trade-offs associated with the initial establishment of each laboratory function should always consider the cost of quality control as a potentially significant factor. This consideration also insures proper consideration of the basic role of quality control.

The testing that takes place in a vendor's plant inevitably has an effect on acceptance; therefore, quality control is automatically involved. Test results requiring verification at the vendor's plant can most readily be accomplished in conjunction with associated inspection requirements. Except in very rare cases, this responsibility is always assigned to quality control. One is inclined to wonder why, in many cases, the buyer's management may fail to recognize a similar need for quality control in its own plant or may minimize the need.

To the extent that it is feasible and economical, necessary testing of incoming parts from vendors is accomplished as part of the receiving inspection activity. The responsibility for this testing usually and logically is assigned to the quality control function. Wherever possible, however, receiving inspection is supported or serviced by other groups. In other words, whenever tests of incoming vendors' products require the use of laboratory equipment, major test facilities, or expensive test equipment, none of which can be economically duplicated solely for receiving inspection they will be conducted by the department that has the equipment as a service to receiving inspection. On the other hand, equipment procured primarily for the evaluation of vendors' products, regardless of size or cost, should be assigned to receiving inspection.

To implement a philosophy regarding the role of quality control in factory tests, such testing should be considered in three distinct phases. First, certain tests are strictly associated with the build cycle and with the inspection of the manufactured article. Next come tests that are related solely to the processing of manufactured articles at some point within the manufacturing cycle. This phase includes all physical and chemical processes such as heat treating and plating and is the paramount feature of process industries. Finally, the acceptance test phase includes all activity designed essentially to test the performance of manufactured product, whether it be material, parts, sub-assemblies, components, sub-systems, complete systems, or combined systems.

Much of the testing connected with the basic manufacture of articles is also closely associated with the inspection of these articles, if not an integral part of it, so it is logical that this testing be made part of the responsibility of the inspection function. Examples of this are best illustrated by the type of equipment commonly used today for this purpose and commonly found in inspection quarters. A list of such equipment would include conductivity or eddy current meters for hardness testing; dermitron equipment, optical gauges, and vidigauge equipment for thickness measurements; optical, brush, or electronic comparators for finish measurements; continuity meters, hi-pot machines, and circuit analyzers for various electrical measurements; and numerous others. It would also include such stalwart fixtures as Rockwell hardness testers, magnaflux equipment, X-ray, many types of dye-penetrant equipment and various pressure testing devices. Of more recent vintage, it may include elaborate measuring machines for coordinate or rotary measurements, ultrasonic testers, and infrared measuring devices. The continued development of new and exotic test equipment for inspection purposes indicates that inspection is in the testing business to stay.

In some manufacturing processes the results can never be verified completely. For these, in-process controls are required for acceptance. In some cases there are so many variables, each having variable interactions with the others,' that it is impossible to determine accurately what the individual output will be. A typical example is the bonding process used to produce bonded panels for aircraft; another is welding. In both, the strength of each individual attachment cannot be fully determined without destruction. The results of such processes can be accepted only on the basis of controlling each known variable and of periodically requalifying the entire process through the destructive testing of samples.

Whether required for business economics, acceptance of product, or both, the process controls encountered in industry today include almost every conceivable type and method of testing or measurement. Examples are environmental controls for time, temperature, pressure, and cleanliness of materials, equipment, and atmosphere; chemical, physical, and electrical tests of process materials and product; and tests for the continued certification of equipment and people. Certain tests are designed into the process; others are performed with equipment available in the processing area; yet others require outside support, such as a materials testing laboratory.

Whenever new processes are being developed or new methods of processing materials are being sought, the need for process controls and methods to measure the results should be rccognized from the start. If sufficient attention is not given to these needs early in the process development, ultimate implementation may be delayed unnecessarily. If quality control is not in a position to "buy" the results, neither will, a prospective customer be in a position to know what he is getting.

In the area of a factory that is designated strictly for acceptance testing, there will be sample testing of outgoing products, 100 percent testing of each product, or a combination of both. When there is both, it probably means that quality control is sampling the output of manufacturing tests and is assuring management that only acceptable products are flowing out the door. When sample testing alone is being performed, it probably means that the product must be destroyed to be tested, as in the case of ordnance products. In this instance, the smart company will be having such sample testing performed by quality control on the basis of a statistically sound plan assuring all customers that their requirements are being met fully. In all other instances, where there is 100 percent testing the problem of test monitoring may exist to some degree.

As previously mentioned, calibration is not only a significant factor to all testing but a major test operation in itself. Calibration of test equipment and instruments is needed so that product performance measurements can be traced back to a national standard against which all accuracies must be determined. There is no other way to validate the achievement of any performance criteria. Inability to produce this traceability in industry can compare with the inability of a top antique or art dealer to trace and prove his merchandise's origin. There may be exceptions, of course, such as products intended only to provide physical stimulation or sense of feeling.

Calibration is generally established as a laboratory function and usually involves more than one level of standard instruments. Prime standards are those that are directly traceable to the National Bureau of Standards in Washington. These are usually kept in a controlled environment are periodically revalidated by the Bureau of Standards, and are used to transfer accuracies to working standards. Working standards are those instruments which are used periodically to calibrate all test equipment in use throughout a company. The frequency of calibration must be determined by a careful analysis of the capacity of each piece of equipment to retain accuracy in use. Quality control's role in calibration can be that of an enlightened leader or of a vital monitor.

In sum, it can be seen that the role of quality control can take on many different aspects and its value in testing can be varied. If it has not become a respected technical function its ultimate value in testing will be limited. On the other hand, if quality control as a complete entity can be developed into a dynamic, technically sound, and useful force throughout the company, its value will be unlimited. In testing alone, quality control has the potential for making significant contributions to a company's performance image and overall cost effectiveness. The wisdom of effectively utilizing quality control to achieve this potential must be recognized by each company for itself.

❐